DogLife ❧ Lifelong Care for Your Dog™

# CAVALIER KING CHARLES SPANIEL

Loren Spiotta-DiMare

# CAVALIER KING CHARLES SPANIEL

Project Team
Editors: Mary E. Grangeia, Stephanie Fornino
Indexer: Dianne L. Schneider
Design: Patricia Escabi
Series Design: Mary Ann Kahn, Angela Stanford

TFH Publications
President/CEO: Glen S. Axelrod
Executive Vice President: Mark E. Johnson
Publisher: Christopher T. Reggio
Production Manager: Kathy Bontz

TFH Publications, Inc.
One TFH Plaza
Third and Union Avenues
Neptune City, NJ 07753

Printed and bound in China

11 12 13 14 15 16   1 3 5 7 9 8 6 4 2

**Library of Congress Cataloging-in-Publication Data**
Spiotta-DiMare, Loren.
  Cavalier King Charles spaniel / Loren Spiotta-DiMare.
     p. cm.
  Includes bibliographical references and index.
  ISBN 978-0-7938-3604-8 (alk. paper)
  1.  Cavalier King Charles spaniel.  I. Title.
  SF429.C36S65 2011
  636.752'4--dc22

                    2010014938

This book has been published with the intent to provide accurate and authoritative information in regard to the subject matter within. While every reasonable precaution has been taken in preparation of this book, the author and publisher expressly disclaim responsibility for any errors, omissions, or adverse effects arising from the use or application of the information contained herein. The techniques and suggestions are used at the reader's discretion and are not to be considered a substitute for veterinary care. If you suspect a medical problem consult your veterinarian.

Note: In the interest of concise writing, "he" is used when referring to puppies and dogs unless the text is specifically referring to females or males. "She" is used when referring to people. However, the information contained herein is equally applicable to both sexes.

*The Leader In Responsible Animal Care for Over 50 Years!*®
**www.tfh.com**

# CONTENTS

Introducing the Cavalier . . . . . . . . . . . . . . . . . . . . . . . . . . . .6

## PART I: PUPPYHOOD

1: Is the Cavalier Right for You? . . . . . . . . . . . . . . . . . . . . .22

2: Finding and Prepping for Your Cavalier Puppy . . . . . . . . . . . .32

3: Care of Your Cavalier Puppy . . . . . . . . . . . . . . . . . . . . .48

4: Training Your Cavalier Puppy . . . . . . . . . . . . . . . . . . . .60

## PART II: ADULTHOOD

5: Finding Your Cavalier Adult . . . . . . . . . . . . . . . . . . . . .80

6: Cavalier Grooming Needs . . . . . . . . . . . . . . . . . . . . . .90

7: Cavalier Nutritional Needs . . . . . . . . . . . . . . . . . . . . .102

8: Cavalier Health and Wellness . . . . . . . . . . . . . . . . . . .114

9: Cavalier Training . . . . . . . . . . . . . . . . . . . . . . . . . .134

10: Cavalier Problem Behaviors . . . . . . . . . . . . . . . . . . . .144

11: Cavalier Sports and Activities . . . . . . . . . . . . . . . . . . .160

## PART III: SENIOR YEARS

12: Finding Your Cavalier Senior . . . . . . . . . . . . . . . . . . .182

13: Care of Your Cavalier Senior . . . . . . . . . . . . . . . . . . .188

14: End-of-Life Issues . . . . . . . . . . . . . . . . . . . . . . . . .200

50 Fun Facts Every Cavalier Owner Should Know . . . . . . . . .208

Resources . . . . . . . . . . . . . . . . . . . . . . . . . . . . . . . .210

Index . . . . . . . . . . . . . . . . . . . . . . . . . . . . . . . . . .213

# INTRODUCTION

# INTRODUCING THE CAVALIER

There's something innately appealing and irresistible about spaniels. With the exception of the curly-coated breeds who have their own charming qualities, spaniels have silky coats in a beautiful array of colors, soft drop ears, and warm, expressive eyes. But even more attractive than their appearance is their unsurpassed devotion to people.

Although Cavalier King Charles Spaniels are recognized as toy dogs by the American Kennel Club (AKC), they retain many of the attributes of their larger sporting spaniel cousins. Established in 1884, the AKC is the oldest and largest purebred dog registry in the United States. The organization currently registers 168 breeds, with an additional 11 in the Miscellaneous Class awaiting recognition. Cavaliers have become quite popular over the years. Out of the 168 registered AKC breeds, they ranked 25th in popularity in 2009 as compared to 58th in 1999.

Breeds are classified by the American Kennel Club (AKC) in seven groups: Sporting Dogs, Hounds, Working Dogs, Terriers, Toys, Non-Sporting, and Herding Dogs. Each group designates what the dogs within in it were originally bred to do. For example, the Sporting Group consists of dogs who hunt: the pointers, setters, spaniels, and retrievers.

When prospective pet owners begin to consider the breeds of dog that appeal to them, appearance is usually first on everyone's list. I know I like a certain type and look. My sister once commented, "Your dogs match." To which I replied, "You think that's a coincidence?" I'm highly attracted to spaniels and setters, and I prefer red, red and white, chocolate, and tricolor coats. Plus I enjoy how attached they become to their owners and their joyful, playful spirits. Not all of my dogs are purebreds, but they all have sporting breeds in their ancestry and retain the traits I admire. Which brings me to the topic of behavior versus appearance.

It's important for pet owners to select a breed with an energy level and set of behaviors that are compatible with their own. Sporting dogs are very active. Although I don't hunt, I do enjoy watching my gang harmlessly hunting backyard birds. Woody, our field-bred setter, is especially breathtaking doing the job for which he was bred. I also like walking my dogs and dabbling in various canine sports such as obedience, agility, and flyball. So I'm able to channel their exercise needs with these activities. If you are a couch potato and prefer reading to hiking, a sporting dog is not for you. On the other hand, if you admire the traits of the hunting spaniels but would prefer a smaller and a little more sedate companion, the Cavalier King Charles Spaniel, which is classified in the Toy Group, may be perfect for you.

## BRIEF HISTORY OF THE DOMESTICATION OF THE DOG

Cavalier King Charles Spaniels are easy to spot and easier to love. They are without doubt the consummate canine companion. What makes these toy spaniels so special, aside from their beauty and delightful nature? Perhaps it all begins with their unique history.

As most dog lovers are aware, dogs descend from wolves, who live in packs within a hierarchal society. The leader, or alpha, heads the group followed by his subordinates. Dogs make excellent companion animals because they view their human families as a pack—a social arrangement they innately understand and accept. Pet parents take on the role of pack leader and establish house rules for their canine companions to follow.

While not everyone has agreed over the ages that wolves are the ancestors of dogs, DNA tests actually prove the theory to be true. With this new technology, scientists have been able to collect DNA samples from dogs around the world. Their tests reveal a direct genetic link to wolves.

Interestingly, in her new book, *Animals Make Us Human*, Temple Grandin has a slightly different take on the social lives and behavior of wolves. Grandin, who has a Ph.D. in Animal Science and teaches at Colorado State University, is one of the most accomplished autistic adults in the

Cavalier King Charles Spaniels are classified by the American Kennel Club in the Toy Group.

country today, and she believes that her hypersensitivity to sensory stimuli seems to have given her a special understanding of and affinity for animals. She professes that most wolf research has been conducted in captivity, where unrelated wolves are thrown together and have no choice but to form a pack. Grandin says that in the wild, wolves actually live in nuclear family groups (basing her claim on the work of L. David Mech, who studies wild wolves living on Ellesmere Island in Canada). So wolf cubs learn to respect the leadership of their parents, not a pack leader. Hence she believes that dogs, who are genetically wired to wolves, need to respect a human parent. To me, it's a bit of semantics. A small family group is still a pack. Someone has to be in charge, and whether considered a pack leader or parent, that someone needs to be you.

Keep in mind that a puppy is not a child. This is especially important for first-time dog owners to understand. To raise a well-adjusted adult dog, you need to know the innate nature of dogs and teach puppies in a manner that simulates canine language. (We'll discuss more on this topic in the training chapters.)

# EARLY DEVELOPMENT OF THE CAVALIER

Over time, evolving dog populations were selected for various traits by their human benefactors and willingly adapted to their surroundings.

## The Spaniel as Hunter

Spaniels developed an especially strong attachment to people because they have hunted beside humankind for centuries. In fact, there are references to these dogs as far back as 17 CE. Dr. Johannes Caius, a recognized authority on the subject, penned *Of Englishe Dogges* and divided the spaniels into two groups: those who hunted primarily on land and those who hunted on water. Usually the larger, stronger breeds were utilized around lakes and streams while their smaller cousins worked the fields.

Originally, nets were used when hunting but were ultimately replaced with guns. The large, long-legged pointers and setters were bred to be far ranging, but spaniels were expected to "quarter" (sweep) the field in a zigzag pattern in close proximity to the hunter. Once game was spotted, they'd "flush" (spring at it), forcing the bird to take flight, then "hup" (sit) while the hunter fired. When given the release command, the dog would fetch and retrieve the downed bird to his master's hand.

True partners, the hunter and his spaniel formed a close relationship. This bond extended to the home front as well, as spaniels like nothing better than to be near their human family. In fact, many of the breeds are referred to as Velcro dogs. Having lived with three of the sporting spaniels myself, the English Springer, Welsh Springer, and Field Spaniel, I can attest to the truth of this "where you go, I go" attitude. My guys follow me from room to room, sleep beneath my desk as I write, and one of my Welshies walked right into the shower with me when I forgot to close the door!

Although other small breeds, possibly the Japanese Chin, Tibetan Spaniel, or Papillion, were involved in the development of Cavaliers, most likely they inherited their strong devotion to people from their sporting spaniel relatives.

You should be your dog's "pack leader."

The Cavalier most likely inherited his strong devotion to people from his sporting spaniel relatives.

## The Spaniel as Lapdog

During the Tudor age and later throughout the reign of the Stuarts in England, toy spaniels were quite capable of hunting small game alongside their masters, but their true calling was to fill the role of lapdog. In fact, they were bred by British royalty specifically for this purpose. While the middle and lower classes needed dogs able to earn their keep, i.e., herding, hunting, or guarding, the aristocracy could afford to have dogs solely as companions. The ladies of the day especially enjoyed their little canine comforters, and indeed they were often referred to as "comforter spaniels." Offering something for everyone, the Cavalier was also quite capable of frolicking with children, acting as a playmate and companion.

Aside from fulfilling all of these important roles, toy spaniels served other useful purposes. They drew fleas away from their people, sparing them from contracting disease, and they were literally used as lap and foot warmers. So it's no wonder that Cavaliers were much-beloved members of the family.

The reciprocal adoration between Cavalier King Charles Spaniels and their people has been well depicted and documented in vintage paintings throughout the centuries. Toy spaniels are frequently seen in family portraits, out in the field, and in portraits of their own. In fact, *The Vision of St. Eustace*, a painting created in 1440 by Antonio Pisanello, showcases several animals, including two small spaniels. Reproduced in William Secord's book *Dog Painting*, the canine subjects have relatively flat heads, with their ears set high, almond-shaped eyes, and long muzzles. This type of spaniel is later also depicted in works of art created by many of the great master artists including Hogarth, Landseer, Stubbs, Titian, van Dyck, and Vermeer.

## BREED HISTORY IN ENGLAND

While in power from 1660 to 1685, King Charles II played a pivotal role in the development of his namesake breed. Several of his cherished Cavaliers were always at his side. So smitten was he that it's said he proclaimed that no toy spaniel would ever be denied access to public buildings, including Parliament! He also allowed his bitches to raise their litters in his personal bedroom chambers.

Actually, it was a family affair. Charles' brother, James, also loved Cavaliers, as did their father, Charles I. The siblings agreed that James would continue their breeding program in the event of Charles II's death. The story recounted through the ages is that a dozen of Charles' adored spaniels were at his bedside when he died at the age of 54 in 1685.

James took the throne for several years as James II, but then William III and Queen Mary II rose to power in 1689. They preferred Pugs, and over time the Cavalier's popularity began to wane. However, the Duke of Marlborough had become interested in Cavaliers through his acquaintance with King James II and later continued his own breeding program at Blenheim Palace. He particularly liked the red and whites, who eventually became known

King Charles II played a pivotal role in the development of his namesake breed.

The name "Cavalier King Charles Spaniel" was selected to differentiate the breed from the "King Charles Spaniel."

as Blenheims. Several Dukes of Marlboro continued the Palace breeding program until the early 1900s.

Queen Victoria, who was in power from 1837 to 1901, was also a dog lover and besotted with several breeds. But she had an especially close attachment to her favorite, Dash, a Cavalier-type spaniel. Dash appeared in a number of Landseer paintings on his own and alongside his royal person.

However, over time, due to the influence of the Pug and other small Oriental breeds, a new type of toy spaniel began to emerge. This variety had a domed skull, undershot jaw, shorter face, and larger protruding eyes. This dog ultimately became the King Charles Spaniel, known as the English Toy Spaniel in the United States. The original, longer-faced type may have been lost in

antiquity if not for Roswell Eldridge, a wealthy American who traveled to England in 1925 to import some of the small spaniels he admired in the paintings of old.

Alas, Mr. Eldridge was disappointed when he arrived. The flatter-faced dogs had become popular, and the originals depicted in paintings were next to impossible to find. Undaunted, Eldridge created a challenge for breeders: to develop the best female and male resembling the spaniels who had lived during King Charles II's time and later were referred to as Blenheim spaniels. Winners would win a cash prize of 25 pounds (a handsome sum) at the annual Crufts dog show for the following five years. The desired type of spaniel was then illustrated by Sir Edwin Landseer's painting of a long-nosed toy spaniel. Eldridge required "Blenheim spaniels of the old type as shown in pictures of Charles II's time: long face, no stop, flat skull, not inclined to be domed, with spot in centre of skull. The First Prizes in Classes 947 and 948 are given by Roswell Eldridge, Esq., of New York, and will be continued for five years. The Prizes go to the nearest to type required." Many breeders laughed at or were totally put off by the idea, especially those involved in perfecting the King Charles Spaniel with its roundish, Pug-like head. But a few breeders were intrigued and took up the challenge. Purists say that only long-nosed toy spaniel individuals were bred to bring back the old type. But others believe the Papillon, Cocker, and possibly Welsh Springer contributed to the recreation of the breed.

In 1926, only two bitches and two dogs were shown. In 1927, there were three entries in each class. Waif Julia exhibited by Amice Pitt received the prize for best bitch. Pitt went on to be involved with Cavaliers for the next 50 years. And like Eldridge, she had an instrumental influence on the development of the breed.

## Formation of the Cavalier King Charles Spaniel Club

The year 1928 became a substantial one for Cavaliers. Five dogs and nine bitches were entered in the Crufts show. Ann's Son, a Blenheim bred and owned by K. Mostyn Walker, won the dog class. The Cavalier King Charles Spaniel breed club was formed soon after, with Mostyn Walker as chairperson and Amice Pitt as secretary. The official name "Cavalier King Charles Spaniel" was selected to differentiate the breed from the "King Charles Spaniel." "Cavalier" referred to medieval knights who had existed in the middle ages serving the royal families.

During the club's first meeting, Ann's

Son stood on a table for all to see and to serve as a model for the breed standard (guidelines describing the ideal characteristics, temperament, and appearance of a breed), club members brought their vintage spaniel paintings along, and it was agreed that Cavaliers would always remain natural, i.e., no trimming to spare them the flights of passing fancy that often occur in the dog world. Still, Kennel Club recognition did not come swiftly or easily, so Cavaliers continued to be shown through other canine societies.

In the United States, the Cavalier is considered a newer breed.

## Recognition by the Kennel Club

Ann's Son went on to win the Cavalier dog class three years in a row. Sadly, Eldridge never had the opportunity to see the most prestigious winner of his challenge, as he died in 1927. And yet his legacy to the breed lives on.

World War II took a toll on the Cavalier, as it did with many other purebred dog breeds. From 1940 until 1945, there were only 60 Cavaliers registered. After the war, a group of 14 Cavalier devotees pulled together on behalf of their beloved breed and petitioned the Kennel Club again for recognition, which was finally granted in 1945.

From their tumultuous beginnings, interest in Cavalier King Charles Spaniels has soared. Today Cavaliers are one of the most popular dogs in the United Kingdom. When reviving the old long-muzzled type, breeders took some artistic license and perfected a softer look. The snout is not as long and narrow and the eyes are round and quite soulful.

## BREED HISTORY IN THE UNITED STATES

In the United States, the Cavalier is considered a newer breed. In 1952, Lady Forwood of England presented her American friend, Sally Lyons Brown of Kentucky, with a black and tan pup. It's thought that there were six other Cavaliers in the country at the time. Brown became entirely devoted to the breed, added more to her canine family, and sought recognition from the AKC.

To become recognized, Brown was told that a club of Cavalier devotees had to be formed, dog shows held, a standard compiled, records kept of pedigrees, and in general she had to generate greater interest in the breed. She took up the task and formed the Cavalier King Charles Spaniel Club-United States, Inc., in 1954. Club members created a strict code of ethics to protect their breed from commercialism and exploitation. Dogs could not be sold to commercial breeders or at auction. A female could not be bred too often, and so on. Breaking these mandates was considered a serious offense and punishable by being dropped from the club and banned from further breeding.

But there was also a very social aspect to the club. Shows were held in a variety of fancy locations, including estates, hotel ballrooms, and polo fields. There was a nice camaraderie among handlers and none of the stiff competitiveness that can be seen in the show world.

In 1962, Trudy Brown-Albrecht, Sally's sister-in-law, took over the presidency and was actively involved with the breed until her death in 1983. Because the club was so well focused, members became quite content to carry on without AKC recognition (other than being a part of the Miscellaneous Class, which allowed them to compete in obedience trials).

## Recognition by the AKC

In 1992, realizing the growing popularity of the Cavalier, the AKC decided to recognize the Cavalier in the Toy Group and invited the Cavalier King Charles Spaniel Club-United States, Inc., to become the breed's national parent club. You might say that the invitation set off fireworks among the club membership. Some members felt that they were quite capable of continuing as guardians of the breed on their own, while others believed that AKC recognition was now inevitable and who better to form the new parent club than long-standing devotees of the breed? The latter, a group of 12 people, accepted the AKC's invitation and formed the American Cavalier King Charles Spaniel Club, Inc. (ACKCSC), in 1993. On January 1, 1996, full recognition was

The Cavalier King Charles Spaniel became the 140th AKC breed in 1996.

granted and the Cavalier King Charles Spaniel became the 140th AKC breed.

## INFLUENTIAL PEOPLE AND MEMORABLE DOGS

Both national Cavalier King Charles Spaniel clubs still exist today. Some fanciers are members of both, while others have a strong affiliation with one or the other. The CKCSC-USA, commonly referred to as "The Old Club," is primarily composed of companion-animal devotees rather than breeders and handlers. However, the club does hold two to three dog shows throughout the country on a monthly basis in one of four regions. The CKCSC-USA has about 1,500 members and still maintains its own stud book, awards championships, and registers litters.

The ACKCSC is recognized by the AKC as the parent club. It's much smaller, and most of the approximately 400 members are breeders. There are approximately 33 "Member Clubs" across the country, primarily for the purpose of holding shows, health clinics, and educational programs. The standards developed by each club are slightly different.

In 1996, Ch. Ravenrush Gillespie, a Blenheim, won the first-ever Best in Show in an AKC-sanctioned show. The win took place in Little Rock, Arkansas, soon after Cavaliers were granted permission to participate in AKC shows. To add to the excitement of the newly recognized breed, in 1997 Ch. Partridge Wood Laughing Misdemeanor, a Ruby, won Best of Breed and a group placement at the

Producing exceptional Tricolors was a goal of the Sheeba Cavaliers breeding program.

Westminster Kennel Club Dog Show—the Super Bowl of dog shows in the United States.

## Holyoke Cavaliers

Many people have contributed to the continued development of the Cavalier King Charles Spaniel in the United States, but a few truly stand out. Originally involved with Cocker Spaniels, Bettina Sterling of Holyoke Cavaliers became smitten with the breed in the late 1970s but didn't actually acquire her first until 1987. Since she'd been showing her Cockers in obedience she was happy to show her Ruby

Cavalier in conformation and obedience when asked by the Cav's breeder. "Twenty-three years later, I'm still infatuated with this sweet and loving breed," Sterling says.

In the very first Holyoke litter, there was a beautiful Blenheim puppy named Ch. Holyoke Pistol Pete. He went Best Puppy in Show at the CKCSC-USA, at nine months. When Sterling became involved with the AKC parent club, Pete finished in three shows and won multiple Best of Breed placements. In her second litter, a black and tan female, Ch. Holyoke Black Magic, finished in five AKC shows. Magic and Pete produced Ch. Holyoke Infra Red, who finished rather quickly and went on to win multiple Best of Breed, Award of Merit, and group placements.

All in all, there have been more than 35 Holyoke Champions, and Sterling is heavily involved with the ACKCSC, holding numerous positions.

## Pinecrest Cavaliers

In 1990, Ted and Mary Grace Eubank bought their first Cavalier, Regis Chelsea. Mary Grace entered a few fun matches and was soon bitten by the show bug. Eventually, she bred Chelsea to Ch. Rutherford Elliot of Shagbark and produced her first champion, Ch. Pinecrest Santa's Pleasure. Over the years, Pinecrest became one of the top breeders of Cavaliers. Both Eubanks were affiliated with the CKCSC-USA club, and Mary Grace became one of the founding members of the ACKCSC. In 2008 there were 39 Cavaliers entered in the Westminster Kennel Club Dog Show. Ch. Pinecrest Orchard Hill Rock the Boat, "Rocky," won Best of Breed.

## Rattlebridge Cavaliers

Meredith Johnson-Snyder of Rattlebridge Cavaliers was also one of the founding members of the ACKCSC. Originally a German Shepherd breeder, Johnson-Snyder discovered the Cavalier in 1989 and became completely smitten. That year she purchased a finished Champion, Ch. Werrington Buoyancy, from Australia. "Bounce" became her foundation sire and produced some spectacular dogs when crossed with domestically bred lines.

Ch. Rattlebridge Masterpiece, "Rubens," stands out above the rest, as he won seven all-breed Best in Show titles. Sadly, Rubens died at an early age from heart arrhythmia, which is an irregular heartbeat. Johnson-Snyder was devastated by the loss of her special companion and vowed to help improve the overall health of Cavaliers through her breeding program.

## Sheeba Cavaliers

Karin Ostmann of Switzerland began breeding Cavaliers in her native land 27 years ago. "I fell in love with a painting of little land spaniels. I then saw the breed at the Crufts dog show and was totally smitten," Ostmann recalls and shares why she is so fond of the breed. "Cavaliers are the perfect companion dog. Sweet and gentle in nature, they can adapt to pretty much any environment. If an owner is an avid jogger, the Cavalier will have lots of fun running alongside. If you are older or for any reason have trouble getting around, the Cavalier is perfectly happy to keep you company. Cavaliers enjoy anyone willing to spend time with them. They love children and grandmas equally, are happy to run around in the snow or swim in the lake. It's amazing how many things you can enjoy with your Cavalier."

After moving to the Midwest, Ostmann continued her Sheeba breeding program. One of her original goals was to perfect Tricolors. Her successful endeavor came to fruition with BISS Ch. Sheeba Special Edition "James," who was the CKCSC-USA's top stud dog for three years: 1999, 2000, and 2003.

Ostmann fondly remembers two of her early favorites: "Moggy, the coolest dog ever and the mother to my top sire James. And my cute little man Ch. Telvara Top-Kopy was not just a great show dog but also a wonderful sire. Most of my dogs today go back to these two dogs in one way or another."

When asked about her concerns about the future of the breed. Ostmann is pragmatic. "I had to learn that I can only do so much and help as many people as possible to do the same. We are dealing with nature, and nature has strange ways to teach us many lessons. Medical research has given us amazing insight into our breed and there is so much more to learn. I think that there are many people out there who truly care about this breed, and as long as we are willing to learn and make the right decisions, the breed is in good hands."

## Laughing Cavaliers

Barbara Garnett-Wilson grew up in England and moved to the United States in 1965. Her original Cavalier was a gift, but later she imported her first show dog from

Cavalier breeders take breeding their dogs very seriously.

England in 1982. However, her foundation sire, Ch. Alansmere Rhett Butler, "Rebel," would initiate her true place in the Cavalier world. Rebel was the sire of many CKCSC-USA and Canadian champions. Another standout Laughing Cavalier, Ch. Partridge Laughing Misdemeanor, as previously mentioned, was the first of his breed to win Best of Breed and a Group Placement at the Westminster Kennel Club Dog Show in 1997. Many from the Laughing line have earned national and international championships.

Totally devoted to her breed, Garnett-Wilson has written several books about them. Her two most recent are large, impressive volumes: *The Cavalier King Charles Spaniel: In Fact and Fancy* and *The Cavalier King Charles Spaniel: A Tribute in Art.*

## Orchard Hill Cavaliers

After spending 20 years showing and breeding Shetland Sheepdogs, Erica Venier decided to downsize to a smaller breed, and Orchard Hill Cavaliers was founded. She has been in the breed for 14 years. Today, her daughter Rachel assists in the breeding program.

"We were attracted to the gay, fearless temperament, an athletic sporting spaniel in a portable toy package," Rachel says. "He's a dog that can easily go for an hour hike with you, but he's happy to rest on a pillow when in the house. This distinguishes him from some breeds that have the need to work deeply bred into them and tend to be more 'busy' if not given a job to do."

Orchard Hill began when Erica Venier contacted the late Joy Sims of Bramble

Cavaliers. "Her willingness to mentor and my ability to learn made a good combination," Venier explains. "Although I would have loved to buy a Blenheim bitch right from the start, I instead purchased a black and tan male because he was a dog of exceptional quality and I knew I would be able to prove my merit by showing him. Within a short time, my first Cavalier had earned three championships and became CKCSC-USA/Am./Can. Ch. Bramble Coco at Orchard Hill. I was then able to buy a lovely Blenheim bitch, our foundation bitch CKCSC-USA/Am./Can. Ch. Bramble Royal Heritage at Orchard Hill. She in turn produced three successful daughters known as "The Party Girls," who are in every pedigree we have today.

"By taking a seemingly slower route, I was actually able to progress more quickly by initially purchasing only the most healthy, beautiful dogs and breeding on from them. From our small breeding program we have produced all-breed Best in Show, National Specialty, and Specialty Winners, including the Tricolor bitch CKCSC-USA/AKC Ch. Orchard Hill Never Grow Up and the Blenheim bitch CKCSC-USA/Am./Can. Ch. Orchard Hill Easier Said. Our newest youngster is the Specialty-winning Blenheim bitch Ch. Orchard Hill Ingenue, J.W."

Mother and daughter intentionally keep the breeding program at Orchard Hill small and currently limit themselves to Blenheims and tricolors. Their goals are to produce typey, healthy Cavaliers that will succeed as loving pets and in the show ring as well.

As with other devoted breeders, the Veniers do have concerns about their beloved breed. "The current popularity of Cavaliers is a great cause for concern among reputable breeders," Erica Venier says. "Whenever a breed becomes wildly popular, that breed suffers by being bred indiscriminately by nefarious characters simply for financial gain. I firmly believe that the goal of a committed breeder must always be to produce a better animal than the parents and to 'First, do no harm.' As reputable breeders, we know that we are reaching this goal when we are recognized by our peers in the show ring. Breeding typey, healthy dogs is a huge responsibility that should never be taken lightly. After all, our Cavaliers are depending on us."

# PART I

# PUPPYHOOD

# CHAPTER 1

# IS THE CAVALIER RIGHT FOR YOU?

*Happiness is a warm puppy.*
—Charles M. Schulz

My dogs love people and seem convinced that our guests have arrived solely to visit them. So I'm accustomed to the company of warm, friendly dogs. And yet even I was taken by surprise the first time I entered the home of a Cavalier breeder. She had six of these little spaniels of varying age ranges, from two adolescents to a senior matriarch.

The entire crew greeted me with unsurpassed enthusiasm and gusto. No sooner did I sit down than all six leapt into my lap without a moment's hesitation—hugging, wiggling, and kissing. Try as I might, I'm not sure that my writing skills allow me to adequately describe the greeting. But suffice it to say, it left an impression and was a true testament to the outgoing nature of the breed.

Soon after my visit with the breeder, I started rally (a newer form of obedience competition) class with one of my mixes, Junior. I quickly spotted Emma, a Blenheim Cavalier. She was certainly cute—I have yet to meet a Cav who isn't—but what impressed me the most was her incessantly wagging tail. I don't think that

long, silky floor duster stopped once, whether she was working the course, waiting her turn, or standing by while her person chatted with another student.

## BREED CHARACTERISTICS

The constantly wagging tail is a signature trait among Cavaliers. They are without question happy little dogs and very adaptable too. They can enjoy life in a city apartment, a small home in the suburbs, or the posh accommodations and grounds of a country estate. They're also sensitive enough to make excellent pets for seniors and hardy enough to play with children, plus they adjust to every age group in between. Unlike many of the other toy breeds, Cavaliers are not big barkers and don't tend to be yappy. Easygoing and willing to please, they're a good choice for both experienced and novice dog owners.

Regardless of their family situation, Cavaliers have one stringent requirement. They must be given plenty of attention. After all, these dogs were bred specifically to be companions. To deny them human companionship is disallowing them to fulfill their destiny. For those who work full-time away from home and party hardy after hours, the Cavalier is not a suitable choice. (Actually, if you live this kind of lifestyle, you should consider another type of pet altogether.) Nor is the breed a viable option for those who prefer a more independent or less devoted dog. And Cavaliers should certainly not be kept outdoors! Underfoot or in a warm lap is where they are meant to be.

Couples and parents with full-time jobs outside the home need to give ample consideration to meeting a puppy's needs before adopting one. You can't expect a young pup to spend ten hours alone, five days a week, and become a well-adjusted dog. So who will visit during the day while you're at work? Do you have a friend, neighbor, or relative you can count on each and every day? If you have children, do they come home right after school or are they off to soccer games, ballet classes, and other activities?

A pet sitter may be the best option during the workday because a puppy should go out at least twice: at lunchtime and then again in mid-afternoon. I've used sitters for more than 20 years and always line one up if I plan to be out of the house for more than four hours. I also employ live-in sitters when we travel. I'm most comfortable with this arrangement as it's the professional pet sitter's job to care for pets and she takes the responsibility seriously. (Note: Because the Cavalier

Cavaliers must be given plenty of attention.

is so people-oriented, some breeders will not sell their pups to those who are not home at least part of the day.)

When I'm at home, I'm a great napper and find having my dogs with or near me especially restful. So when we adopted our first small breed, Topo Gigio (a mix who looks suspiciously like a spaniel), my only prerequisite was that he be strong and sturdy enough to jump up on the bed or couch—a feat that can be either impossible or dangerous, with high risk of injury, for many small breeds. I'm happy to report the Cavalier, largest of the toy breeds, is quite capable of joining you at naptime.

I don't allow our dogs to spend the night in the bedroom except for an occasional treat and certainly not all five at once. (Okay, truth be told, I have been known to give in during a thunder and lightning storm. But usually the dogs have their own beds in different areas of the house.) However, as my favorite trainer, Linda, once said to me, "Your house, your rules." So if having your dog sleep with you is your preference, that's fine too. And

there's probably no better bed buddy than the comforter spaniel. Evelyn says of her Cavalier, Hope, "I think she has me well trained. I said I would never let a dog sleep with me. She sleeps every night curled against my side. I can't even explain how that happened."

Jenn, who owns three Cavaliers, elaborates on the breed's devotion and sleeping habits by sharing some stories about Cooper. "If you want to feel needed, this is the perfect breed. Mr. Roo (one of Cooper's many nicknames) will do anything to be with me. If he could go everywhere I go, he would be content. He sleeps every night by my side, with either his paw or his head on me, so I won't disappear in the night. He follows me from room to room. This may sound off-putting to many, but there is nothing quite like the greeting I get from Roo when I come home. He assaults me, kissing me, barking with enthusiasm. He reattaches himself. He's about the most loyal dog you could ever want to meet."

## APPEARANCE

The Cavalier has a special look among spaniels. His ear set, snout, and large round eyes give the breed a unique gentle expression. He also has a luxurious silky coat, elegant long, feathered ears, and a plumed tail.

If you are interested in a more detailed description of the Cavalier's structure and appearance, you can refer to the official standard of the Cavalier King Charles Spaniel as it appears on the parent club's website (www.ackcsc.org).

## General Body Structure

Cavaliers are solid, longish, and relatively low to the ground. They also have a long natural tail with plenty of feathering.

## Sleeping With Dogs

There is nothing wrong with having your dog sleep on the bed with you if all is going well—that is, if he is in a balanced and stable frame of mind and respects you as his leader. However, if you're experiencing dominance or aggression issues, such as your dog demonstrating possessiveness when you move in the bed or try to leave or get in it, then human bed privileges must be taken away from him immediately. Dogs, being pack animals, always sleep together, so it's a natural thing for them to do. People sleeping with their companion dogs is fine as long as there are no behavioral issues.

## Size

A well-bred Cavalier should stand between 12 and 13 inches (30.5 and 33 cm) at the withers (top of shoulders) and weigh 13 to 18 pounds (6 to 8 kg), although it's not uncommon to see well-proportioned members of the breed who are larger or smaller.

## Head and Neck

The head should be proportionate to the body, not too big, not too small. In a mature dog, male or female, the head should have the appearance of being flat between the ears. In reality, it's not; it will have a slight rounding if you feel it, but because of the fur and the "devil horns" of fur that often appear right next to the ears, it looks flat.

There should be the appearance of an elegant but not really long neck. Many of the dogs can look "stuffy," meaning their head seems to go right into their shoulders. You want to see a neck, although most people

The breed's long, silky, feathered ears are a distinguishing feature.

rarely think about it, and there is no desired measurement.

## Ears

The breed's long, silky, feathered ears are a distinguishing feature. They certainly contribute to the Cavalier's overall "adorable" presence.

## Eyes

The eyes are the hallmark of the breed. They should be large, round, and dark brown, giving a "melting" expression, meaning they melt *you*! They should not be light brown in color or have any white. They also have darkened pigment around the eye, giving the impression that the dog is wearing mascara.

## Feet

When I've spotted Cavaliers around town, I've often wondered about their fuzzy bedroom slipper feet (untrimmed paws). But as I learned in researching the history of the breed, these dogs are expected to have a natural appearance, which specifically means no trimming or clipping except for the hair beneath their toes on the underside of the paws.

## Coat

The coat should be soft and silky, not curly. Wavy is acceptable. An undercoat is also found in this breed, but it is not dense and is usually seasonal. Most Cavaliers "blow coat" (shed heavily) about once a year. Older dogs who have been spayed or neutered can (but do not always) develop a very fluffy coat.

Cavaliers are slow to mature—puppyhood can last two or more years.

## Colors

The Cavalier is bred in four striking colors: Blenheim, Black and Tan, Ruby, and Tricolor. The Blenheims, the most popular coloration, have patches of chestnut red set on a white background. Some have a diamond-shaped red mark on the top of their heads. Referred to as the "Blenheim spot," it's considered a desirable marking in this color variety. Black and Tans are solid black with tan points (circles of color) above their eyes, as well as splashes of tan on their cheeks, inside of the ears, chest, legs, and beneath their tails. The Ruby is a solid chestnut red. Tricolors are white with black markings, plus tan points above the eyes and bits of tan on the cheeks, inside the ears, and under the tail.

## SUITABILITY AS A PET

A well-bred Cavalier loves everyone, young and old. When Dr. Rafael Pajaro, a board certified internist, decided to open a private practice he aspired to have a family dog he could bring to the office. The doctor's wife and office manager, Pam, explains,

"We wanted to build a practice where people come to a welcoming and relaxing environment. We feel great medicine can be provided in a home-like atmosphere." Indeed, Pajaro Medical, with its comfortable, welcoming decor, has the feel of home, not a sterile medical office.

And how does Odie, the Pajaros' two-year-old

Black and Tan Cavalier fit in? "He's our official greeter and therapy dog," Dr. Pajaro says. "He lessens our patients' fears and anxieties about seeing a doctor. Everyone loves him." It's not surprising—who could resist such an adorable welcoming committee of one? "When a patient arrives, Odie runs up to him wagging his tail, smiling, and clamoring to get attention first," Pam says. The Pajaros specifically selected a Cavalier as their official office greeter. "We first fell in love with the breed on our honeymoon in Italy. They were house pets in the Palazzo where we stayed. They were amazing and we never forgot them," Pam recalls fondly. "After

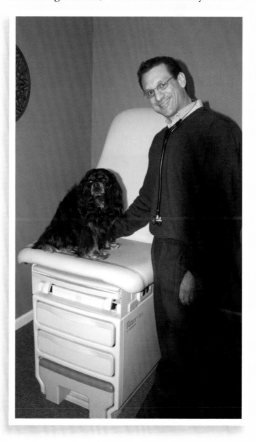

Dr. Pajaro and official patient greeter and therapy dog, Odie.

much research, we also decided on a Cavalier based on a recommendation from a dog trainer after outlining our needs for the office," Dr. Pajaro adds.

And how does Odie like his job? "There are office pets who sleep in the corner and then there is Odie, who makes each person who walks through the door feel special. He loves everyone," Pam says, then adds with a laugh, "I think most of our patients come to see Odie."

## Environment
One of the Cavalier's most appealing traits is his ability to adapt to various lifestyles. These portable toy dogs can enjoy life in a small urban apartment, a home in the suburbs, or the rambling mansion and grounds of a country estate. They are just as happy to parade down Park Avenue in New York City as to wait with you at the bus stop to walk your children home from school along a country lane.

## Exercise
Cavaliers don't require as much exercise as their larger spaniel cousins, but they do benefit from a daily walk and playtime in the yard. A moderate amount of exercise would best describe their needs.

## Grooming Requirements
Cavaliers are relatively easy to groom because they do not require trimming. However, their silky coats do shed considerably, and they are prone to getting mats under the ears and legs if not groomed thoroughly on a regular basis. Brushing and combing a Cavalier several times a week would be a good investment of your time

## Training Tidbit

Although intelligent and easy to train, Cavaliers are so friendly, inquisitive, and independent-minded that they should never be allowed off leash unless they're in a securely fenced area.

to maintain his beautiful coat—but a quick once-over every day would be even better.

## Health Issues
Unfortunately, Cavaliers are genetically susceptible to several health problems, including juvenile cataracts (loss of transparency in the eye lens), syringomyelia (malformation of the skull), mitral valve dysplasia (heart defect), patellar luxation (kneecap slides out of place), and hip dysplasia (abnormal development of the hip joint.) Those devoted to the breed are working diligently to correct these problems.

## Hunting Instinct
Cavaliers are often described as having a big-dog personality in a small-dog package.

Because of their sporting spaniel heritage, they are curious and athletic dogs. That hunting instinct can be channeled in numerous ways, from playing fetch and flying disc to competing in obedience, agility, tracking, and other canine sports—or just in creating their own fun.

Karen reports

### Want to Know More?
Cavalier health issues will be explained in more detail in Chapter 8: Cavalier Health and Wellness.

Because of their affinity for people, Cavaliers excel as canine therapists.

that her Cavs, Emma and Gracie, are up for just about anything. "They love the snow. They're both out there chasing each other around and rubbing their faces in it. They come in with snowballs all over them— sometimes larger than golf balls. You can hear them clicking on the tile floor. Sometimes Emma can barely walk but she can't get enough of the snow. That is what I love about the breed; they are little dogs who are not afraid to do anything. They are a big dog in a little package. They will hike, run on the beach, play in the snow, and not be afraid to do it."

## Trainability

Perhaps not the Einsteins of the canine world, Cavaliers are nevertheless bright little dogs.

Add in their desire to please and the fact that they are highly food motivated and you have a dog who is relatively easy to train. However, because they are friendly and inquisitive and seem to have no sense of fear, they will eagerly run after a jogger to say hello or chase a squirrel across the street, regardless of traffic. They're not a dog to turn on a dime when called and will often turn a deaf ear until they're ready to come back. Hence, breeders advise that Cavaliers should never be allowed off leash unless they're in a securely fenced area.

Alison, who owns two Welsh Springer Spaniels and a Blenheim Cavalier, Tizzy, is convinced that the Cav is bright enough to learn from observation. She shares some around-the-house training advice: "You must, must, MUST take care in what your puppy sees—either what other dogs do, or what YOU might be doing. He will immediately sop up the information and use it, not necessarily well. I had to keep the big dogs away from the windows when I had fence repair and clearing to do lest they get the idea to dig at the fence line.

I recently took advantage of the thawed ground to go after some old tree roots that, with the ground settling around them over time, had gotten in the way of mowing. I dug at them with a wrecking bar, cultivator, and saw, and forgot to tuck my Cavalier away in the house. I was working furiously at the roots and looked up to see Tizzy working just as furiously on a hole of his own, with his little fuzzy paws now firmly packed with clay and mud and a joyously proud look on his face, so pleased he could "help" too!"

## Sociability

Because of their true affinity for people, Cavaliers excel as canine therapists. And there are many opportunities these days for people and their pets to participate in pet therapy—a very worthwhile endeavor. For example, some Cavalier owners enjoy visiting patients in nursing homes and hospitals, while others prefer participating in *Children Reading to Dogs* programs that take place in schools and libraries. I've observed the latter myself, and it's quite touching.

### With Children

Cavaliers are wonderful with children, whether they be youngsters within their own families or new acquaintances. The breed is small enough to be a nice-sized companion yet sturdy enough to be a true playmate.

Cavaliers enjoy the company of other dogs. Best friends Slim and Emma.

Frankly, I think that Cavaliers and children are kindred spirits.

Jody, who has two Cavaliers and is very active in agility, shares this story. "They are incredible with kids. This past weekend we were at an event and a little girl was practically mauling Chevy. While I could tell he would rather she sit politely, he tolerated all of her attention." And I'm willing to bet he was smiling and wagging his tail all the while. (Note: Some breeders will not sell their pups to families with children younger than six, as inquisitive little hands may not yet fully understand that a Cavalier is not a toy.)

## With Other Dogs

Cavaliers seem to especially like the company of other Cavaliers. As a whole, the breed gets along very well with all types of dogs. In fact, Karen, who owns Emma, the Blenheim from Junior's rally class, adopted her to keep Slim, her Golden Retriever, company. "I was looking for a companion for Slim, who doesn't really like other dogs," Karen says. "I wanted a small breed that would act like a big dog but in a small body.

When I was researching, I read that Cavaliers get along with other dogs and are submissive, so I thought that Slim would be okay with one." And it worked out very well as the then nine-year-old Golden accepted Emma very quickly. A few years later, Gracie, another Blenheim, joined the family. "They all get along really great," Karen reports. "Slim now has company instead of being alone when I go out. They have also kept him acting young. He is still active at 14 years old. He's very gentle with them, and they all like to cuddle up with each other."

## With Other Pets

Cavaliers usually do well with other pets. Quite a few share their homes with cats. Emma is especially kind to various little creatures.

> ## Multi-Dog Tip
> Very social, a Cavalier will benefit from the company of another dog—ideally another Cavalier!

Karen says "Emma loves all animals and is very gentle with them. I remember one day we were outside and a bird flew into the glass on our door. Emma went over to the bird and was kissing it and finally the bird got back up and eventually flew away. She was so gentle with it—like she was helping it. Now she is always looking for birds to befriend. She also likes to play with baby bunnies."

Emma is probably an exception when it comes to befriending wild critters. Gracie is more likely to dispatch them, which shows that Cavaliers have differing degrees of hunting instinct and prey drive (desire to chase). Many Cavs can be just as birdy as their larger spaniel cousins and go crazy when they see backyard birds. Chipmunks, mice, squirrels, and other small, furry animals will also cause their prey drive to kick in.

I often read books advising owners of sporting dogs not to have pet birds. But I've found that my gang, with minimal training, learns to respect my parakeets and finches and keep their distance. However, I certainly wouldn't push my luck and let the birds out of their cages when the dogs are nearby.

My husband has an Amazon parrot, Loro, who once nipped Chelsea, our first spaniel, on the nose when she put her paws up on his cage. She learned her lesson and never went near him again. So I think that with a little training and common sense a Cavalier and birds could coexist peacefully.

# CHAPTER 2

# FINDING AND PREPPING FOR YOUR CAVALIER PUPPY

I f there's anything cuter than a Cavalier King Charles Spaniel puppy, I don't know what it is. Those little round expressive faces and soft, fluffy ears are just irresistible. And I don't think you could ask for a more attractive color selection.

Bringing a puppy into the family is a large undertaking, with inherent responsibilities not the least of which is the time commitment. To raise a happy, well-trained, well-adjusted dog takes time. There is no way around it. But the joy of watching your pup grow up is immeasurable.

People often ask me how I manage a multi-pet household. My answer is always the same: "The enjoyment has to outweigh the work." For me it does. But if that simple formula is not true, there really is no point in sharing our homes with companion animals. We owe it to them to provide the best life possible.

## THE PUPPY OPTION

I love the "firsts" with a puppy. The first time he climbs the stairs, jumps into the car on his own, or performs a new command and is so obviously proud of himself. The true pleasure of raising a dog from puppyhood is establishing your own house rules and having

him fold into your lifestyle. Some folks prefer to have their dogs live on the first floor, while others allow them the run of the house. Many families invite their companions to join them on the furniture; others insist that all four paws remain on the floor. As long as the rules are fair and consistent, you can come up with whatever you like and your Cavalier pup will quickly adapt.

My dogs and I are up at 6:30 am. We head outside for a romp in our 2-acre fenced yard. Then we go back to the house to play with toys. I always make sure that they have some time to visit with my husband before he leaves for his office. Then I prepare breakfast for everyone. Afterwards, the dogs take their morning nap in the family room and kitchen and I walk up to my home office on the second floor. By late morning, I take a break and we head outside again. At noon, Lily, our spaniel puppy, has lunch and the older dogs have their snacks. Time for another nap, and so it goes throughout the day.

If I'm lounging around and can keep an eye on the dogs, they have the run of the house. Or depending on the weather and my schedule, I may pop them into the car while I run errands or go for a walk in the neighborhood or a local

The true pleasure of raising a dog from puppyhood is establishing your own house rules and having him fold into your lifestyle.

park. Usually I try to include everyone, but sometimes they take turns accompanying me.

Dogs thrive on routine, and having one is also very helpful when we travel and my live-in pet sitter takes over.

## FINDING YOUR PUPPY

Once you have decided that you are interested in a Cavalier, your work begins with finding an experienced and reputable breeder. Searching for a good breeder is important with any purebred dog but especially so with Cavaliers because of their genetic health issues. That's not to say that you can't find a healthy puppy who will live a full long life, but dealing with a Cavalier breeder who focuses on health, longevity, and temperament is essential.

So let's talk about breeders for a moment because not all breeders are created equal. There are many ways to find dogs these days, and I can attest to the fact that there are some truly beautiful puppies for sale on websites. But an attractive website does not ensure a responsible breeder. In fact, there are quite a few categories of breeders and breeding facilities. If you're reading this book, you are obviously a devoted dog lover who wants what's best for your pet. We'd like to think that all people in the dog world feel the same way, but sadly it's just not true.

### Backyard Breeders

Backyard breeders just want to sell puppies, perhaps mating their family female with a neighbor's male. They are not familiar with the various lines of dogs and probably not aware of or concerned about genetic health screenings. They may enjoy the process of breeding and selling dogs but rarely or never become involved in the fancy or with the show world or breed clubs. As a result, they could well be breeding dogs that should not be bred to one another, which could lead to puppies with health and behavioral problems.

To be fair, some backyard breeders probably really do love dogs, treat them well, and raise the pups in their homes. But there are others who are just trying to make some extra income and may keep these adorable housedogs in overcrowded, unsanitary kennels. You should easily be able to spot the different types of backyard breeders. But always remember, breeding dogs should never be taken lightly.

There are far too many unplanned canine pregnancies leading to a high percentage of dogs being euthanized. Breeding should be left to those devoted to the process and interested in the lives of all the dogs they breed.

## Puppy Mills

Puppy mills are large-scale operations that raise all breeds of puppies in deplorable conditions, like chickens literally housed in coops stacked on top of one another. They may have wonderful websites, but do your research! Puppy mill pups are very likely to have health and behavior problems. Avoid puppy mills at all costs. (Note: Some folks intentionally adopt puppy mill survivors. I greatly admire these people. But you need to be fully prepared for the challenges and possible heartache you may face.)

Experienced and responsible breeders are involved with dogs to perfect their breed and leave a legacy.

## Commercial Breeders

Commercial breeders usually do not specialize in a specific breed. They sell to brokers and in quantity to fill demand. Their involvement with dogs is all about business.

## Hobby Breeders

Hobby breeders are interested in the betterment of a specific breed. They are devoted to their dogs and seek mentors with more experience. They show and trial their dogs to demonstrate their worth. As a group, hobby breeders are very concerned with health and temperament issues and have appropriate genetic health tests performed.

## Experienced Breeders

Experienced and responsible breeders are involved with dogs to perfect their breed and leave a legacy. They are usually very involved with their breed club and act as mentors to newcomers by writing books and articles and perhaps sponsoring seminars. These breeders are in the dog fancy for the long haul and have been breeding for decades. They are very strict about placing their puppies and follow the development of each pup over the years. These are the folks who want to receive your Christmas card with one of their pups front and center in the family photo.

## By the Numbers

Reputable Cavalier King Charles Spaniel breeders usually don't release their pups until they are 12 weeks of age.

## How to Find the Right Breeder

To find a reputable breeder, start by visiting the two national club websites: Cavalier King Charles Spaniel Club-USA (www.ckcsc. org) and the American Cavalier King Charles Spaniel Club (www.ackcsc.org). Each has a list of reputable breeders who do everything possible to breed healthy, structurally sound pups with good temperaments by carefully researching various lines, having genetic health tests performed on their breeding dogs, and evaluating the pups in each litter. There are very few guarantees in life, but these measures greatly place the odds in your pup's favor for a long and healthy life.

You will realize immediately whether you have found a reputable breeder by the questions asked of you. If you feel the breeder's questions are akin to those for adopting a child, you will know that this breeder has the best interests of the pups at heart. You're off to a good start.

- Your potential breeder will probably begin by asking whether you live in a house, apartment, or condo, and whether you own or rent. If you rent, the breeder will probably request written permission from your landlord allowing you to have a dog. Then you will be asked whether someone will be home a good portion of the day. If you head to an office, the breeder will want to know what arrangements will be made to have someone visit the puppy and allow him outside for potty breaks. Because Cavaliers are so people oriented, having enough human interaction is especially important. In fact, some breeders will not sell to prospective puppy buyers who work full time outside the home.
- The breeder will want to know whether you have a fenced yard or are planning to install a fence. If your answer to both is no, he or she will ask what type of exercise plan you have in

Finding a breeder who focuses on health, longevity, and temperament is essential.

mind for the pup. (Note: Having a fenced yard does not mean that your pup will self-exercise. It merely provides a safe environment for you and your Cavalier to play.)

- The breeder will most likely ask about your history with pets. Have you owned other dogs and for how long? Have you raised a puppy before, and do you currently have another dog or other types of pets currently in the home?

- The breeder will certainly want to know whether you have children and how many and how old they are. Chances are that if you live locally, your entire family will be invited over to see how they interact with the breeder's dogs.

- Some breeders will inquire whether anyone in the household smokes because there have been studies proving secondhand smoke can affect dogs. All will ask where your dog will be kept when you're not at home.

- Sometime during the conversation the breeder will ask why you have chosen the Cavalier King Charles Spaniel and also whether you prefer a male or female or a particular coat color.

Now it's your turn. You have every right to ask the breeder your own list of questions.

- I'd begin by asking how long the breeder has been breeding Cavaliers and whether he or she participates in the various dog sports and has titles on any of the dogs.

## The Rule of Sevens

Responsible breeders practice the Rule of Sevens, exposing the pups to a minimum of seven different items in seven categories before they are seven weeks old:

1. Seven surfaces: grass, tile, carpet, wood floors, cement, sand, dirt, etc.
2. Seven different types of bowls and plates: ceramic, stainless steel, plastic, glass, flat kitchen plate, aluminum plate, paper disposable plate, etc.
3. Seven people
4. Seven different environments: the yard, car, bank, library, vet's office, book store, neighbor's home, etc. (Obviously not a dog park, large chain pet store, or any other location where they could pick up doggy diseases prior to being fully vaccinated. And it's best to keep your puppy off the floor when visiting stores and other buildings that allow dogs.)
5. Seven different toys: rubber, fabric, plush, hard plastic, etc.
6. Seven different sounds: music, television, bells, sirens, vacuum, etc.
7. Seven types of doggy attire: collars, harnesses, sweaters, leashes made of different materials, etc.

---

- I'd also want to know how long some of the breeder's dogs have lived, say perhaps the grandparents and great grandparents of the next litter of pups.
- Then, and probably most important, I would ask whether the following genetic health tests have been performed on the dogs used for breeding, as well as the stud dog's family:
  - heart tested by a board-certified cardiologist
  - eyes cleared by a board-certified ophthalmologist
  - patellar luxation checked by a regular vet or orthopedic vet
  - hips cleared by the Orthopedic Foundation for Animals (OFA) for hip dysplasia

Assuming that all of these tests have been routinely performed, I'd request a copy of the most recent test results.

I think you should feel some sense of chemistry with the breeder because you will probably have a relationship with that person for the lifetime of your dog. You should always feel comfortable reaching out to your breeder if you have concerns about your Cavalier's health and/or behavior.

### Talk to the Breeder

Here's what Diane, who has been breeding Cavaliers for 15 years, has to say on the subject: "I think the most important thing I want people to realize is we work very hard at this. We are human and not perfect, neither are the dogs. We really want everyone to have that perfect puppy, but some things are just out of our control.

"I urge anyone who gets a dog from a reputable breeder to stay in touch with that breeder. We really want to hear from you. We want to know about the antics of your dog, the successes, the failures, the happiness, and the heartbreak. We care about each and every puppy we have ever bred throughout his life.

It's important to share health information with us so that we are more informed to make decisions about future breedings.

"In my experience, I think people who seek out this breed are good hardworking people, just like us, and we all want the same thing: to own and raise sound, well-balanced, happy dogs. Talk to your breeder."

## PICKING THE PERFECT PUPPY

When it comes time to select your puppy, be aware that some breeders will insist on picking the perfect puppy for your family. If you have the option of choosing your own pup, observe the energy levels of all of the individuals in the litter. There are four energy levels: low, medium, high, and very high. You should always pick a puppy with the same energy level as you and your family, or one energy level lower.

As you observe the litter, look for the pup with the most balanced personality. There will probably be a range of temperaments, from the most dominant to the most submissive. Look for the puppy who is active but will also sit down and rest at times. Many people make the mistake of falling for the shy and withdrawn (most submissive) pup because they feel the urge to "rescue" him. This puppy

As you observe the litter, look for the pup with the most balanced personality.

may not be the best choice for a first-time, inexperienced owner, as he will need a lot of confidence building and not an owner who feels sorry for him.

On the other hand, you may be attracted to the pup who is running around and trying to dominate all the others by pushing them out of the way because he appears to be the most fun loving and spirited. This may be the alpha puppy. So unless you are a balanced, calm, confident leader yourself, avoid this little spitfire, because no matter how cute, tiny, and cuddly he is, if you don't take on the role of leader from the get-go, the puppy will try to seize control of the pack, causing problems down the road.

## Show-Quality Versus Pet-Quality Dogs

Because Cavaliers are slow to mature, it can be difficult to determine show potential in young pups. Generally speaking, however, these are the dogs whose attributes closely fit the breed standard and show the greatest potential to win at dog shows. Pet-quality puppies fall short in this regard for reasons such as an incorrect bite or markings that do not conform to the standard. For example, in the Blenheim, too much white or ticking (freckles) would be considered faults. However, pet-quality pups are just as wonderful as their show-quality siblings—usually only the very experienced eye can tell the difference.

### Puppy Prices

And how much can you expect to pay for a Cavalier puppy? In metropolitan areas in

Before bringing your new Cavalier home, puppy-proof your home and yard to ensure his safety.

and around New York City, Boston, Chicago, and so on, $3,000 is a common price. As with many things in life, the cost of purchasing a Cavalier pup is based on supply and demand. For starters, Cavaliers have small litters—three or four pups on average. In addition, puppy prices help reputable breeders recover the costs of ongoing health tests and campaigning their dogs in the show ring throughout the country.

Beware of the bargain-priced puppy, which in the Cavalier breed would be less than $1,000. Chances are breeders of these pups are not performing the health tests that are so important in this breed. You may save money with your purchase but could accrue a lot of veterinary costs, as well as heartbreak, down the line.

In many breeds there is a different price range for show- and pet-quality puppies. Pet-quality puppies are equally wonderful dogs but may not have what it takes to win in the show ring. Because Cavaliers develop more slowly than other breeds, it's almost impossible to ascertain whether they are show quality at 12 weeks. So the price is the same. Breeders will sometimes hold on to pups who they think have show potential and later sell them only to experienced show homes.

## BEFORE PUPPY COMES HOME

Assuming that you have a month or so to prepare for the arrival of your new puppy, it's time to get ready. The first thing I do is order pet health insurance. Generally, if you opt for a wellness plan, it will cover accidents and wellness exams the next day. But there is usually a 30-day waiting period on illness. That's why I like to order plans in advance.

## Puppy-Proofing the Home and Yard

Next I inspect the yard to make sure that there are no escape routes in our fence, and I walk through the house to see whether there are any exposed lamp cords or knickknacks on tables the pup could knock over or steal. Decorative pillows may need to be placed out of reach for awhile. The same goes for plants. In short, imagine all of the possible trouble your pup could get into and avoid temptations by removing or covering them up.

Puppies are naturally curious, with extremely quick reflexes. An inadvertently misplaced paper clip or hair tie or an electric bill that floated to the floor will be found interesting to your puppy and likely end up in his mouth. Be extraordinarily attentive and observant when your new pup comes home. Do not leave the puppy unsupervised to explore on his own.

## Setting Up a Schedule

Because dogs thrive on routine, you should set up a schedule for your puppy as soon as he joins the family. Plan what time he will be fed, go outside to potty, exercise, play, and sleep, and make sure all family members will stick to the schedule and be responsible for these chores every day. Doing this will help your Cavalier adapt to his new home and family and facilitates housetraining as well.

## Supplies

I've often felt sympathetic toward parents of young children as they head to the beach laden with all of their gear. Though I must tell you, I don't look much different packing for a trip with the dogs! My list consists of food, dog dishes, collars, halters, leashes, beds, crates, and toys. In short, these are all of the items you will need whether you're home or taking a vacation with your pets. Best to start shopping before your puppy arrives.

### Bed or Cushion

You'll also want to purchase an appropriately sized dog bed or crate cushion. I prefer those made of sturdy fabric without zippers. When Topo was young, he was so small that the puppy bed we already had was too large for him. My husband solved the problem by buying him a brand new powder-blue cat bed. It was perfect. A Cavalier pup is about the same size as a kitten, so look in both the dog and cat sections of the pet store during your shopping spree.

### Clothing

Some folks enjoy dressing up their dogs just for fun. I view canine clothing in a more practical way. My dogs have raincoats for heavy rain and winter

Squeeze cheese or pet-manufactured liver, chicken, peanut butter, or mint-flavored treats that can also be squeezed from a can onto your hand make a quick and easy training reward for a puppy. Just a dab is all you need.

coats for cold, snowy days. Believe me, with five dogs, this type of clothing really helps with cleanup afterward.

Because Cavaliers have quite a bit of feathering and easily accumulate snowballs, you might want take a tip from Pat. "When it snows, Penny shows her pluckiness by romping through snow deeper than she is tall. However, she is soon full of ice balls, which are not easy to remove. Solution: boots and a sweat suit with arms in it. When I put the boots on, she lies on her back with all four paws in the air until I bribe her off the couch with a treat. She forgets that she has the boots on and looks like a little clown flapping her feet."

We live in the Northeast and brought Topo home in February. When I took him outside to our large enclosed yard on his first day, I was very excited. We didn't have snow, but I wasn't sure whether he'd ever seen grass and was eager to watch him explore. I put the little 3-pound (1.5-kg) chocolate ball of fluff on the ground and he started to shiver. Exploring was the last thing on his mind—he wanted to get back into the warm house. So later in the day I set off to the pet store to buy him a winter coat. He's outgrown it now, of course, but has a new one. Do keep the time of year in mind. If you're picking your puppy up in a cold or very rainy

season, it's probably best to plan ahead and purchase any necessary clothing in advance.

### Collar/Harness

There are many types of collars available on the market today. A young puppy (12 to 24 weeks) would be better off in a well-fitted harness. A buckle collar also may be used to get your pup accustomed to the feeling of something around his neck. When he gets older, you can switch to a collar and leash for walks, or if you prefer you can stick with the harness.

If you decide to use a collar, check it weekly to make sure it's not getting too tight because puppies at this age grow rapidly. I prefer an adjustable nylon snap buckle collar for this reason. Harnesses can be the same type—an adjustable nylon buckle style. Also, there are now some wonderful vest-type harnesses with leash buckles on them. Whichever you choose, make sure it fits properly. Too loose and your dog can wriggle out of it, too tight and it can rub on the skin and cause sores.

### Crate

Next I head to the basement to dust off an appropriate-sized crate. This box-like structure, which represents a den to a dog, can be made of plastic, wire, or fabric, with a door that could be locked if necessary.

**Plastic:** Plastic crates are durable and easy to keep clean. They have a wire door and usually a few air holes covered with wire to provide adequate circulation. These are the type used by airlines to transport pets and are very popular at home since they are affordably priced. However, they can lend themselves to destructive chewing by young pups or adult dogs who have not been previously exposed to crates.

**Wire:** Wire crates are made completely of wire. They break down for transport and are easily carried. They also give the dog the most visibility. This can be both an advantage and a disadvantage. A mellow Cavalier will be just fine in a wire crate. For the very active individual who needs his down time, too much visibility may translate into too much stimulation. A crate that blocks off more household activities would be a better choice.

**Soft-Sided:** Soft-sided crates are made of fabric. They are lightweight and break down easily. They're excellent for vacation travel. However, they should be used only for crate-trained adult dogs. Puppies and adults unaccustomed to crates can chew them.

Most trainers recommend the use of a crate because it helps the housetraining process tremendously and serves as a safe haven when your pup cannot be supervised. If you have never owned a dog before, you may be uncomfortable with the idea of crating. You might even think that it's cruel. But actually a dog is a den animal and, when properly introduced to a crate, will appreciate its den-like features. However, no dog should be crated for hours on end. The crate is meant to provide security for the pup and peace of mind for you—it is not a prison.

The crate should be set up in an area where the family frequently gathers. It should never be in an isolated room like the basement. Always remember a dog is a pack animal. He needs to be with the group. Also, many breeders expose their puppies to crates (and exercise pens) early on so that the pups accept them easily in their new homes.

Let's not forget car travel. Most dogs love riding in the car but should always be safely secured. A crate is a favorite choice. For

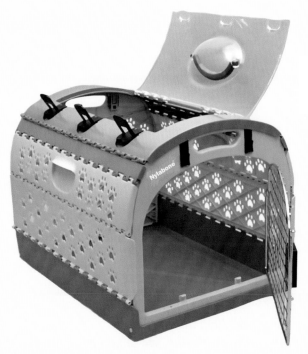

The crate serves as a safe haven when your puppy can't be supervised.

the Cavalier, a doggy car seat is also quite appropriate. Or if you prefer, you can use a harness with a leash attached to the seat belt. All of these options will keep your pup from being thrown around the car in case of an accident.

## Exercise Pen

With my older dogs, I relied solely on crate training, but these days I like to use both a crate and an exercise pen, or ex-pen. An ex-pen is a wire metal pen that is set up in the house or outdoors. It gives the pup a little more freedom but still keeps him out of harm's way when you're not available to keep a constant eye on him.

I set up a crate in our family room and an exercise pen in the kitchen. The ex-pen has a bed on one end and a piddle pad on the other. Lily spends most of her unsupervised time in her pen. But whenever we are in the family room with the other dogs, watching television, reading, or just relaxing and Lily needs some downtime, I place her in the crate so that she can be with the pack.

## Food and Bowls

Remember to purchase dog food and food and water bowls. Prior to picking up your pup, ask the breeder what type of food he is accustomed to being fed. Dry, moist, a combination of both? Then purchase enough of the exact same brands to last you a few weeks.

Bowls come in every size, color, shape, and material imaginable. Breeders generally recommend stainless steel bowls because they are the safest and can go in the dishwasher to be well cleaned and sanitized. Ceramic bowls are attractive, but they are more porous and can harbor bacteria and mold. Plastic bowls are not recommended at all because many are made with chemicals that may have long-term carcinogenic effects. It's best not to take a chance.

## Grooming Supplies

The Cavalier has a beautiful silky coat, so you'll want to maintain it with regular grooming. Buy yourself a slicker brush, comb, and scissors for cutting mats out and trimming between the puppy's paw pads. It's also nice to have a grooming table. Because the Cavalier is a small breed, you can also use the center island in your kitchen if you have one. However, without the benefit of a grooming table arm to keep your pup from jumping off, plan on having someone assist you. I would also place a nonskid mat on the countertop.

## Identification

When your pup has been with you for a few days and you've come up with a name, head back to pet store to order a name tag for his collar. It will include his name, and your name, address, and phone number. Hopefully, your Cavalier will never run off, but if he does, having a name tag should help get him back home.

In the early 1990s, tattooing dogs was a popular way of creating a permanent form of identification. While it is still available, there is a more modern option that is usually the first choice for toy dog owners: microchipping. A small transponder no bigger than an uncooked piece of rice is implanted in the dog's shoulder. The transponder has an identification

*Want to Know More?*

For more detailed information on grooming your Cavalier, see Chapter 6: Cavalier Grooming Needs.

number that can be read by a scanner. Most animal control officers, animal shelters, and the vets who implant the chips have scanners, so a lost dog can easily be identified. Implanting the chip is quick and no more painful than the prick of an injection.

## Leash

A 4-foot (1.2-m) thin leather or nylon leash is fine for short jaunts around the neighborhood. Most people buy leashes that are too long and either drag on the ground or can get caught on something, possibly causing serious injury. If you start a puppy training class, your instructor may recommend a 6-foot (1.8-m) leash.

## Toys

Don't forget to welcome your puppy to your new home with some toys to play with. Be sure that they are safe and durable. Nylabone chew bones, which come in different textures, are good choices. Fabric bones designed to be moistened and placed in the freezer are comforting for teething puppies. Rope toys are also fun for chasing and chewing. Plush and lambs wool toys are usually favorites. Just make sure that they are well made and not easily torn apart.

# BRINGING PUPPY HOME

Finally, the big day arrives and you're off to pick up your new puppy. Your crate is set up. Food and water dishes are ready. Your home and yard are pet-proofed. All you have to do is get him from the breeder.

My husband and I always pick up our new pups together. He drives and I sit in the back seat with the new puppy in a traveling crate alongside me. Don't be surprised if your little guy cries a lot on the way home. He may be accustomed to the crate, but this is his first time away from his mother and littermates.

Welcome your puppy to his new home by providing him with some toys of his own.

Our Woody screeched at the top of his lungs during the entire ride, despite all of my efforts to console and distract him. Luckily, it was only a 40-minute drive.

In addition to picking up your little bundle of joy, you should also leave the breeder's home with several documents.

- **Pedigree Document:** This document outlines your pup's ancestry. It will have a chart of at least three generations of relatives.
- **Medical Records:** This is a list of vaccinations and deworming medications administered to date, plus any other medical treatment your pup may have undergone.
- **Registration Application(s):** These are applications to either or both national Cavalier clubs.
- **Sales Contract:** The contract should include a purchase price; health certificate from a veterinarian completed within seven days of taking your pup home; whether spay/ neutering is mandatory, and if so at what

age either should be performed; and a stipulation that the dog should be returned to the breeder if the owner is ever unable to continue to care for him. (If your Cavalier develops a genetic health problem early in life, there are pet protection laws outlining compensation requirements from the seller. These laws differ from state to state.) Buyer beware. Read your contract carefully.

It should take only a few days for your puppy to accept his new surroundings and integrate into the family.

• **Other Paperwork:** Often the breeder's personal recommendations for feeding and housetraining are part of the puppy package.

## When You Arrive Home

When you arrive at your home, take your puppy wearing his buckle collar and new leash to an area of the yard where you want him to relieve himself. Use a command such as *hurry up, bathroom, potty,* or whatever you prefer. When your pup performs, praise him lavishly and bring him into his house. Let him explore a room or two—usually the kitchen and/or family room. Let him have a little snack and some water, then place him into his crate or ex-pen for a nap.

## Meeting the Neighbors

Everyone in the neighborhood will probably want to meet your puppy, but it's best to give him a few days to settle in and become accustomed to his new environment.

## Playtime

You will probably want to play with your puppy a lot too. But keep it low key for a while and let him nap as often as he needs to. You may want to set up a crate in your bedroom so that he can be near you during the night. Don't be surprised if your Cavalier cries the first few nights. Again, he is not accustomed to being alone. Your breeder should give you a toy or small blanket that bears the scent of his family. Place this in his crate because it will comfort him. A ticking clock nearby may also help at bedtime because it mimics the sound of the mother dog's heartbeat.

## Nighttime

By 12 weeks, the age most Cavaliers are sent off to their new homes, your puppy should be able to sleep through the night. But if he falls asleep for several hours and wakes up crying, it may be time to head outside for a potty run.

## Puppy Classes

It should take only a few days for your new puppy to accept his surroundings and integrate into the family. These are happy times as he explores his new world and begins to learn your house rules. If there is a puppy kindergarten class in your area, sign up and get started. Puppy classes are wonderful for socializing your new pup and teaching him basic commands.

## WHAT ABOUT TWO?

Normally I would not advise pet owners to adopt two puppies at once because they may form a stronger bond to each other than to you. And if you're a novice, I still think it would be best to bring in one pup first and then perhaps add another a year or two down the road if you're interested in having more than one.

On the other hand, with Cavaliers being such social creatures, they may well bond to you and another pup at the same time. There are some benefits. They will create an actual dog pack for play and companionship. Separation anxiety could be averted because the pups will play and roughhouse together and learn bite inhibition by testing out their teeth on each other and not on family members. They can

## *Multi-Dog Tip*

Introduce your new puppy to your older dog(s) on neutral ground. A friend's yard is ideal. Just be sure to confirm that the lawn has not been treated with pesticides.

also sleep together, which will make them feel more secure at night, most likely avoiding whining or crying at bedtime.

An experienced dog owner will know how to help the puppies develop their independence and still have a close relationship with their sibling and the humans in the family. As long as the owner takes on the appropriate leadership position needed in a stable pack (humans and dogs together), the puppies will grow and mature perfectly well. The one thing a pet parent of two young pups cannot do is expect them to exercise and police each other. They will still need a daily structured walk, individual training, and close supervision when they are interacting. Most important, an owner must use leadership skills to set the proper rules, boundaries, and limitations needed to raise healthy, happy, and fulfilled dogs.

I'm told that Cavaliers are very much like potato chips—it's hard to have just one.

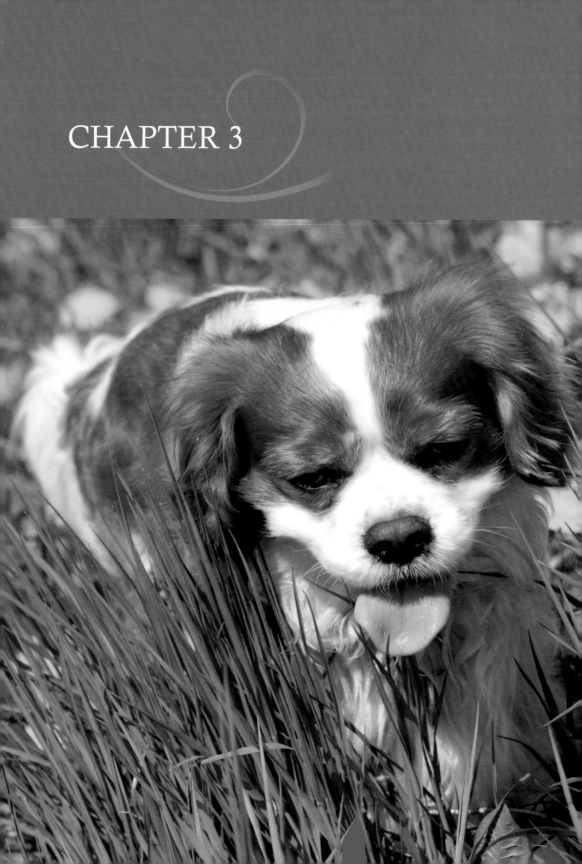

# CHAPTER 3

# CARE OF YOUR CAVALIER PUPPY

Ahh, the puppy phase; so much fun and so much mischief. After raising our Irish Setter, Woody—who chased everything that moved, from bees to cars to helicopters, raced circles around our family room banking his turns on the couch at five o'clock each evening, required 17 trips to the vet the first year, and is largely responsible for most of my gray hair—I swore I'd never adopt another puppy. And sure enough, our next dog, Rory, was three years old when he joined the family. But in time I mellowed, memories of all of Woody's craziness subsided, and we adopted three puppies in relatively short succession.

I learned a lot from raising Woody, though. First, how important it is to assess the energy level of the breed of dog you're interested in, and once you have decided, to try to select a puppy within a litter with an energy level that matches your own. I also learned to let go of and adjust my expectations and love the dog I had even if he was not the one I dreamed of.

A few years after Rory came along, we decided to look for a tricolor English Springer or English Cocker pup. Eight months later I found Junior on PetFinder.com, a national website of dogs and puppies available for adoption through rescue groups and animal shelters.

He was listed as a pointer mix but looked very much like a tricolor spaniel (though time and a DNA test proved otherwise). Junior is actually a Border Collie/German Shorthaired Pointer/Doberman Pinscher mix. Surprisingly, with all of those high-energy breeds in his background, he was a very calm puppy. (The polar opposite of Woody, who, by the way, matured into a wonderful, loving, well-behaved adult dog.) Junior seemed to have an old soul in a young body. His demeanor was a welcomed relief. After gaining all those gray hairs with Woody, I often said about Junie, "I deserve this puppy."

Hopefully, your new Cavalier puppy is a perfect match. But if not—don't be discouraged. You can still create a wonderful and lasting bond. Let the journey begin.

## FEEDING

Because there are so many pet food choices these days, it's best to seek advice from your vet or breeder regarding proper nutrition and feeding. Generally, you should begin by feeding your new pup the food to which he is already accustomed. Dogs react strongly to sudden dietary changes and often develop diarrhea. Because you will be in the early stages of housetraining, a pup with an upset

The proper care of your puppy during his first few months ensures that he will become a healthy, well-balanced adult.

stomach is the last thing you need. If over time you wish to change his diet, do so gradually, adding just a small amount of the new food to the original. Increase the amount of new food over several days and eliminate small portions of the original food. As previously mentioned, dogs thrive on routine, which includes when meals are offered. So setting up a consistent schedule for feeding is equally important.

## Changing Food Requirements

Breeders usually start weaning puppies at around four to five weeks of age. That's about the time they can stand, walk, and start to lap up liquids. It takes them about a week to figure it out. Sometimes mothers with small litters want to nurse their puppies longer, which is fine; they are really the ones to decide. But when the puppies' teeth begin to come in, the mother usually loses interest in nursing them. Most of the time, the first foods offered are warm soupy combinations of baby food, oatmeal, or rice-type mixtures. Some breeders add small amounts of canned dog food. Others take regular puppy food and soak it in warm water until it gets mushy, or they may add a little puppy milk replacer and offer it in a shallow bowl. For the most part, baby puppy food should be about 30 percent protein and fed three times a day.

By the time the puppies are eight weeks old, they can chew pretty well, and the food balance of water and solids will start to change to a more kibble-based diet. Kibble is probably the easiest and most nutritional food for a young puppy, though some people prefer to start a home-cooked or raw diet and feed it for the entire lifetime of the dog.

At about 10 weeks, a gradual switch is made from baby kibble to a puppy kibble, which is still offered three times a day. At about six months, meals should be reduced to about ½ cup (113 g) twice a day. At one year, ¾ cup (170 g) of adult food, which has lower protein levels, split into two meals a day is appropriate. Once my adult dogs are down to two meals a day, I like to give them a snack at lunchtime—usually just a biscuit or a couple of baby carrots.

## GROOMING

The key to raising your Cavalier so that he will enjoy being groomed as an adult is to begin when he is still a pup. If introduced in short, positive sessions, he should accept being brushed, combed, and bathed readily. Grooming your Cavalier also gives you a special time to bond with him, as well as an opportunity to do a quick health check of his eyes, ears, paws, and skin looking for any signs of a problem. As your pup becomes accustomed to being handled, you should both find grooming sessions quite relaxing.

### Handling

To get your puppy accustomed to being handled, start by placing him on a grooming table. You might want to do this with the help of an assistant if he is particularly squirmy. Gently rub his paws while praising him and offering a small treat. I like to use tiny bite-sized biscuits, a dab of squeeze cheese on my fingers, or the squeeze treats made by pet food manufacturers available in various flavors. My dogs love these. I imagine yours will too.

Next, take a peek in his ears. Lift his lips

and run a dab of doggy toothpaste across his gums. Most likely he will think you are playing a game, and as long as you keep the session short while offering a lot of positive praise and treats, he will enjoy the attention. Five minutes is all you need for the first few sessions, then build up to 10 minutes, and so on.

### Bathing

Puppies don't usually need bathing, but you can begin to get your Cav used to the process in much the same manner. Because puppies are small, you can introduce your pup to his first baths in the kitchen sink. Be sure to place a nonslip mat at the bottom to give him some traction and lessen his fear. Again, an assistant would be helpful. Spray your pup with warm water and work in a small amount of shampoo. After gently lathering up the coat, rinse it thoroughly. Don't forget the praise and treats. Be quick and efficient. Next, place your pup on a grooming table or your countertop and towel him dry. You can use a hair dryer meant for dogs, but some puppies will react strongly to the sound. So work quickly. Your assistant can help by distracting your puppy with treats.

More detailed information on grooming and bathing will be covered in Chapter 6: Cavalier Grooming Needs.

## By the Numbers

At 12 weeks of age, a Cavalier pup should be fed three times a day.

## Training Tidbit

Have food rewards at the ready when grooming to provide a positive association with the process.

## Brushing

While he's a puppy, your Cavalier's coat will be short. So begin with brief brushing sessions using a soft puppy brush. Eventually, you will also need:

- a mat raking tool
- a pair of grooming shears (scissors)
- a shedding tool
- a small pin brush
- a small slicker brush
- a straight comb

Remember, as with anything else you expose your puppy to for the first time, reward him with treats while you groom him so that he will always associate the process with a positive experience. Gradually increase the time of each grooming session, introducing your other tools until your Cavalier will remain still for a longer period. If you want to follow the breed standard, the only trimming you will need to do is with the hair between your pup's paw pads on the bottom of his feet.

## HEALTH

To start life off right with your new puppy, you need to focus on his health needs. At home that means providing the best-quality diet you can, as well as plenty of water, safe and comfortable living accommodations, and the appropriate amount of exercise and mental stimulation for his age. And it should go without saying that you will also need to provide excellent veterinary care.

## Finding a Vet

Without question, your Cavalier puppy will become an important member of your family. Just as parents take the utmost care in finding a competent pediatrician, "puppy parents" need to be equally selective in choosing a veterinarian. These well-trained professionals have numerous roles and responsibilities: diagnostician, clinician, dermatologist, dentist, and surgeon to name just a few. And dogs don't have the advantage of human patients who can explain where it hurts or why they don't feel well.

Ideally, you should find a vet before your pup comes home. Seek recommendations from your breeder and fellow dog owners, and visit several veterinary hospitals beforehand. Many have websites that will provide a virtual tour before your actual tour of the facility.

During each visit, note the level of cleanliness. Vets who take pride in the presentation of their facilities will also take pride in the care they give your pet. Also, prepare a list of questions:

- What medical and surgical services are offered?
- How many vets work at the hospital?
- Do the vets solely practice traditional medicine or are holistic remedies (vitamins, homeopathy, acupuncture, etc.) also provided?
- What are the hours of operation?
- How much time is allotted for each appointment?
- Are after-hours emergency visits available?
- Is someone on duty should your pet need to spend the night?
- What is the hospital's policy on responding to client phone calls? (immediate, within a

few hours, in the evening, etc.)
- Are other services offered, such as boarding and grooming?

When we moved from the suburbs to the country, the most difficult part of the move was leaving my vet behind. I had been a client for 14 years and thought he walked on water. When we reached our new home, I tried several vets at two hospitals before finding one at a third facility with whom both my dog and I were comfortable.

My current vet has fabulous clinical, diagnostic, and surgical skills. He speaks slowly and calmly, patiently answering my handwritten list of questions. Thus, I never feel rushed. Since I've been writing about dogs for more than 30 years, I imagine I'm more in tune with canine health issues than many pet owners. So believe me when I tell you, I take my dogs' health very seriously and always have plenty of questions. I'm not left to sit in the waiting or exam room unless there's something more serious happening with another patient, which is certainly understandable. I find the level of faith I have in my vet and his staff is invaluable. Plus, the hospital is just nine minutes from my home. Having a vet you trust in close proximity is also a plus when there's an emergency. Rory developed pancreatitis at one point and needed subcutaneous fluids twice a day. Because he too, like the Cavalier, is a Velcro dog, I didn't want to leave him at a specialty hospital for an extended stay. So I dutifully ran him up to my vet's office twice a day for the length of his treatment. He was less stressed, and it wasn't that difficult for me to do this because the hospital was nearby.

It's also helpful if you are comfortable with the technicians and receptionists who work with your veterinarian. I know everyone on staff at my vet's office by first name and have an easy rapport with each of them. It adds to my comfort level knowing that everyone who comes in contact with my dogs will be kind to them. Of course, with five canine patients, I'm at the vet's far more frequently than the single-dog owner. I often joke that I'm moving in, or at the very least should have my own parking space!

## The First Checkup

It's a good idea to take your pup to the vet within the first week of his arrival. Assuming that the puppy appears healthy, this will be a wellness visit. Plan to bring the health records provided by his breeder and a stool sample to be checked for parasites.

Usually upon arrival, a vet tech will weigh your Cavalier before you meet with the veterinarian. Once in the examining room, the vet will perform a canine physical as well as answer your questions. Specifically, she will

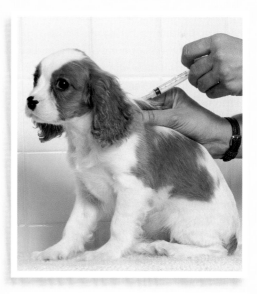

Ideally, you should find a vet before your puppy comes home.

## Pet Health Insurance

Pet health insurance has become widely available and can be invaluable. As a multi-breed owner, all of my dogs have their own policies. I find this coverage more than pays for itself and gives me tremendous peace of mind. No one wants to make a medical decision for their beloved pet based on a lack of funds. Preventive medicine, sickness, and emergency care are all covered, depending on individual policies.

When pet insurance first became available, Smokey was eight years old. We toyed with the idea of obtaining a policy but decided against it. A few months later, Smokey suffered a life-threatening illness. Veterinary bills reached $5,000. From that time on, I have purchased pet insurance for each of my dogs. I bought a policy for Rory, who was already an adult, a month before he came home. Six months later he began having cluster seizures—a serious form of epilepsy. It was a stressful time to say the least, with numerous trips to the vet for tests and evaluations. Another six months ensued before we were able to bring the condition under control. I'm now happy to report that Rory has not had a seizure in more than five years and because of insurance, I never once had to worry about his vet bills.

examine his eyes, ears, teeth, and genitals, checking for any abnormalities. She will listen to his heart and lungs as well as palpate his abdomen. By running her hands over his body, she will check for lumps, rashes, and/or parasites. She will then administer vaccinations appropriate for your pup's age.

Flea and tick control and heartworm prevention should be discussed. Products to deal with these parasites will be dispensed at the end of the exam.

Those vets who take their time during the pup's physical without rushing through will be thorough in finding any problems. While clinical skills are important, so is a calm and reassuring bedside manner. An owner must feel comfortable with the vet and trust that questions will always be patiently answered and the best possible medical care provided. If you don't walk away from the visit with a good feeling, make an appointment at another clinic the following week.

## Vaccinations

Vaccinations have protected our beloved pets from serious illnesses such as parvovirus, distemper, and rabies for decades. They have also reduced the incidences of these diseases.

Puppies need vaccinations every three weeks starting at five to seven weeks of age until they reach between 14 and 17 weeks of age. It's important not to take your Cavalier pup to playgrounds, kennels, dog parks, or any other public areas until this initial vaccination schedule is complete. A booster shot will be given one year later.

Vaccines fall into two primary categories: core (universally recommended) and noncore (optional or not recommended at all). The core vaccines are distemper, hepatitis, parvovirus, and rabies. Noncore viruses include bordetella, coronavirus, leptospirosis, Lyme disease, and parainfluenza. Explanations of the diseases these vaccinations are manufactured to prevent appear below.

**Bordetella:** Bordetella is an upper respiratory tract infection caused by a bacterial agent, *Bordetella bronchiseptica*. Bordetella is implicated in causing "kennel cough." Clinical signs include a dry, raspy cough, nasal discharge, signs of depression, and a decrease in appetite. Antibiotics and cough suppressants are used to treat this condition. This disease is highly contagious and can be contracted easily from infected dogs. Bordetella vaccinations are usually required before leaving your dog in a boarding facility.

**Coronavirus:** Coronavirus is a virus typically seen in puppies 6 to 16 weeks of age. The disease is very similar to parvovirus, causing vomiting, diarrhea, and depression. However, this virus is rarely fatal. Your Cavalier could contract coronavirus from the feces of an infected dog. In minor cases, no treatment is advised. In more serious situations, fluids given into the vein or below the skin may be administered. Antibiotics may also be used if there is evidence of sepsis, which is bacteria in the blood.

**Distemper:** Distemper is a deadly disease that can develop in dogs of all ages but will affect the young more severely. This disease is typically characterized by a high fever with concurrent respiratory and gastrointestinal distress. Hardening of the foot pad or nose can occur as well. Many dogs who appear to have survived distemper go on to develop seizures, paralysis, and muscle tremors. The distemper virus is airborne, and your pet would become exposed through his nasal cavity. The prognosis for this disease is poor. Treatment consists of constant supportive care while the animal is kept in a warm, draft-free environment. Fluids are administered

if he's dehydrated, and anticonvulsant medication is given if seizures are occurring.

**Hepatitis:** Hepatitis is a virus that causes liver failure. This is typically seen in unvaccinated dogs. Clinical signs include fever, depression, vomiting, abdominal pain, and abdominal distension. Ingestion of urine, feces, or saliva of infected dogs is the main route of infection. Prognosis is varied, and supportive care is the only treatment.

**Leptospirosis:** Leptospirosis is a bacterial infection that typically causes kidney failure. Clinical signs include fever, painful abdomen, discolored urine, and depression. This disease can affect many other organs as well. Your Cavalier can become infected by coming in contact with urine from an infected dog. This disease is contagious to humans as well and can be fatal. While people can recover with

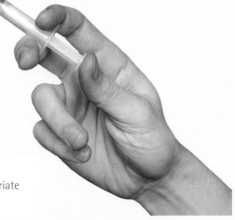

The vet will administer vaccinations that are appropriate to your Cavalier's age.

aggressive antibiotic treatment, fatalities have occurred. If caught early in dogs, antibiotics can shorten duration. With more advanced cases, supportive therapy will be needed to compensate for abnormal blood, kidney, and liver function. If there is severe liver disease, which has led to a bleeding disorder, a transfusion will be needed. Because leptospirosis is contagious to other animals and people, the utmost care must be taken by caregivers when handling the afflicted dog.

**Lyme Disease:** Lyme disease is a bacterial infection that causes joint swelling, pain, fever, and depression. Internal organs are also affected. The deer tick carrying the *Borrelia burgdorferi* bacteria transmits this disease. Lyme is transmitted through the saliva of a tick that bites your dog. Good tick control helps reduce the incidence of this disease. Lyme is treated with antibiotics.

**Parainfluenza:** Parainfluenza is another disease that can cause kennel cough. It is highly contagious through nasal secretions or coughed-up mucus. It is rarely fatal and most dogs recover uneventfully. Treatment includes supportive care and cough suppressants.

**Parvovirus:** Parvovirus is a deadly virus that can affect dogs of any age. Typically, severe illness is most often seen in puppies 6 to 16 weeks of age. Clinical signs include vomiting, depression, anorexia, and severe bloody diarrhea. Rapid dehydration and death can occur without rigorous treatment. This disease is usually fatal without extensive supportive treatment. Dogs who survive parvo can shed the virus in their stools for about ten days, so it's possible for your Cavalier to contract this disease from feces carrying the virus from an infected dog.

**Rabies:** Rabies is a deadly viral disease that affects all mammals, including humans. This virus affects the central nervous system and causes aggressive behavior, seizures, dementia, and death. This disease is always fatal, so your Cavalier must always be vaccinated against it. Raccoons, skunks, and bats are common animals that can transmit rabies to your dog. Contact your veterinarian immediately if your pet has been exposed to an ill wild animal. (Note: The frequency for administering the rabies vaccine is mandated by the government and can vary from state to state.)

As your puppy grows up, there will be different options for vaccinating him. Although inoculations are extremely important and beneficial, the frequency of administration has come under scrutiny in recent years. Many veterinarians and pet owners believe that overvaccinating can weaken the immune system and open the door to serious degenerative health problems. Also, vaccine manufacturers are learning that many of their products provide immunity for several years, making the long-standing practice of vaccinating for all diseases annually unnecessary. Therefore, some veterinarians elect to follow the 2006 guidelines outlined by the American Animal Hospital Association (AAHA): a three-year interval for core vaccines and annual inoculations for noncore if indicated.

Others opt to test titer levels on a yearly basis, which determines whether each vaccine is still providing immunity. If only one level has begun to drop, the dog will be given a booster for that particular

## Want to Know More?

For more detailed information on illnesses that can affect the Cavalier, see Chapter 8: Cavalier Health and Wellness.

Cavalier puppies may be prone to a few health conditions, such as heart murmurs and juvenile cataracts.

disease. When all protective levels remain high, revaccinating may be postponed.

Still other veterinarians feel that more research needs to be done overall, and if titer levels have begun to drop, the animal is in essence unprotected. They further believe that the protection provided by routine vaccinations far outweighs the small percentage of dogs who have had serious reactions or illnesses related to them. Therefore they have the most confidence in and continue to recommend the annual schedule.

It's important to look at the individual and his risk of exposure. Obviously, a dog who travels or boards frequently may benefit from more frequent vaccinations than the dog who always stays at home. Pet owners should discuss the various options with their vet and select the best protocol for their dog.

Usually, vaccinations are give in a 5-in-1 or 7-in-1 combination, which means that the dog is being vaccinated against five or seven diseases at one time. Some pet owners prefer to break up these combination vaccines and give them separately or in smaller combinations, usually one month a part. Although reactions to vaccines are uncommon, some dogs have such reactions as facial swelling, hives, continual vomiting, lethargy, and difficulty in breathing. Serious reactions such as these

## MVD

Mitral valve dysplasia (MVD), also known as mitral valve disease, occurs when there is a defect in one of the four valves of a dog's heart. The malformed valve is unable to close properly, and blood begins to flow backwards. This backflow keeps the proper amount of blood from circulating throughout the body and it spills back into the heart. Over time the dog can develop congestive heart failure—fluid buildup in the lungs.

Although MVD occurs in a number of dogs after the age of ten, an unusually high percentage of Cavaliers develop MVD before they are five. It is the leading health concern in the breed.

For more information about MVD, visit http://www.cavalierhealth.org/mitral_valve_disease.htm.

usually occur prior to leaving the vet's office after receiving the vaccine. More common and expected vaccine reactions are local swelling and pain at the injection site, lack of energy for a few hours, and sometimes a mild fever. It's not unusual for some vaccines to cause local swelling that may last up to several days. The swelling is typically hard and not painful and will over a couple of weeks reduce in size and eventually disappear. If it does not, you should have your veterinarian check this area to make sure that the lump is a normal reaction to the vaccine given. If your pet has had a serious reaction to a vaccine, it is important to notify any new veterinarians who may be vaccinating the dog in the future. There are different medications that can be given to dogs prior to vaccinations to make their reactions less severe or nonexistent.

## PUPPY-SPECIFIC HEALTH CONDITIONS

There are a few health conditions that may strike Cavalier puppies, including heart murmurs and juvenile cataracts.

### Heart Murmurs

Because Cavaliers have a higher than average occurrence of mitral valve disease (MVD), heart murmurs are always a concern. However, it's important to know that not all murmurs are a sign of trouble. Those in young Cavalier pups can eventually disappear.

### Juvenile Cataracts

Like people, dogs can develop cataracts in their eyes, which means that the lens loses its transparency. Cataracts usually develop later in life. However, some Cavaliers have a genetic predisposition to juvenile cataracts, which occurs in younger dogs as early as six months old. The condition can lead to blindness by the age of two. Fortunately, poor lenses may often be treated surgically.

## SPAYING AND NEUTERING

All pet dogs should be spayed or neutered. These surgeries cut back on unwanted pregnancies, which also helps with pet overpopulation. Spaying can prevent breast cancer and pyometra (life-threatening uterine infection) in females, plus do away with messy heat cycles. Neutering eliminates the male's need to wander in search of romance and decreases fighting and testicular cancer. Owners are sometimes concerned that spaying or neutering will lead to obesity. Because these procedures do greatly reduce testosterone and estrogen levels, which affect metabolism, it's important to discuss appropriate diet and exercise with your vet after your pet has been surgically altered. Personality will not change, and both males and females will be equally happy and fun-loving.

## Spaying Your Female

Your Cavalier will come into her first heat between four and eight months of age. It is now recommended to spay your female dog prior to her first heat cycle. Doing so dramatically reduces her risk for breast cancer as an adult female dog. However, it does not reduce her risk as much if you spay her after her first, second, or third heat cycle.

When a female dog is spayed, both ovaries and the entire uterus are removed. This will prevent her from coming into more heat cycles, thus eliminating the possibility for pregnancy and pyometra, a uterine disease. It also eliminates the risk of ovarian and uterine cancer.

## Neutering Your Male

Neutering your male Cavalier should be done as early, as well, between four and six months of age. During the procedure, the testicles will be removed. Neutering reduces unwanted male dog behaviors: leg lifting on furniture, mounting, and roaming. In addition to eliminating testicular cancer, it also reduces the risk of prostate disease and reduces the incidence of perianal tumors and perineal hernias.

## Rules for Post-Altering

When your dog leaves the hospital, you will be advised to keep him calm and on leash while he recovers. No jumping on furniture, climbing up stairs, playing with other animals or children, etc. Stitches will be removed 10 to 14 days after surgery.

You may be imagining how people feel after a surgery—perfectly content to stay in bed, rest up, and give their bodies a chance to recover. However, dogs bounce back in an amazingly short time. Be prepared.

Lily was spayed recently. The surgery took place in the morning and I brought her home at 5:00 pm the same day. She was groggy the first night and a good patient. By the next morning, she was full of beans and ready to go. I kept her in her ex-pen most of the time and worked at the kitchen table as much as possible. In the evening I let her lounge in a soft crate to be near my husband and her brothers. When everyone walked out of the room one night, she managed to unzip the crate and race up the stairs after them. A few days later, I left her with Woody in the kitchen safely locked behind our doggy pocket door, which is more than waist high on a tall person. I no sooner reached the second floor than I heard an odd banging. Within seconds, Lily had scaled the pocket door (a first), dashed up the stairs, and looked at me with great glee. I was counting the days until she fully recovered and the stitches would come out.

So plan ahead, set up safe recovery areas, and expect the unexpected.

# CHAPTER 4

# TRAINING YOUR CAVALIER PUPPY

Early training is very important if you wish to have a friendly, well-behaved adult dog. When basic commands are combined with socialization, daily exercise, a healthy diet, and regular grooming, a puppy will grow up to be a true companion—one whom you will be proud of and who will become an important part of your family.

There's a certain level of skill to raising a puppy to respect you as his pack leader and become a good canine citizen. It takes some creativity, consistent daily practice, and an abundance of patience, love, and lip-smacking treats to train and reinforce good behavior. Human guidance is essential in helping your puppy learn appropriate behaviors. When your puppy has had a few days to explore and acclimate himself to his new surroundings, it's a good idea to invite friends and family over to interact with the new arrival. Short, informal gatherings help a puppy learn that human handling is a pleasant experience.

## INTRODUCTION TO TRAINING

Most people think of training as the basic commands (*sit, stay, come, down, heel*) we learn to teach our dogs in obedience school.

But there is another, more fundamental, meaning to the word. Training also represents *discipline*—the rules, structure, and boundaries that all dogs need to survive.

Discipline sometimes conjures up negative feelings in some people because they think that we're talking about punishment. That's not the case. You see evidence of discipline throughout nature. It means survival to animals—it's the distinction between a time to hunt, a time to migrate, a time to rest, a time to play, etc. Discipline is watching an alpha wolf eating first while the rest of the pack members stand back waiting for their leader to give them the sign that he is finished and they can now eat. Discipline does not mean punishment—discipline means survival.

In our homes we need to give our puppies rules, structure, and boundaries because they are genetically programmed to look for them so that they don't throw their own or our lives into chaos. They want to know what their limitations are and how to behave in their new pack. If you don't provide these things for your puppy, he may start exhibiting unacceptable behaviors. You may find that your puppy's housetraining is "iffy," his response to your commands is "iffy," and he will do those things

Training represents the rules, structure, and boundaries that all dogs need to survive.

only "if" he decides he wants to.

So think of training as life training—teaching your puppy the appropriate way to fit into his new pack. When you bring your puppy home, the first things he will be questioning are: who is here, am I safe, and who is in charge? Once you have established leadership, you can teach your dog anything you like. Commands are really the icing on the cake.

## The Importance of Positive Training

You'll want to use positive methods when training, which means positive verbal praise and appealing rewards, such as affection, a special toy, or a tasty treat, to motivate and reward your puppy for learning correct behaviors. Punishment should *never* be used

when teaching your puppy right from wrong. If you find yourself becoming inpatient or frustrated, stop training on a happy note and resume the lesson at another time

Consistency and timing are the two most important aspects of reinforcement training. Your puppy will benefit from your ability to be especially consistent in your training methods.

## How to Find a Trainer

There are several ways to find a qualified private dog instructor or reputable dog obedience training program. Word of mouth is a good place to start. If you acquired your puppy through a local breeder, she should be a good resource. Your puppy's veterinarian may also be able to recommend a local kindergarten puppy training class with a good reputation. In fact, some veterinary practices host training classes for their clients right on the premises.

Local obedience clubs, animal welfare centers, and large pet supply stores often offer dog training classes. In addition, reach out to neighbors, friends, and family members for honest and reliable referrals if they own a dog you admire.

As you embark on your search for a competent instructor or suitable training program, it's important to know that it's not a requirement to be certified or licensed to become a professional dog trainer. However, what certification will indicate is that a training facility and the trainers on staff are dedicated to the profession and have a willingness to continue with their professional education for the benefit of their clients. To learn more about the qualifications of dog trainers and/or behaviorists you plan to interview, visit the websites for the Association of Pet Dog Trainers (APDT), the Certification Council for Pet Dog Trainers (CCPDT), the National Association of Dog Obedience Instructors (NADOI), the International Association of Canine Professionals (IACP), and the Animal Behavioral Society (ABS) to become a more educated dog owner and consumer.

## Multi-Dog Tip

If you have adult dogs in the family, allow your pup to watch them performing commands because it will hasten the training process.

surroundings through exposure to all sorts of sights, sounds, smells, people, places, objects, and other dogs.

There are two forms of socialization. The first actually starts before your puppy comes home. At 3 to 4 weeks of age and up until 12 weeks, when a Cavalier puppy is ready to join his new human family, his sensory and motor skills are developing at a very fast pace. Puppies discover that they can run and communicate both vocally and with distinct body postures. Puppies become much more interested in their littermates and engage in entertaining and rowdy play, such as biting, chasing, and wrestling. This type of play helps a puppy learn what is appropriate behavior and, in contrast, inappropriate behavior. Once your puppy arrives home, socialization should continue with other dogs, but it is also important to socialize your puppy with people, places, and things.

## SOCIALIZATION

The importance of early socialization cannot be overstressed. It's a facet of training where your puppy is exposed in a positive way to new experiences that will challenge his curiosity and intelligence but not make him fearful. Your puppy needs you to help him adjust to his

## How to Socialize

It's really quite simple. The key to ensuring that your puppy is comfortable in

Word of mouth is a good place to start when trying to find a qualified private dog instructor.

different settings, meeting strangers, including other dogs, and not fearful around unfamiliar objects, visible or tangible, is to ensure that your puppy is exposed to all of these elements on a daily basis. It's very important to start this process following your puppy's homecoming and while he is still young. If your puppy is not exposed to new situations early on and in a positive manner, he may be fearful when exposed to new objects and experiences in the future.

Once he's home, socialization should continue with the puppy's first trip to the veterinarian. At the vet's office your puppy will be exposed to several compassionate strangers who will give him lots of attention. A helpful tip is to try to divert your puppy's attention while the vet is administering that first vaccination. Offer your puppy a treat so that he's not focused on the pinch of the needle. Afterward, a warm hug and soothing words of admiration will also help him know that he is safe and that nothing all that terrible has happened.

After your puppy's first trip to the vet, it's time to expose him to other people and objects. Under your close supervision, let your puppy explore his new home and the objects around him. Introduce your pup to family and friends, small children, and other family pets. Remember to always keep some tasty treats available when introducing your puppy to someone or something new so that he associates these experiences with positive rewards.

Interactions between dogs and young children should always be supervised, and both must be taught how to treat each other appropriately.

If you have a safe and secure fenced-in yard, let your puppy explore the world outdoors. Keep a watchful eye on him at all times. When he's accustomed to a collar and leash, slowly expose him to objects you might encounter on a walk around your own neighborhood. The things we take for granted, such as a fire hydrant, trash can, a child's bicycle, or passing car, can all be quite terrifying to a puppy. If the puppy shows fear in approaching those objects, turn the encounter into something fun. In a cheerful, enthusiastic tone, encourage your puppy to investigate and offer a treat to reward him for his bravery.

As your puppy gets older and a little bolder, take him with you to as many safe places as possible where he will have more opportunities to advance his socialization skills. At a local park he might encounter baby strollers, joggers, skateboarders, squeaky swing sets, and a game of catch or flying disc. Go out of your way to introduce your puppy to people who appear different in some way, whether in height, skin color, or manner of dress—especially people wearing hats or eyeglasses or someone with a mustache or beard.

I take my puppies to the local bookstore, camera shop, library, doggy gift shop, and any other business where they are welcome. I always carry small treats in my pockets and ask people who stop to admire them to please offer a treat. In no time, my puppies love to shop, so to speak, and meet people. (Note: If your pup has not received all of his puppy vaccinations, don't take him to dog parks, large chain pet stores, or other locations where dogs congregate. Stick with the shops and facilities listed in this section and keep your pup off

## Want to Know More?

For intermediate cues to teach your Cavalier, see Chapter 9: Cavalier Training.

the floor. Once all his shots have been given, you can venture out to more locations.)

You may need to wait to start puppy class because vaccination paperwork from the vet is required. If it's not, select another dog training school.

## CRATE TRAINING

By nature, dogs, like their not-so-distant relatives, wolves, have an inborn instinct to seek a den. By using a crate, you are providing your puppy with his own "room" and thus taking advantage of his innate tendency to keep his "room" clean. If the crate is appropriately sized for your puppy, he will be reluctant to soil it. Thus you not only will have provided safe and secure sleeping quarters but also will have started housetraining your puppy. A puppy kept in his crate for a reasonable length of time will learn to hold his bladder and bowels until he is let outside to eliminate. Consistent use of a crate will help your puppy adapt to a regular schedule for elimination.

A general crate-training formula is as follows: A pup should be kept in a crate for only one hour for every month old he is plus one. For example, a three-month-old pup should not be confined for more than four hours. However, because small dogs have small bladders, I would suggest one hour for one month, i.e., for a three-month-old pup, no more than three hours.

There are also other benefits to crate training, such as helping to reduce separation anxiety and to prevent young puppies from getting into mischief when they cannot be supervised. A crate can also be a mobile indoor dog house that can be relocated from one room to

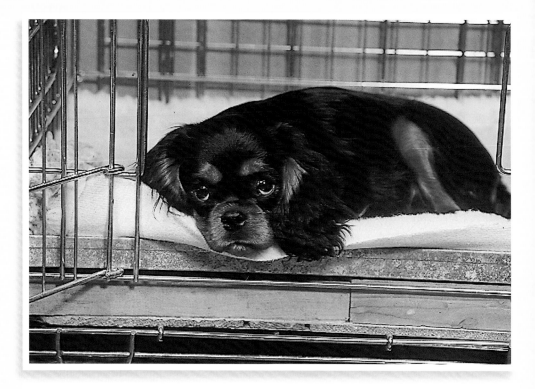

Where you put the crate is one of the most important aspects of crate training.

another and is also ideal for safely transporting your puppy by car or (if of an airline-approved type) for longer trips by plane.

Crate training should always be a positive experience and provide a pleasant environment for your puppy. It should *never* be used for the purpose of punishment.

## Crate Size

First, let's review the basics. It's assumed that you purchased a crate for your puppy according to the size he will become when fully grown. The breed standard for the height of a full-grown Cavalier King Charles Spaniel is 12 to 13 inches (30.5 to 33 cm) at the withers. Weight is proportionate to height and will fall somewhere between 13 and 18 pounds (6 and 8 kg). Given that the height and weight may vary slightly from the breed standard, your crate should measure no less than 24 inches long (61 cm), 18 inches wide (45.5 cm), and 21 inches (53.5 cm) high, which is typical for a dog weighing somewhere between 11 and 25 pounds (5 to 11.5 kg).

If you opt to be a bit more conservative, ensuring that your adult Cavalier will have enough space to lie down, turn around comfortably, and have at least 3 to 4 inches (7.5 to 10 cm) of additional headroom when sitting or standing, the next bigger size of crate or kennel might be a better fit. Try the 30 inch long (76 cm), 21 inch wide (53.5 cm), and 24 inch (61 cm) high crate. If you opt for the slightly larger crate, it should come with a crate "divider panel," which will allow you to adjust the living area inside the crate as your puppy grows into his adult size. If you are uncertain, do not forget that your breeder will be the best person to recommend an appropriate-sized crate.

## Crate Location

Location, location, location. Some owners prefer to place the crate in the bedroom so that the puppy is not separated from them overnight. Dogs are pack animals and prefer to sleep with their human pack. However, other owners prefer to locate the crate in the kitchen, where the family gathers most frequently and where there's usually easier access to the outdoors. Or if you're like me, you can set up more than one crate in the house.

## Crate Design

Now that you have selected a location for your crate, let's consider the interior design. Begin by making the crate a comfortable, warm, and inviting den by placing a well-fitting crate pad or cushion over the floor of the crate. You want to be sure to use something that is easy to wash in the event that your puppy has an accident, and you want it to be chew resistant.

## How to Crate Train

Chances are your puppy has been exposed to a crate in his first home and will readily recognize it as a safe place. But if not, here are the steps to follow to introduce the crate properly:

1. Leaving the door open, let your puppy explore the inside of the crate. With your puppy watching you, toss several pieces of irresistible treats inside the crate. If he goes inside after the treats, praise him cheerfully.
2. If your puppy hesitates and does not enter on his own, try placing a treat in the crate but where he can get to it while standing outside the crate. Praise him as he eats the

treat. Gradually toss the treat farther inside until your puppy willingly goes inside to retrieve it. If that doesn't work, then gently pick him up and place him inside, reassuring him with praise and showing him the treats. Don't shut the door.
3. When he's finished gobbling up all of the treats and you have his attention, call your puppy enthusiastically and praise him when he comes to you.
4. Repeat steps one through four for several minutes. When your puppy enters the crate, begin to introduce a cue word or phrase such as "Go to your room" every time he steps inside his crate. Eventually, he will learn to go inside the crate on the verbal command.

If your puppy seems to enjoy this repetitive game and shows no signs of anxiety, try closing the door but for no longer than a minute. Conclude the session by opening the door, calling him to you, and praising him lavishly. As you go about your day, stop periodically to take some time to repeat this exercise. Always conclude these brief training sessions with praise. Gradually increase the time you keep your puppy contained in the crate with the door closed.

Many reputable trainers suggest that puppies be fed inside their crates with the door shut. If your crate is located in or within close

## *Making the Crate Enticing*

Another trick for motivating your puppy to want to go into his crate and stay a while longer is to place a yummy edible Nylabone in there for him to chew on. This will, without doubt, make your puppy recognize that his crate is a wonderful place to be.

The key to effective housetraining is to establish a consistent routine that is followed throughout the day.

proximity to the kitchen, mealtime is another way to associate the crate with something your puppy looks forward to and enjoys. When your puppy finishes his meal, give him about 15 minutes to digest, then take him outside to eliminate. If he begins to complain by whining, yelping, or hitting the crate with his paw, discourage this behavior with a firm though not loud "No!" Wait for your puppy to quiet down before letting him out.

I prefer to wean my dogs off their crates when they are reliable in the house and are no longer having accidents or chewing on things that don't belong to them. Depending on the dog, they are usually ready for full house privileges by 12 to 14 months. Because Cavaliers are slow to mature, it may take longer. You should be able to gauge by your dog's behavior.

Some dog owners prefer to use a crate throughout their dog's life, either with the door open or in the same manner they established when housetraining. All of these lifestyles are acceptable as long as the use of a crate is not abused. Remember, your house, your rules.

## HOUSETRAINING

Housetraining could suggest a variety of polite indoor etiquette. However, when it comes to puppies, housetraining, by and large, refers to eliminating outdoors. Teaching a puppy that eliminating indoors is not acceptable takes time, patience, and regularity and, depending on the age of your puppy, could take weeks but more likely several months. The key to effective housetraining is to establish a consistent routine that is followed throughout the day. It is a commitment the entire family must be dedicated to making to help your puppy succeed.

## How to Housetrain

First, select an outdoor "soiling area" where you and other family members will repeatedly take your puppy to eliminate. Always use the same door and identical route outside to the designated soiling area. *Never* let the puppy outdoors by himself, even if you have a fenced-in yard or enclosure. Young puppies do not like being left alone, and if you want to ensure success, you need to observe him about to relieve himself and while he's eliminating so that you can immediately offer the appropriate cue word and praise when the job is done.

Once outside, observe your puppy closely.

When he has the urge to go, he will begin to sniff the ground and circle. As he is doing that, softly repeat a simple word or phrase such as "Hurry up!" or "Potty!" to coincide with the act. Repeat the cue word or phrase until he actually begins to relieve himself. When he starts to eliminate, switch your cue word to praise, like "Good boy!" "Good Potty!" "Bravo!" or "Hooray!" until he's finished.

The housetraining schedule on page 70 is an example of what is meant by establishing a consistent routine. If you follow a schedule such as the one described, your puppy will become housetrained in no time. Times are approximate—you may need to adjust them to fit your daily routine. This sample schedule is based on three meals a day, spaced about five hours apart (7:00 am, 12:00 pm, and 5:00

Food rewards are helpful in the training process.

# Puppy Housetraining Schedule

| 6:30–8:00 am | Upon waking, take your puppy outdoors to his soiling area or for a brief walk.<br>Feed your puppy his breakfast. Offer fresh water.<br>Wait 15 minutes and then take your puppy outdoors to his soiling area.<br>Put your puppy into his crate along with a special treat. |
|---|---|
| Mid-morning | Take your puppy outdoors to his soiling area or for another walk.<br>Afterward, play with your puppy indoors for about 15 minutes.<br>Return your puppy to the crate. Offer a special treat. |
| 12:00–1:00 pm | Take your puppy outdoors to his soiling area.<br>Return indoors to feed him his second meal and offer fresh water.<br>Wait 15 minutes. Take your puppy to his soiling area. Return indoors.<br>Put your puppy into his crate along with a special treat. |
| Mid-afternoon | Offer your puppy water and then take him outdoors to his soiling area or for another walk.<br>Return your puppy to the crate. Offer a special treat. |
| 5:00 pm | Take your puppy outdoors to his soiling area. Return indoors to feed him his third (last) meal and offer fresh water.<br>Wait 15 minutes and take your puppy outdoors to his soiling area.<br>Return indoors and allow your puppy to play in the kitchen in a secured area where he can be watched while dinner is being prepared. |
| 7:00–7:30 pm | Walk your puppy briefly.<br>Return home and play.<br>Return your puppy to his crate or a secure area where he can be watched. |
| Before bed | Take your puppy outdoors to his soiling area or for a brief walk.<br>Return your puppy to his crate for the night. |

pm). Ensure that you feed your puppy the same time each day. Once your puppy reaches five to six months of age, you may do away with the noon meal and transition him to two meals daily.

During the crate training and housetraining period, you can plan to be outside with your puppy every two hours. Remember, after waking, eating, and playtime, you need to bring your puppy to his soiling area or out for walk. Be observant—if you see him starting to pace or sniff or circle indoors, pick him up and get him outdoors pronto!

## Accidents

When you go about cleaning up after an indoor accident, be sure to use a good enzymatic cleaner to thoroughly eliminate not only the stain but the odor. If you do not clean the area well and eliminate the odor, your puppy may be tempted to use the exact same area again. Enzymatic cleaning solutions especially formulated for pets may be found at any pet shop. Do not use cleaning agents formulated with ammonia. Ammonia actually smells very similar to pet urine and may attract your puppy back to the same indoor spot to eliminate.

Your puppy's capability to be successful depends on your commitment to adhere to a routine that will enable him to achieve the desired behavior.

## BASIC OBEDIENCE COMMANDS

Basic obedience commands create a simple language between pet owners and their dogs. Once these commands are firmly established and reliably followed (and assuming there are no behavior issues), life with dogs is very enjoyable. Because we have 2 acres of fenced property, having dogs who respond to the

## Training Tidbit

Never call your Cavalier to come to you if you plan to trim his nails or give him a bath, or for any other task he may perceive as unpleasant.

word "come" is very important. I can send everyone out for a romp and when I want them back, call out "Come!" from the back door. Before you know it 20 paws are running through the mud room. I often ask everyone to sit and hand out treats. Then we go about our day.

## Come

Come is regarded as one of the most important and useful commands to teach your puppy to obey. More importantly, coming on command, especially under dire circumstances, could save his life. Come and here are often referred to as recall commands, which is the ability to recall your puppy when he is off leash.

Puppies are capable of learning the come command at a very early age. Think about it: Your puppy already knows to come to you, even without being formally trained. For instance, when he hears his meals being prepared, a bag of treats being opened, or the squeak of a favorite toy, he's expecting something good is about to be bestowed upon him. This is how you want the come command to be viewed every time your puppy hears the word. The goal of teaching the recall is to train your puppy to come to you readily and freely because he wants to. Why? Because you are the most exciting and desirable reason to stop what he is doing and eagerly return to you.

Teach your Cavalier to come to you no matter the circumstance.

To ensure that your puppy views you as amazing, there is one fundamentally important rule you must abide by at all costs. Never, ever call your puppy to come to you with an angry tone in your voice to discipline or punish him—*never*. Not for house soiling, destructive chewing, barking, or anything else. By the same token, never call your puppy to you for something that he may perceive as being unpleasant, such as getting his nails clipped, for a bath, or for administering medication. In these instances, go and get your puppy. The *come* cue must always be associated with something positive. Remember, you want your puppy to perceive you as being nothing less than exciting and pleasurable.

### How to Teach *Come*: Method 1

There are a few ways to introduce the *come* command to your puppy. The first will require the help of a family member or friend to assist you.

1. While the other person gently restrains your puppy, call his name enthusiastically, along with giving the *come* command.

2. As your "assistant" releases him, continue to praise enthusiastically as he bounds toward you. Have the assistant clap hands or gently tap the floor to make the exercise more exciting.

3. When he reaches you, praise and reward him with several treats or engage in play with a favorite toy.

4. Repeat this again, except this time, it's your turn to restrain your puppy while your

assistant calls his name along with the *come* command.

5. Repeat the exercise several times.

You can also try a variation of the same game with the entire family sitting on the floor in a large circle. Each member of the circle will take turns calling your puppy to come and rewarding him with a treat or his favorite toy when he obeys. Remember to end the game before your puppy gets overexcited, tired, or bored.

### How to Teach *Come*: Method 2

A second way to begin *recall* training is to start when your puppy is not really paying attention to you and distracted with something else.

1. Call your puppy's name enthusiastically, along with the *come* cue. For example, "Fido, come!"

2. As he turns to run in your direction, clap your hands and give him verbal praise, such as "Good boy!" to keep him engaged.

3. When he reaches you, praise him again and reward him with a few small treats so that he knows that he did the right thing and to keep him interested in you. Doing this frequently will help a dog to associate the verbal *come* command with the action of running toward his owner and being praised and rewarded.

4. Repeat this several times either inside or outdoors in a safe and secure fenced area.

### How to Teach *Come*: Method 3

A third way to start teaching your puppy to come is with a leash and collar.

1. Again, while your puppy is distracted, say his name, followed by the *come* command in a cheerful, upbeat tone. You may make a sound or movement such as clapping your hands and take a few steps backwards.

2. As soon as your puppy starts to come

toward you, cheer him on and encourage him.

3. If he doesn't start to head in your direction, lightly tug on his leash to encourage him to move toward you. At the same time, say his name followed by the word "come." Always keep your voice upbeat and enthusiastic.

4. When he comes to you, offer him a few treats as his reward.

5. Continue to practice this for several sessions.

### Sit

The *sit* is one of the very first and easiest commands to teach a puppy. Because Cavalier puppies, due to size, are already close to the

## *Putting the* Sit *to Good Use*

Two simple steps will help you get off to a good start in puppy training. First, ask your pup to sit when you are about to feed him. Place the dish down and say "Okay." If he jumps at his food bowl before you say "Okay," pick it up immediately and try again. He should not have his meal until you give him the release. Don't worry; he'll catch on very quickly. When my Woody started testing my leadership as a youngster, teaching the polite *sit* at mealtime helped me readjust his thinking in an easy, positive manner.

Another tip is to exit and enter the house ahead of your puppy: leaders always go first. You can ask your pup to sit and then move out ahead of him. This practice spares you the crazy mad dash for the door and possibly tripping over your whirlwind fur ball.

ground, they almost automatically have to sit to look up at you. By following these easy steps, along with an enticing tidbit, your puppy will quickly learn to obey this basic command.

### How to Teach *Sit*

1. With a handful of your puppy's favorite treats, start by catching his attention.
2. When he gets a whiff of his treats and comes in closer to investigate, hold one of the treats over his nose.
3. As he begins to raise his head, draw your hand up over his head and toward his back. As he begins to sit down to reach the treat, say "Sit."
4. As soon as his little bottom hits the floor, praise him enthusiastically with a cheerful voice and give him the treat.
5. Repeat several times. Remember to give the command and your praise with a treat as soon as his bottom hits the floor.

As your puppy catches on, begin to introduce the hand signal for *sit*.

1. Place the treat in one hand, between your thumb and index finger. With your palm open and facing up toward the ceiling, slowly raise your hand, the one with the hidden treat, slightly above your puppy's head and introduce the cue word "sit."
2. When your puppy looks up to follow the treat, he will likely rock back into a sitting position.
3. Mark the *sit* with a lively "Yes!" and promptly offer your puppy the treat.

The *sit* is one of the very first and easiest commands to teach a puppy.

# The Find It Cue

While walking with your puppy on a loose leash, get his attention and toss a soft treat or piece of kibble on the ground slightly ahead of you. Use the cue phrase "find it!" Your puppy will find this fun walking game a reason to check in and be more attentive to you and what you are doing. If you are able to create some excitement and curiosity, your puppy will look forward to his walk and what surprises may be in store for him.

## Down

Teaching your puppy the *down* command typically comes after you have taught *sit*. *Down* is useful when you want your puppy to lie on the floor and stay put in one place for a longer period—longer than you would expect your puppy to sit comfortably.

Remember, *down* means to lie on the floor. Don't confuse it with the *off* command, such as when you want your puppy to stop jumping up on you or to get off the couch. The *off* means that all four of your puppy's paws should be firmly planted on the floor.

### How to Teach *Down*

1. Start with your puppy in a sitting position.
2. Hold your puppy's favorite treat a couple of inches (cm) in front of his nose. Move your hand down toward the ground.
3. As your puppy begins to follow the treat toward the ground, say "Down."
   Your puppy should follow the movement of your hand along with the treat. As soon as his belly hits the ground with his front legs stretched out in front of him, praise him with "Good boy!" or "Good down!" and offer the treat.
4. Repeat this action over and over in short training sessions.
5. Your goal is to build an association between the verbal command *down* and the act of your puppy's lying down.

Eventually, after several practice sessions, you can begin to introduce the hand signal for *down*, along with the treat.

1. To do this, place the treat in the palm of your hand, securing it with your thumb.
2. With your palm facing down, lower your hand toward the ground. Your puppy will follow the scent of the treat while watching your hand lower toward the ground.
3. As your puppy begins to follow the treat toward the ground, say "Down."
4. As soon as his belly hits the ground with his legs stretched out in front of him, praise him with "Good boy!" or "Good down!" and offer the treat.
5. Repeat this action.

Keep training lessons short but repeat them often. Five-minute sessions four or five times daily will keep the newly learned skill fresh in your puppy's mind but will also keep him from becoming bored.

## Walk Nicely on Leash

Teaching your Cavalier puppy to walk nicely on a loose leash may not sound difficult. After all, you're not dealing with a heavyweight. But don't let his size fool you. Even a Cavalier, with a low center of gravity, can tug unpleasantly on the leash. If you want your puppy to be viewed as a refined, polite canine citizen, teaching him how to walk nicely on a loose leash is a very good place to start.

Playtime, which offers opportunities for socialization, is an important part of puppy kindergarten.

### How to Teach Walk Nicely on Leash

You can begin indoors or outdoors, where there are certain to be more distractions and reasons for your puppy to want to pull at the end of the leash.

First fill your pocket with some of your puppy's dry kibble. If you are afraid of overfeeding, use a portion of his breakfast, lunch, or dinner for practicing loose leash walking. The kibble will be used as a reward for walking nicely.

Once again, use a cue word or phrase such as "Let's go" and start walking with your puppy on your left side. Don't worry if he strays in front of you or to your right, as we are not at the stage where we want to teach *heel*, which always has the dog positioned on your left. The objective of this lesson is to simply walk nicely without pulling.

1. Begin walking. Watch your puppy closely—if he begins to pull, stop dead in your tracks.
2. Resume walking only when the leash is loose. Every time your puppy begins to pull, stop.
3. This can be frustrating not only for the puppy who is on a mission but for you as well. Remember, this is a training exercise, not quite yet a walk as you might be expecting.

Another option to keep you moving is to change direction on your puppy if he begins to pull.

1. Simply turn around.
2. Shortly before doing so, try using the phrase "about turn." This will eventually alert your puppy that you are about to change direction.

3. Try changing the pace and mixing it up a bit. Varying the speed at which you are walking will teach your puppy to pay greater attention to you. When he is walking nicely at your side, offer him a piece of kibble and tell him cheerfully what a good job he's doing.

4. Encourage and praise your puppy as you walk together on a loose leash. Don't be shy about talking to your puppy. Positive feedback sends him a signal that you like what he's doing. He will soon associate loose leash walking with the praise and realize that this is the behavior you are looking for.

## PUPPY KINDERGARTEN

A puppy kindergarten training class is a very popular introductory class for young puppies. It allows them to socialize and helps the owner better understand their new addition. Course content generally covers topics such as understanding puppy behaviors, effective communication, basic grooming needs, learning to correct typical puppy problems such as mouthing, chewing, jumping, and housetraining, and allows owners to ask questions and share their experiences in a group setting where everyone is in the same boat, so to speak. Puppy kindergarten also covers the basic commands, such as *sit, down,* and *come,* and allows the puppy to play with other puppies in a safe and secure area under the watchful eye of the instructor.

Before you sign your puppy up for puppy kindergarten, I recommended that you visit several different classes as a spectator. It's best to attend without your puppy so that

you and the class are not distracted by a restless, fidgety puppy while you're trying to observe.

Examine the training area. Is it clean, warm, and well lit? Is there a reasonable ratio of students to the instructor? Typically, puppy kindergarten classes are limited to no more than eight puppies. Does the instructor have an assistant? Is the duration of the class no longer than one hour? Anything longer could become stressful for your puppy.

Is the instructor upbeat and cheerful? How does he or she interact with the owners and puppies? I've noticed that some trainers are great with dogs but less patient with people. Both you and your pup should enjoy the class! Also study how the instructor answers an owner's questions. How does the instructor react to a puppy and owner who may be struggling? By being patient and kind? Most important, is everyone having fun?

I personally prefer taking classes with puppies because the exposure to other puppies is very important. Teaching your puppy to tune out distractions and follow your commands is also a big part of the training experience. I usually employ private trainers if I need help with a specific problem.

# PART II

# ADULTHOOD

# CHAPTER 5

# FINDING YOUR CAVALIER ADULT

*Acquiring a dog may be the only opportunity
a human ever has to choose a relative.*
—Mordecai Wyatt Johnson

Not everyone is set up for or wants to start out with a puppy. Cute as they are, puppies are demanding and time consuming. I'm at an advantage because I work at home and can take a break every three or four hours to interact with my dogs. We play in our fenced 2-acre yard, go for walks in the neighborhood or, if I need to run quick errands, pop everyone in the car to enjoy the ride. It's one of the wonderful perks of being an author. But few of us have this luxury.

## WHY ADOPTING AN ADULT IS A GOOD IDEA

For seniors or those who don't have the time, the high energy and destructive tendencies of a puppy might just be too much work. Adult dogs are generally calmer and easier to be around. And there are other advantages in bringing a mature dog into your life. For one, you will know exactly what he looks like and how much he weighs. His personality is already developed, he has life experience living with a human pack, and most likely he will be

housetrained. Depending on his circumstances, he may even have obedience training. If he is a rescue, he will be grateful to have a forever home, and you may well have saved his life.

Prospective owners interested in obtaining an adult dog have a few options: adopting from a breeder, shelter, or rescue. Breeders may have a retired show dog, a former stud who has been neutered and needs a pet home, or a female no longer used for breeding. You can find breeders by visiting the websites of Cavalier clubs and then e-mailing those in your area, expressing your interest in adopting an adult dog. If they don't have an older dog available, you can ask that they keep you in mind if they hear in their circle of canine friends of any Cavalier adults who need to be placed in pet homes.

Because Cavaliers have become so popular, chances are there are some right in your community. If you spot one, ask the dog's owner for information about his breeder.

You can also check to see whether there is a dog breed directory in your area. In my state, the New Jersey Federation of Dog Clubs publishes a Breeders and Rescue Services Directory biennially. Friends of mine, a two-career couple, were interested in adopting an adult Golden Retriever. They wrote to each

Adopting an adult Cavalier provides a viable alternative to anyone who cannot handle the high-energy demands of a puppy.

Golden breeder in the directory expressing their desire to have an adult, described their previous dog-owning experience, mentioned that they had a fenced yard and that the husband particularly enjoyed taking long walks in the neighborhood. Although this couple worked full time away from home, they planned to hire a pet sitter to visit the dog during the workday. Sure enough, a wonderful breeder contacted them when she was ready to place Surry, a female she no longer planned to breed. It turned out to be a wonderful match.

Years later, this same couple, now with a young son, wanted to adopt another adult Golden. It took some time to find the right dog, but then Chloe arrived. Her original owner passed away and she was being fostered by her breeder. Although different in type and personality from her predecessor, Chloe too has become a much loved member of the family.

Attending dog shows is also a good way to network. You might chat with Cavalier handlers after they have come out of the ring and express your interest in adopting an adult Cavalier. It's important to always have your ears and eyes open—you never know when the perfect opportunity might present itself.

## ADOPTING AN ADULT FROM A BREEDER

Cavaliers are considered adults between the ages of two and seven. Many people have adopted adult dogs from breeders, and the matches have been very successful. I have had this experience myself. We adopted our current spaniel, Rory, from his breeder when he was three years old. At the time, Smokey, our Field Spaniel, was well into his senior years and Woody, our Irish Setter, was a playful adolescent with too much energy for Smokey. We decided that Woody needed a canine buddy his own age to play with.

I started contacting breeders of several spaniel breeds. I had a list of requirements. The dog needed to be between one and three years of age. He had to be well socialized with dogs and people, as he would be moving into a multi-dog household. Plus, we frequently host doggy play dates.

By luck, when I contacted the then-secretary of the national Welsh Springer Club, she had just decided to place one of her own nine dogs. Rory was a conformation champion who had also participated in hunt tests. He was a sweetheart of a dog. Unfortunately, one of his half-brothers just didn't like him and would start fights. Neither dog was neutered at the time, and Rory's breeder had to keep the two separated. Because we had raised a female Welshie previously, we were delighted with the prospect of having another. Rory was neutered and we brought him home two months later.

Rory has been a wonderful addition to our family. Smokey accepted him immediately,

A responsible breeder will interview you at length to make sure the right dog is chosen for you and your family.

and Woody came around in about a week. The two became fast friends. They would hunt the backyard birds together—Woody pointing and Rory flushing. They'd chase and play with their balls and enjoy wonderful games of tug-of-war. Smokey enjoyed observing their antics from the deck.

If you purchase an adult dog from a breeder, the purchase price is often less than for a puppy. Usually, after a dog has completed his show career or is no longer needed for breeding, a breeder's first priority is to find the dog a wonderful forever home.

While interviewing breeders for this book,

## By the Numbers

Cavaliers are considered adults between the ages of two and seven.

If you purchase an adult dog from a breeder, the purchase price is often less than that for a puppy.

I came across an adorable four-year-old male Ruby Cavalier in just this situation. Such a temptation! But I've vowed that I will have no more than five dogs at one time. Otherwise I'd be unable to provide the type of life I want each of them to have. But you can bet I'm networking to help find that Ruby a nice forever home.

## Breeder Interviews

If you are interested in adopting an older dog from a breeder, call several in your area. Visit as many as possible. The breeder will want to get

to know you, and there will be interviews and applications to fill out.

Cavaliers are very happy and versatile dogs and make the transition easily from one family to another as long as you have given the breeder enough information to understand your lifestyle. Proper placement for success is always important. A dog who has been raised in the country may have a difficult time transitioning to a bustling city, and vice versa. A dog who has had people at home with him all day might not be happy in a new situation where everyone heads off to work or school each morning. Trust the breeder to want to select the best possible family for the dog. If you are fortunate, there will be a match out there for you.

## Terms and Conditions

Breeder contracts may vary. A breeder may wish to have the dog neutered or spayed while still in her care. If not, the contract will probably outline a time line for this important surgery. Other terms will deal with recommended veterinary care, i.e., vaccinations, special types of exams for Cavaliers (eye and heart testing, for example), plus dietary and grooming requirements. They may also require that the dog be returned should you ever decide you cannot keep him. Most breeders will want to check in on their dogs from time to time, so keep in mind that this may be a long-lasting relationship, but one from which you may benefit in having an ally and expert resource in your pet's care.

## ADOPTING FROM RESCUE GROUPS AND ANIMAL SHELTERS

When considering adopting an adult dog, there are two other adoption options: rescues and shelters. A canine rescue group fosters unwanted, abandoned, abused, or stray pets and attempts to find suitable new homes for them. There are single-breed and all-breed rescues. These groups do not euthanize. Essentially, the major differences between shelters and rescue groups are that shelters are usually run and funded by the local government and have a kennel, while rescue groups are funded mainly by donations and comprise volunteer foster families.

Cavalier Rescue USA is a well-known Cavalier rescue group affiliated with the national club, Cavalier King Charles Spaniel Club-USA (www.ckcsc.org). Located throughout the United States, it has a large range of adults available for adoption. According to a current representative, 325 Cavaliers passed through rescue last year in comparison to only 13 dogs in 1999. Sadly, the very thing that early members of the USA club feared has happened: The breed has become very popular and fallen into the hands of puppy mill and commercial breeders. That, plus easy-access Internet sales by these groups, has increased the need for rescue. Most of the dogs available are young to middle aged (two to five years old). The national parent club, American Cavalier King Charles Spaniel Club, also has a rescue division. Visit it at www.ackcsc.org.

Two other adoption options are to contact local shelters and all-breed rescue groups in

## Why Dogs Are Relinquished

There are three primary reasons why dogs are relinquished: their owners have misjudged the amount of time raising a dog requires; the owner's life circumstances have changed (birth of a first child, divorce, return to full-time work); and canine health issues arise that owners are unable or unwilling to pay for.

Just because a dog has not worked out in his first home does not mean that he can't be a perfect addition to yours. Many people I know have had wonderful experiences adopting adult dogs from rescue groups.

# Sample Adoption Questionnaire

- Number of people in home: adults: ____ages: ____ children: _____ ages: _____
- Why do you want to bring a new dog into your home?
- Is everyone in the household in agreement on adopting a new dog?
- When will you be ready for your new dog?
- Do you rent or own?
    Type of housing: House ___Apartment___Condo___ Townhouse___
- If rental, landlord's name and phone:
- Are animals permitted?
- How long have you resided at your present address?
- Are you planning to change residence in the near future? If yes, please explain.
- Do you have a yard?
    Dimensions of yard:___
    Fenced in?___ Height of fence?___
    Not fenced in?___ Partially fenced?_____
- Where will your dog be exercised?
- How much daily exercise will you provide?
- How long will your dog be left alone during the day?
- Where will your new dog be kept while alone?
- Do you own a crate?
- Have you ever crate-trained a dog?
- Will you be crating your new dog?
- Do you understand that your new dog may develop some issues as he/she adjusts to his/her new home?
- Will you tolerate the following issues during that adjustment period? If no, please explain.
    Housebreaking accidents ___Chewing ___Barking/whining ___
- If these issues do not get resolved in a reasonable amount of time, what will you do?
- What do you consider a reasonable amount of time?
- Have you ever taken a dog to obedience training?
- Will you attend training classes with your new dog?
- How long have you been searching for a new dog? Where have you searched?
- Why did you choose this particular dog?
- Does anyone in your household have any known allergies to dogs?
- Is anyone in the household fearful of dogs?
- Has anyone in the household ever been bitten by a dog? If yes, please explain.
- Do you have animals now? What kind? (List breed/age/sex.)
- Are they neutered or spayed? If no, please explain.
- How will they react to a new dog in the home?
- List any animals you have had in the past; include name, breed, and sex. How long did you own the pet/s?
- Why do you no longer own the pet/s?
- Have any of your pets ever been lost? Hit by a motor vehicle? If yes, please explain.
- A dog can live 12 to 18 years. Are you financially prepared and willing to give this animal the medical care he/she requires for his/her lifetime?
- Please list 2 references (nonfamily members):
    Name: _____Relationship:_____ e-mail:_____
    Name: _____Relationship:_____ e-mail:_____

*Courtesy of Rawhide Rescue.*

When adopting an adult dog from a rescue or shelter, try to find out as much about your prospective new pet as possible.

your area. Ask to be placed on a call list when a Cavalier comes in. You may not be able to adopt a dog as soon as you'd like, but with patience and the right timing you will find him.

## Do Your Homework

When adopting an adult dog from a rescue or shelter, try to find out as much about your prospective new pet as possible. Why was he relinquished? How old is he? Is he neutered? Crate trained? Housetrained? What commands does he know? Has he been raised with children? How does he get along with other animals? Does he suffer from separation anxiety?

## Paperwork and Criteria

If you have found a good match, it's time to start the paperwork. Most rescue groups have strict adoption procedures that can include completing an application to adopt, checking a veterinary reference, and conducting a phone interview and/or a home visit.

The sample adoption questionnaire on page 86 from Rawhide Rescue, the group that fostered our spaniel, Lily, will give you an idea of what to expect:

If you are approved to adopt a particular dog, you will be expected to sign a contract. Some of the terms may include that you:

- allow a home visit by a volunteer from the group

- never relinquish the dog to a pound or shelter but return him/her to the rescue if you can no longer keep him/her
- purchase an identification tag for your new dog within the first 24 hours of possession
- notify the rescue immediately if the dog is lost
- have the dog checked by your veterinarian within seven days after adoption
- provide medical care at your own expense for any health conditions, as well as provide routine yearly exams for as long as you own the dog

Know that each rescue group has its own adoption process, and what is true for one may not be true for another. The bottom line is that they're all doing their best to place their charges in forever homes.

Animal shelters also have adoption applications that may include some additional types of questions. Some examples are:
- Are you interested in a guard dog?
- Do you want a dog to hunt or herd with?
- Are you looking for a dog with a playful or laid-back personality?
- Do you plan to participate in any canine sports such agility, flyball, or obedience?
- Would you be interested in adopting a dog with special needs?

Once a match has been made, a contract outlining the owner's responsibilities and commitment to their new pet will need to be signed.

## Fees

You will incur a nominal fee when adopting

Before bringing an adopted dog into your life, make sure that you are willing to invest the time and money necessary to fulfill all his needs—both physical and emotional.

your Cavalier from either a rescue or shelter. However, the adoption fees usually don't cover the significant costs involved, which include traveling to pick up a dog in need, providing veterinary care, vaccinations, spaying/neutering etc. But they do help rescues and shelters to continue the important work they do.

## Potential Issues

When you bring home an adult dog who has been housetrained, don't be surprised if he has accidents. He may be nervous, insecure, confused, or marking. Actually, there are myriad reasons why he may slip up.

When Rory moved in, he marched through our living room and promptly lifted his leg on my grandfather's antique coffee table, which sits on a lovely oriental rug. I was quite shocked. Rory had been a house dog, so I certainly wasn't expecting any housetraining surprises. But in actuality, I did have a problem for about six weeks. So I acted as though Rory was a puppy and set about to housetrain him as if it were all a new concept. Eventually, his earlier training kicked in, and he has been fine ever since.

Unexpected chewing is another problem you might encounter. Rory had a habit of stealing things. One day he met me at the door with a puffy lip. I immediately thought

## Training Tidbit

Give your adult Cavalier time to adjust to his new home, and have patience. Even though housetrained, he may have accidents during the first few weeks.

### Multi-Dog Tip

Introduce your new dog to your resident dog in neutral territory. Use a crate with the new dog until you are certain that the dogs have accepted one another.

that he had been stung by a bee and quickly opened his mouth to investigate. Instead of a bite, I found a wooden spoke caught between his teeth and pushing against his lip. It was easy to remove and Rory hadn't been harmed, but it took me a while to figure out where the spoke had come from. It belonged to my husband's backscratcher that he kept in his dressing room! Eventually, Rory's puppy pranks subsided too.

I called Rory's breeder a few times to get her take on his unexpected behavior. Any reputable breeder will want to help the dog adjust to his new home. So don't be bashful about asking for assistance. Rescue volunteers also want their placements to work out. If you are experiencing any kind of health, training, or behavior issue, call your rescue representative immediately. Don't allow a problem to escalate and risk having to return the dog. Have patience; your new Cavalier may just be going through an adjustment period.

Don't be surprised if, after time passes and your Cavalier has become a true member of the family, you find yourself looking for another. Most people I interviewed for this book have more than one.

# CHAPTER 6

# CAVALIER GROOMING NEEDS

If you've had your Cavalier since puppyhood, hopefully you started getting him accustomed to grooming early on. If you're working with an adopted adult, it may take a little longer for him to adjust to the process. Just remember to keep initial grooming sessions short and positive.

For the Cavalier's long, silky coat to remain in exquisite condition, he should be brushed thoroughly at least once a week. The natural oils of his coat will attract dirt and grime, and the feathering on his ears, chest, legs, and tail will undoubtedly collect all sorts of outdoor debris such as grass cuttings, leaves, and twigs. If this debris is not removed from his coat immediately, it can give way to tangles and mats, those thick, interwoven masses of hair that are difficult to separate and comb through. Mats can irritate the skin and lead to infection if not removed.

If you plan to groom your Cavalier yourself, consider a lesson from your breeder, if local. It's very beneficial to have a one-on-one private tutorial before you go it alone. Either way, you will need the following basic tools:

- a spray bottle filled with water
- diluted detangler or conditioner for loosening tangles and mats
- a small slicker brush
- a small pin brush
- a mat-raking tool
- a shedding tool
- a straight comb
- a pair of grooming shears (scissors)
- nail clippers

## BRUSHING AND COMBING

Now that you have the necessary equipment, you are ready to groom your Cavalier, following these few simple steps.

### How to Brush and Comb

Thoroughly brush your Cavalier's coat with either the slicker brush or pin brush to remove loose or dead hair. The type of brush you choose will depend on your dog's coat. The fluffier or thicker the coat, the better off you will be with a slicker brush. If your Cavalier's coat is silkier, a pin brush will work just fine. If your Cavalier has a very full coat, you might find it more manageable to brush the hair in layers or sections, starting at the bottom and moving up to the top coat. If brushing causes static electricity, lightly mist the coat with water beforehand. Just be sure to remove any tangles or mats before wetting the hair.

Gently comb through the coat to remove any tangles. Use a spray bottle filled with a diluted solution of conditioner or detangler to untangle any stubborn tangles and mats. Sometimes a mat-raking tool, specifically designed to break up mats, will help you remove them more effectively than a slicker or pin brush.

When you brush, begin at the head, paying close attention to the ears. (Note: Brushing the underside of the ears and checking them for debris is probably the most important part of grooming a Cavalier.) Then work your way down to the left front leg, followed by the chest, then over to the right front leg. Next move to the left back leg, the underbelly, and over to right back leg. Finish by stroking along the back and finishing with the tail.

Keep in mind that the breed standard is to be strictly followed if you plan to show your dog in conformation, but if your Cavalier will purely be a companion dog, then there is nothing wrong with a trim if that is what you desire. Just be aware that a coat that has been trimmed will, over time, lose its soft silky texture and grow back thicker and coarser.

Be sure to brush your Cavalier well before giving him a bath, as tangles and mats are impossible to separate and remove when they're wet.

## BATHING

Bathing will keep your Cavalier smelling sweet, and his clean, tangle-free coat will be nothing short of splendid. Although Cavaliers are by nature clean dogs, the oils in their coat will build up, trapping dirt and grime. Only a bath will restore the coat to its natural beauty.

Just remember that too much bathing can irritate and dry out the skin and hair. So how do you know how often you should be bathing your dog? More often than not, it comes down to lifestyle and the needs of the individual dog. Cavaliers, in general, should not be bathed more than once a week, but unless your dog is filthy or smells objectionable, a bath every month or two may be quite sufficient.

The first step is to be well organized and keep your bathing supplies together in a handy plastic pail or box. Your container should contain the following:

- doggy shampoo
- doggy conditioner
- towels
- hair dryer
- comb
- cotton balls

If you use this time to clean your Cavalier's eyes and ears, be sure to include these supplies in your bath-time container as well:

- 100% pure cotton (not one made of synthetic materials, as it may be more abrasive to delicate ears)
- saline eye solution and an ear-cleaning solution formulated for dogs

Additionally, some Cavalier owners may wish to use a grooming table for brushing and after-bath drying. Grooming tables are a great way to raise your dog up to a more convenient height so that you do not have to sit on the floor or bend over your dog in an uncomfortable position for long periods.

## How to Bathe

Again, before bathing, be sure to brush your dog's coat thoroughly to remove any tangles or mats. Place cotton balls in your dog's ears to prevent excess water from entering the ear canal during bathing and rinsing.

Use a large utility-size sink, your own bathtub or shower, or a tub made just for pets. Place a nonslip mat on the bottom. It's ideal if you have a handheld sprayer fastened to the faucet, which will allow you to easily wet the coat thoroughly before shampooing and rinse out the shampoo completely afterward.

First, be sure that the water is a comfortably warm temperature by testing it on your hand. Also, monitor the water periodically for sudden temperature changes. Do not use your own personal shampoo on your Cavalier. Shampoos formulated for the pH, acidity, or alkalinity of human skin is different from shampoos formulated for dog skin and may lead to dryness and irritation. (Tip: A dry shampoo, disposable bath wipes, or doggy hair spray found at a pet supply store, which require no water or rinsing, are wonderful alternatives when a quick "on-the-spot" clean-up is required.) Purchase a shampoo especially formulated for your dog. Your breeder can recommend a shampoo and conditioner that works well on the Cavalier's silky coat.

Thoroughly soak your dog's coat, and massage the shampoo well into his skin and coat. Rinse your dog well from tip to tail with clean water to remove all shampoo residues.

Repeat this process with a conditioner. This time, do not massage it into the coat and skin; just work it gently into the coat. This will make the coat more manageable and will remove any tangles that shampooing may have left behind. Read the directions. Some conditioners require rinsing, while others may not.

If you are using a sink or tub, drain the bathwater and towel dry your pet, removing all excess water. Finish drying with a hair dryer meant for dogs. Two tricks to control your Cavalier from shaking and splattering you and the room with water are to hold his neck or an ear with one hand while towel drying and to wrap a small towel around his body and fastening it with a clip across his chest.

When your dog is thoroughly dry, you can trim the hair between his paw pads whether he is a show dog or pet. It will help keep small stones and other debris from

Before bathing your Cavalier, brush his coat thoroughly to remove any tangles or mats.

The Cavalier's long, feathered ears tend to collect dirt and debris. Daily grooming is recommended.

lodging between his pads, which can be uncomfortable. It will also keep him from tracking things into the house.

## EAR CARE

Cavaliers have long, floppy ears that tend to get dirt in them more frequently than the ears of short-eared breeds. Those long ears also limit proper air circulation, which allows moisture to build up in them. A dog's ear canal is L-shaped. Earwax and debris will often collect at the right-angle bend in the "L." This is why

you need to pay special attention to the health of your dog's ears.

Whether you groom your Cavalier yourself or use a professional groomer, it's prudent to inspect those ears at every grooming session to see whether they need cleaning. Your veterinarian will also examine them at every routine checkup to ensure the absence of any potential problems. If your dog exhibits signs of frequent head shaking and/or ear scratching, it might be a sign of a possible ear infection and he should be seen by a veterinarian.

Examine the inside of the outer ear, or ear flap. If you detect a foul odor or see signs of inflammation or redness or excessive earwax in the form of a tar-like discharge, these visible symptoms may be the result of an underlying problem such as a yeast or bacterial infection. If your examination shows only a small trace of wax or dirt, you can easily clean your dog's ears yourself.

## How to Clean the Ears

Soak a cotton ball with a little bit of saline solution or an ear cleanser recommended by your veterinarian. Lightly wipe away any visible dirt from the folds and crevices on the underside of the outer ear, or "pinna," the part of the ear flap that is made of cartilage and covered by skin and hair. Do not try to clean areas of the ear that you cannot see. Gently pull the outer ear flap up and slightly away from the head to straighten out the L-shaped ear canal. If you notice an excessive amount of wax or debris at the opening of the ear canal, squirt a few drops of the saline or ear-cleaning solution into the ear canal. Placing your thumb at the inside base of the ear flap and the rest of your fingers on the outside of the base of the ear, massage the base of the ear for 20 to 30 seconds until you hear the solution squishing

This breed's large eyes—being more vulnerable to irritation and injury—would benefit from routine inspection and care.

around inside the ear canal. This action will loosen any debris located in the ear canal. Allow your dog to shake his head. Then take a dry cotton ball and gently insert it into the ear to gently wipe out the debris that was loosened by the ear-cleaning solution and massaged up out of the ear canal.

Never use a cotton swab to clean inside the ear canal. You could actually cause more harm than good by unintentionally pushing the wax or debris deeper into the ear canal toward the ear drum.

When you have finished, praise your dog and reward him with his favorite treat for a job well done.

## EYE CARE

The Cavalier's large, round, and somewhat protruding eyes contribute to the breed's overall endearing appearance. However, windy and dusty conditions can cause irritation and tearing in these types of eyes, so routine inspection and care is prudent.

## Multi-Dog Tip

It's easy to let at-home grooming slip when you have multiple dogs. If you find you're having trouble keeping up with a routine schedule, a professional grooming service or mobile groomer may be the answer.

## How to Clean the Eyes

Healthy eyes should be bright and clear. If you see mucus buildup in the corners on the lower lid, remove it with a canine eye wipe or a dampened gauze pad or wash cloth. Wipe away from the eye to avoid accidentally scratching the eye ball. A veterinary eye wash can also be used for periodic cleansing. Frequency of use would depend on the individual dog's tendency to tear and should be discussed with his veterinarian.

Some Cavaliers look as if they are always crying because tears spill down their faces. Chromodacryorrhea (tear staining) can have many causes. Sometimes the placement of just a few eyelashes can act like a wick and pull tears onto the fur. The tears can contain a bacterium that is not harmful but turns brown when it hits the air. Some people treat the staining that appears with antibiotics, while others use white vinegar, diluted hydrogen peroxide, eye wipes, or a powder supplement containing a natural antibiotic that is added to food. Results are mixed, and Cavalier owners need to be vigilant to improve cosmetic appearance. Tearing can also be caused by airborne allergens, dryness of the air, food allergies, and other factors. Although some dogs suffer from constant tearing, which may be perfectly normal for them, others may have tearing due to an ongoing sinus or upper respiratory infection, which may not resolve without medication. It's best to have your pet examined by his vet to determine the actual cause so the condition can be treated appropriately.

## NAIL TRIMMING

Most dogs don't like having their feet touched or their nails trimmed. You need to start early when they are puppies, by gently holding and stroking their paws until you can move on to applying light pressure on their paws, toes, and nails. Praise them if they remain calm and offer a treat during the process. With time and patience, your dog will overcome his fear and get accustomed to the process. Some dogs will eventually become so relaxed that they will lie on their side or sit on your lap or a grooming table while you go about trimming their nails.

Others, no matter what you do to desensitize them to the nail-trimming process, may still require some form of restraint. When Woody was only nine weeks old, he'd snap at me when I attempted to trim his nails. I'm not talking about cute puppy nipping but true attempts to bite. I was shocked to see this type of behavior in such a young and otherwise sweet-natured puppy. Things only got worse. By the time he was a few months old, my vet had to muzzle him while two technicians held him down to trim his nails. At that point, I hired a private trainer to help me overcome Woody's resistance to nail trimming. She taught me several behavior modification techniques.

First, she had me place the nail clipper near Woody's bowl at each meal, for positive association. She also told me to touch the clippers to his paws and give him a small treat.

Plus, gently touch his toes with my fingers and offer a food reward. I repeated these measures frequently for several weeks. The results were amazing.

Your Cavalier will need to have his nails trimmed on a regular basis.

In time, Woody would roll over on his back, legs in the air while I trimmed his nails without offering a peep of protest.

Just as it will be helpful to know how to trim your dog's nails, it's just as important to recognize when your dog needs to have his nails trimmed. Like hair, nails grow constantly and will require your help in keeping them short and tidy. Allowing your dog's nails to grow and failing to have them clipped can cause the bones of the foot to spread, resulting in discomfort and eventually permanent damage and lameness.

If you plan to trim your dog's nails yourself, you will need to purchase the right tools. Here's a list of essentials:

• Nail clippers or trimmers. The guillotine type and small scissors type nail clippers are favorites among breeders and professional groomers for trimming the nails of smaller breeds. The scissors type has a slight advantage over the guillotine style because it allows you to see more of the nail and the nail quick in dogs with clear nails.

• Another option is an electric nail grinder, but it's not ideal unless you can ensure that the long hair on your Cavalier's feet does not get caught in the grinder as it rotates. This can be quite tricky. If the hair gets caught, it can be quite painful for your dog and traumatic for both of you.

• A small nail file to file down any jagged edges after trimming.

• A styptic pencil or powder just in case you

Guillotine and small scissors type clippers are favorites among breeders and professional groomers for trimming the nails of smaller breeds.

accidentally hit the nail quick, the tender part of the nail that contains blood vessels and nerve endings, causing the nail to bleed.

If trimming your dog's nails makes you uneasy, do yourself and your dog a favor and take him to your veterinarian or to a professional groomer to have this done. Believe it or not, your dog may actually be better behaved in someone else's capable hands.

If you have the confidence and ability to do it yourself, read on.

## How to Trim the Nails

First, be sure to read the instructions for the nail clipper you have purchased. Even better, you may wish to ask your breeder or veterinarian to show you how it's done. Then you can fly solo.

You may find it easiest to have your Cavalier lie on his back in your lap, tummy up, legs out, or have someone else hold your dog in his or her arms. You can also have your dog standing or lying on his side on a grooming table.

If you are using the popular guillotine type clipper, you will need to cut from the underside of your dog's nail upward, positioning the clipper in the right place, with the short flat side (the one with the two little screws) resting on your dog's pad.

If your dog is squirming, wait until he stops wriggling and squeeze the clipper firmly and quickly. Be careful to stay away from the quick. You will know that you have trimmed enough if your dog's nails do not touch the ground when he stands.

If you're using the scissors type, push the hair back on your dog's paw with your thumb so you can look at the nail from the side. On Blenheims and Tricolors, you can see a section of white and then the quick. You can cut half way down the white section to avoid hitting the quick. It's a little harder to see on a Ruby, but there is still a color differentiation where the quick begins. Black and Tans have darker nails that are the hardest to clip, so trim little bits at a time until you reach 1/16th of an inch (0.16 cm).

If you accidentally hit the quick and cause the nail to bleed, don't panic. Yes, you will feel awful that you caused your dog to yelp in pain, but remain calm and apply some styptic powder to the wounded nail. That will stop the bleeding immediately and will not sting the dog.

## DENTAL CARE

Just like humans, over time your Cavalier

### Toothbrush Alternative

An alternative to using a doggy toothbrush is to wrap a small clean washcloth or piece of gauze around your index finger and rub your dog's teeth at the gum line daily. If the gums appear red and irritated at the gum line, pour a small amount of hydrogen peroxide on the cloth and gently clean the area to help reduce and heal the inflammation.

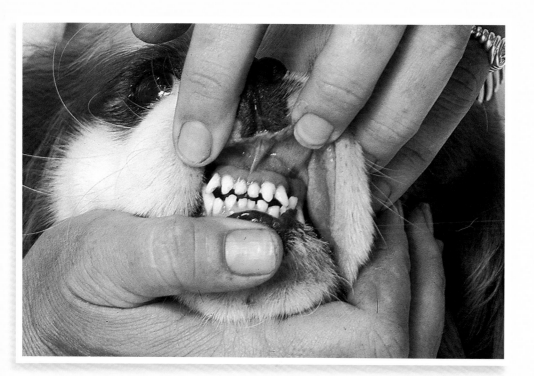

Examine your dog's teeth and gums as part of his regular grooming routine.

will start to build up plaque and tartar on his teeth, especially on the difficult-to-reach back teeth. Plaque is an accumulation of food, bacteria, and saliva. Tartar is a combination of mineral deposits and crystallized plaque. These substances are often the cause of bad breath, gingivitis (inflammation of the gums around the roots of the teeth), tooth decay, difficulty in eating, and discomfort or pain. Gingivitis, if left untreated, can lead to tooth, gum, and bone loss. And worse, poor oral hygiene can also lead to serious systemic health problems. Bacteria from gum disease can spread through the bloodstream and cause heart, lung, kidney, and liver disorders.

Now you might think that feeding your dog dry kibble over wet food is the answer to keeping your dog's teeth clean. Well, actually, dry food does not keep your dog's teeth clean. Surprised? You shouldn't be. How long does your dog linger and chew his food? Most inhale their meals, giving the kibble little time to scrape the tooth surface and clean off the tartar. So you see, eating dry food and hard-as-rock biscuits does very little to clean your dog's teeth. If dry, hard food were the answer, we might opt to include more of it in our own diet if it meant skipping a trip to the dentist! Actually, it's the high starch content in food, including your dog's dry kibble and hard dog biscuits, that contributes to dental disease.

## How to Brush Your Dog's Teeth

So how would you go about cleaning your dog's teeth? Well, if you're lucky enough to have adopted an adult dog who doesn't mind your lifting his flews—those loose flaps of skin on either side of the upper muzzle—to expose his teeth and gums, daily brushing (or at least several times a week) with a toothbrush designed especially for dogs is your best defense against plaque and the bacteria and minerals that create tartar. Otherwise you will have to teach your dog to accept brushing, which normally occurs during puppyhood. Start by getting him accustomed to having his mouth touched. When he's relaxed, say just resting in your lap, let him sniff your fingers, then gently rub your index finger along his gum line. Talk in soothing tones and offer praise.

After a week or two, wrap a clean washcloth with warm water around your finger. Slowly massage the outside of the upper teeth. After a few days, substitute doggy toothpaste for the water. (Note: Don't use human toothpaste because it can cause gastric upset.) If your dog is accepting the washcloth, replace it with a doggy toothbrush. Brush the upper teeth and gums using a circular motion. Eventually move to the lower and inside of the teeth.

## Doggy Toothpaste and Toothbrush

You can brush your dog's teeth with a child's toothbrush or purchase a doggy toothbrush from your pet store or vet's office. There are various types. For example, one has a large soft brush at one end and a smaller brush at the other. Yet another type is actually three sided to help reach around all surfaces of the

You should brush your dog's teeth regularly with a canine toothbrush and toothpaste.

teeth. There are also many doggy toothpastes on the market that can be purchased through veterinarians, pet stores, and catalogs. They're usually made with doggy-pleasing flavors such as chicken or liver. You might want to take care where you keep your dog's toothpaste. I kept ours in the bathroom cabinet since I obviously knew the difference between it and my own. But one weekend while my mother was visiting I happened to walk past the bathroom and overheard her say quizzically, "Chicken flavor?" I burst in on her and exclaimed, "Don't use that, it's for the dogs!"

Since then, I found an alternative to toothpaste: dental sprays. I've discovered several on the market, and the one I use really does keep tartar and plaque at bay. Gels are also available. Cavaliers seem to have a tendency toward dental issues, so daily brushing is still probably your best bet. Your vet will keep a check on the condition of your dog's teeth and recommend a professional cleaning if warranted.

## FINDING A PROFESSIONAL GROOMER

Finding a professional groomer is much like seeking a veterinarian, professional dog trainer, or obedience school. The process starts with the referrals of family, friends, your vet, and other dog enthusiasts in your area.

Once you have acquired the names of several groomers, call first to inquire as to when it might be a good time for you to stop by to visit. If the groomer can accommodate a visit, ask what her experience is with grooming the Cavalier King Charles Spaniel, how long she has been in business, and where she learned her craft.

Take a walk around the salon. Is it clean, well lit, and comfortable? Are the waiting dogs

## Training Tidbit

Ask the groomer whether you can stay during your Cavalier's first few appointments in order to reassure him and offer treats while he's being groomed.

crated or securely tethered? Is there a waiting area for the owner to sit and wait? If clients are dropping off or picking up their pets, is the groomer/client relationship friendly? How does the groomer greet the dog? Ask about the bathing system and dryers. Many groomers will place a dog in a crate with a dryer blowing on him while they set to work bathing another dog. Some groomers use hand-held dryers while the dog is still on the grooming table. Still others do both. Find out what your options are. Ask whether it's possible to make an appointment for a nail clipping only or a simple trim. What are the prices and cancellation fees? Do you feel at ease talking with the groomer and observing the way she interacts with the dogs?

If you are pleased with your visit and have referrals from people you trust, go ahead and book your first appointment. My dogs have no fear of visiting their groomer. In fact, they all seem to enjoy her, especially Woody, who thinks a trip to the dog salon is a grand outing. Rather ironic given his initial reaction to nail trimming.

An alternative to a dog salon is a mobile groomer. These folks drive right up to your house and have everything they need in their truck. It's very convenient although generally more expensive, as travel time and gas are factored into the fee.

# CHAPTER 7

# CAVALIER NUTRITIONAL NEEDS

A well-balanced, high-quality diet is the foundation of a healthy immune system in people as well as in our companion animals. In the past, feeding dogs simply required a trip to the grocery store to pick up some kibble and perhaps tossing in a few table scraps at mealtime. Nowadays, we know better. As we educated ourselves about our own nutrition, we also learned about improving our dogs' diets. Advances in canine nutrition are invaluable and contribute to long life.

There are many feeding choices. How will you decide what's best? That's up to you with advice from your breeder and vet. Or if your dog is experiencing dietary trouble or a more serious health condition, canine nutritionists are also available to assist.

When Chelsea, our first spaniel, was 14 years old, she was diagnosed with cancer. I was afraid to put her through surgery at her advanced age and searched the Internet for alternative treatments. I found a canine nutritionist who was conducting a study on nutritional and other holistic therapies to combat cancer. After speaking with him, I immediately enrolled Chelsea in the program. The nutritionist had me take Chelsea off all commercially prepared

food—even dog biscuits. She was to be fed a totally raw meat/vegetable/fruit diet along with the supplements he recommended. I also remember putting some special oils on her paw pads and using magnet therapy. In just a few days, Chelsea's energy soared. She was literally the Energizer Bunny. Not only that, she had had a pea-size lump in her mouth that faded away. My vet was amazed by Chelsea's reaction to the protocol and was convinced it lengthened her life. She lived to be 15½ and was quite comfortable and content during her last year despite the cancer.

Several years later, when Woody was three he experienced months of stomach issues after I gave him aspirin to alleviate pain for a leg sprain. Traditional medication just was not solving the problem, so I turned to Chelsea's nutritionist. He specialized in treating cancer and other serious illnesses but referred me to his partner. Her protocol of raw food and herbal supplements got Woody back on track. Eventually I was able to reintroduce a better commercially made food than the brand I had been using. Woody has been fine ever since, and he's nearly ten now. When he has an occasional stomach upset, I give him a bland diet of cooked chicken and rice and add the

Essential fatty acids promote healthy skin and a shiny coat.

herbal supplement slippery elm. He always bounces back in no time.

## THE BUILDING BLOCKS OF NUTRITION

Just like us, dogs need a good combination of proteins, carbohydrates, fats, minerals, vitamins, and water to ensure a balanced diet but in different percentages. Each plays an important role within your Cavalier's daily food intake.

### Proteins

Proteins occur in all animal and vegetable matter and are essential to the diet of animals.

Wolves receive the majority of their diet from animals they kill and eat. Today meat is the most natural source of protein for your dog and is more easily digestible than vegetable protein. Protein contributes to overall growth, strong muscles, healthy coats, and strong nails. Recommendations usually are that protein be one of the first three ingredients on your dog food ingredients list. I suggest that it be the first.

### Carbohydrates

Carbohydrates are used for energy and digestion and supply your dog's cells with glucose. They can be found in the form of cereal grains such as rice, wheat, corn, barley, and oats (simple carbohydrates) or whole grains, fruits, and vegetables (complex carbohydrates). The first type of carbohydrates, simple carbohydrates, are easier and quicker for your dog's body to break down and provide immediate energy, while complex carbohydrates take longer to break down but provide a longer, steadier stream of energy.

## Fats

Fats are a very important part of a dog's nutrition because they are required to transport and metabolize vitamins in your dog's system. They're also a source of energy as well as energy storage. Fats are made from fatty acids that contribute to a dog's health in a variety of ways. Some help absorption of fat-soluble vitamins, while others break them down for utilization.

Dogs need a good combination of proteins, carbohydrates, fats, minerals, vitamins, and water to ensure a balanced diet.

## By the Numbers

A dog's protein requirements change at different stages of his life. By the time a pup reaches four to six months his meals can be dropped to twice a day, which is also a good regimen throughout his adult life. Seniors may prefer smaller meals three times a day.

Fats, particularly omega-3 fatty acids, give your dog's coat its healthy shine.

## Minerals and Vitamins

Dogs also need minerals and vitamins to maintain optimum health. Proper vitamin and mineral content will provide their metabolism with the mechanisms needed to process carbohydrates, fats, and proteins. Vitamins are also necessary for good vision and bone growth. Vitamins and minerals help deliver nutrition from food to organs and tissues, they help regulate growth, and they affect many nervous system processes. Minerals are crucial to healthy blood flow and healing in case injury occurs. They also help boost your dog's immune system. Vitamins A, B, D, and E all contribute to your pet's nutrition, as well the mineral supplements calcium, iodine, magnesium, potassium, and zinc.

## Water

Water makes up an important part of your dog's daily intake. Proper hydration is just as important to our canine companions as it is to us. It's best to leave your dog free-range water so that he can drink as he pleases.

Water makes up an important part of your dog's daily intake.

Normal water consumption, however, should not exceed 50 milliliters (a little less than 2 ounces) per 1 pound (0.5 kg) of your dog's weight every 24 hours. For a Cavalier King Charles Spaniel, that is equivalent to about 700 milliliters a day. If you notice your dog drinking far more than that amount daily, it could be a sign of underlying health problems, such as diabetes or kidney and liver problems, so consult your vet.

## WHAT TO FEED

There is a plethora of dog food choices for your Cavalier. You can find them at the grocery store, pet store, veterinarian's office, or even as a special order online. The varieties can seem overwhelming at first, but if you have a good idea of your dog's needs, you will quickly be able to whittle down the selection. There are two main categories of dog food—commercial and noncommercial—plus a variety of special diets, depending on your dog's needs. There are also treats and bones for special occasions.

## Commercial Foods

Commercial dog foods are fed to approximately 80 percent of dogs nationwide. They fall into two main categories: complete diets and incomplete diets that require meat added to them. Within these diet categories, food is categorized as puppy, adult, or senior. From there, the food is broken down into three subcategories: dry, semi-moist, and canned, all with varying moisture content. All commercially prepared food contains a blend of proteins, carbohydrates, fats, vitamins, and minerals. What varies from brand to brand and formula to formula are the percentages and sources of these nutrients.

### Dry Foods

There are all kinds of dry foods on the market. Dry foods, or kibble, are a mixture of ground cereals, meat meal, soybeans, cheese, vegetables, and animal fats, with trace ingredients and preservatives. They are usually presented and fed as meals, biscuits or kibbles, pellets, or expanded chunks. Dry foods are very popular because they are easy to feed and store. They can be fed on their own or moistened with canned food.

With an ever-increasing awareness of the importance of good-quality foods for our pets, some companies are now making foods with meat as the first ingredient and preserving them with vitamins E and C because there have been concerns about traditional chemical preservatives. Read labels carefully and/or seek advice from your vet or breeder so that you purchase the best food possible for your Cavalier.

### Semi-Moist Foods

Semi-moist foods are usually sold in plastic wrappers. They look like chunks, patties, or packets of fresh meat and are made from meat, meat by-products, soybeans, vegetable

## Multi-Dog Tip

If you have more than one dog, give each his own spot in the kitchen so that they can eat their meals peacefully.

## Special Accessories

Because of his long ears, you may want to purchase a spaniel bowl for your Cavalier. It narrows at the top, allowing his ears to fall to either side of the dish and not into the food. Wearing a snood (tube-like hat) at mealtime is another good idea. You can find a snood by visiting www.thesnoodfactory.com.

oils, sugar, and preservatives. Semi-moist foods offer a complete and balanced diet and are highly palatable and easily digested. However, while they look appetizing to the human eye, they contain a high level of artificial chemical additives.

### Canned Foods

Canned foods are significantly higher in moisture than dry or semi-moist foods and are very palatable. They can be fed on their own or in conjunction with dry food. If fed alone, larger quantities would be offered because of the high moisture content. Again, be sure to read labels. Some canned foods are complete meals, while others have only one ingredient such as chicken, beef, or duck. The latter are meant to be combined with a dry food.

## Noncommercial Foods

There has been a wave of interest in noncommercial foods in recent years. Pet owners are cooking for their dogs, buying or preparing raw meals, or mixing traditional and nontraditional foods together. All of these options have merit; you just have to be careful to make sure that your Cavalier is receiving complete and balanced meals each and every day.

### Home-Cooked Foods

For those pet owners who do not want to feed commercial dog food, another option is to offer a home-cooked diet. Some dog owners prefer to make sure that their pet is getting the proper amount of nutrition needed and the best-quality ingredients possible by making the food themselves. If you enjoy whipping up meals for your family and friends, the home-cooked diet might be the way to go. It helps ensure that your dog is getting fresh and wholesome foods, and it is a wonderful way to contribute to your dog's good health. The downside of home-cooked meals is that you may not be offering a balanced diet. So if you go this route, be sure to consult with a canine nutritionist or holistic vet.

### Raw Foods

Another noncommercial dog food diet is the raw, or BARF (Bones and Raw Food), diet. Proponents claim that raw foods retain their natural enzymes and antioxidants, which would otherwise be destroyed by the heat of cooking. Cavaliers on raw foods diet will consume only raw meat and vegetables plus some dairy foods, in addition to bones. Those who feed raw say that their dogs have shinier coats, cleaner teeth, and better overall quality of health.

My personal opinion falls

Special diets are important to consider if your Cavalier has health problems.

somewhere in the middle. After my experiences with Chelsea and Woody, I purchase a dry food designed to be fed along with raw ingredients. It's shipped to my home from the manufacturer. I then add raw hamburger and veggies ground up in the food processor on a regular basis. On occasion I also include yogurt and cooked oatmeal or brown rice. This protocol gives me the convenience of serving a balanced high-quality commercial food plus knowing I am bolstering my dogs' immune system with fresh, wholesome food as well.

## Special Diets

Special diets are important to consider if your Cavalier has health problems. Depending on his particular condition, your veterinarian may suggest a temporary or permanent change to a prescription regimen. This can be a way to control allergies, gastrointestinal conditions, and even kidney problems.

If your dog's health problems are less severe but you would like to keep him looking (and feeling!) topnotch, supplements are considered helpful. Vitamin E can help improve coat quality, while vitamins C and D administered together can help promote the production of collagen, which strengthens tendons and ligaments. B-complex vitamins can help nerve function, while wheatgrass is popular for its healing elements. It's important to note that even if a supplement is considered to be helpful, it is still paramount that you administer the correct dosage. For your dog's well-being, always consult with your veterinarian or a nutritionist before starting your dog on any supplement.

## Bones

Bones can be an important part of a dog's diet because they promote good dental hygiene. If you consistently feed your Cavalier raw bones, you will notice that he has beautiful white teeth with little plaque or tartar. (Never offer cooked bones because they can splinter.) Small bones are a choking hazard even for smaller dogs, while larger bones are more optimal for teeth cleaning. Knuckle and marrow bones are good choices because they are large enough for dogs to really chew. Just don't let your Cavalier ingest too much marrow because it is very rich and can cause diarrhea.

## Treats

Once you have settled on your dog's basic diet, you can also decide on appropriate, healthy treats. These range from commercially prepared dog treats, such as the natural snacks and chews made by Nylabone, to some of the regular snacks you might consume, such as carrot sticks and fruit slices. As with humans, the rule of thumb is moderation. Just as you won't get obese from eating one cookie, your dog won't either. But if your Cavalier is constantly munching on too many biscuits, you will be setting him up for health problems down the road. I like to give my dogs healthy midday snacks.

Try to keep your Cavalier from finding his own ingenious ways to get at extra food. My friend Jacki's ten-year old Tricolor, Abbey Rose, was the culprit in the following story, though Lindsay, her Blenheim sidekick, may have been in on it too. The two were having their

## Training Tidbit

Teach your Cavalier to sit before setting down his food bowl. It's polite and reaffirms your status as pack leader.

afternoon meal in the garage as they routinely do. Usually they bark to come inside after about five minutes. On this particular day, after about 20 minutes with no sound, Jacki went to investigate. She came upon a scene that should have made her angry, but she was too busy laughing. Somehow, Abbey Rose had managed to get the top off a large garbage can and, Jacki assumes, launched herself from a small set of steps into the can. She was covered in tomato sauce and fish. Absolutely covered. The little spaniel didn't seem to realize she was in a bit of a predicament—in fact she was quite pleased with herself. The look on her face could only be interpreted as "Hey mom! Look what I found! Yum!"

## READING DOG FOOD LABELS

Just as you are interested in the quality of food you eat, you should be equally aware of what you are feeding your dog. There are many choices available on the market these days. However, pretty packaging and advertising can be deceiving. It's important to learn how to read and understand the ingredients listed on products you may purchase for your dog.

Dog food ingredients are listed in descending order of their percentage of the total composition of the product. Those with the highest percentages are listed first. The initial four or so are the most important. The

Adult dogs should be fed breakfast and dinner at the same time every day.

best-quality foods are mostly made of meat, not grain.

Ideally the first ingredient listed should be a whole meat protein, i.e., chicken, lamb, beef, etc. Be leery of meat meal and bone meal, as those ingredients are not approved by the Association of American Feed Control Officials (AAFCO) and may contain contaminated meat. Meat by-products should also be avoided because they can contain a mix of beaks, feathers, and feet.

Protein should be followed by vegetables (but not corn or beet pulp) and then a high-quality whole grain such as brown rice.

Less is more with dog food ingredients. Don't be impressed by long lists of ingredients. Food colorings, artificial flavorings, and chemical preservatives should be avoided if possible. In fact, the latter can be particularly detrimental. Avoid foods preserved with BHA and BHT. Opt for those foods that use vitamins E and C. They are often labeled "mixed tocopherols."

The manufacturing of dog food is a complex subject; if you would like more detailed information on reading and understanding labels, search the Internet under "reading dog food labels." You can also visit www. peteducation.com, and look for Dog Food Labels under Dog Articles, which offers a wealth of information on this subject. Also, seek guidance from your veterinarian.

## WHEN TO FEED

Adult dogs should be fed breakfast and dinner. With dry food, you do have the option of free feeding, which means leaving food out during the day for your pet to nibble on at will. Maybe this works for cats, but I can't imagine a dog eating half a meal and going back to it a few hours later. Perhaps some do, but most likely your pet will inhale the food, which is probably too much to take in during one sitting if you thought it would last the entire day. Free feeding is also the fastest way to create a picky eater or the best way for your dog to put on unwanted weight. Cavaliers usually have voracious appetites and should be put on a strictly supervised feeding regimen.

## OBESITY

If you notice that your dog is starting to look chubby or has problems with his mobility, it's important to consult with your veterinarian about the possibility that he may be heading toward obesity. Just as Americans are growing larger, our animals are too. Obesity is becoming more common in all dog breeds. Cavaliers love to eat. Combine that with those beautiful pleading eyes and your dog may be easy to spoil: a sure recipe for an overweight pet. Obesity is usually related to overfeeding. However, there are medical conditions such as hypothyroidism and diabetes that should be tested for in order to determine whether they can be ruled out if your pet is becoming overweight.

How can you tell whether your Cavalier is becoming overweight? Remember the breed standard. Cavaliers are supposed to weigh between 13 and18 pounds. So the first thing to do is get your dog on the scale. Actually, with a small dog the best way to obtain an accurate weight is to weigh yourself first, then weigh yourself with your dog in your arms and subtract your weight to obtain the difference. Unless your Cavalier has an unusually large frame, he's probably getting too heavy if he's

over the ideal weight. You can also stand over your dog and look down over his back to see whether he has a waist. If he looks like a pork roll with legs, it's time to take action. Obesity can lead to other health problems or make certain diseases difficult to treat. In short, obesity can shorten your Cavalier's life. So despite those pleading eyes, do not overindulge your little friend.

If your Cavalier is otherwise healthy but simply overweight, discuss a weight loss plan with your veterinarian. There are special light diets available that should help, as will increasing your companion's exercise program. And watch the treats. A few biscuits at lunchtime may seem harmless, but they add

Once you have settled on your dog's basic diet, you can also decide on appropriate treats.

unnecessary calories, so substitute these with healthy snacks like small pieces of veggies, fruit, or oat cereal.

## OTHER FOOD-RELATED PROBLEMS

Aside from weight gain and obesity, dogs may be prone to other food-related problems, such as digestive disorders and food allergies. And, just like humans, they can become picky eaters for any number of reasons.

## Food Allergies

Well-bred Cavaliers generally are not prone to food allergies. The problem is more commonly seen in puppy mill dogs and other poorly bred dogs. However, signs that indicate a possible allergy are scratching, dandruff, loss of fur, and, in extreme cases, sores that become infected.

The most common food sources for allergic reaction are corn and grains in general, which is why there are many "grain-free" dog foods on the market these days. If corn is listed as

Like humans, dogs can be allergic to certain ingredients in food. Scratching, loss of fur, and dandruff are possible signs.

the first ingredient in a dog food you are considering, don't buy it. Remember the importance of the ingredients list.

Some dogs have reactions to the additives and preservatives in their food. Your vet is the best person to diagnose a food allergy and help you find an alternative diet that will be well tolerated and enjoyed by your dog.

## Want to Know More?

For more information on medical conditions that can affect your Cavalier, see Chapter 8: Cavalier Health and Wellness.

## Diarrhea and Constipation

Your dog's diet is often responsible for diarrhea and constipation. An imbalance of water and food wastes is usually the culprit. Lack of water or the insufficient removal of water from food can trigger these conditions.

There are all kinds of causes for diarrhea, both simple and complex. When not enough water is removed from the food source, stools can become loose, watery, and hard to control. More frequent or bloody diarrhea is a greater cause for concern as it may present the threat of dehydration or indicate a serious health condition. The best course of action is to take your dog to the vet along with a stool sample for evaluation. In some instances, your dog may have chewed on a stick or gotten into the garbage, which has upset the chemical balance in his stomach, resulting in a loose bowel movement or two. If this is the case, feeding cooked plain chicken and white rice often solves the problem.

Constipation is a very minor problem in the breed. When not enough water is in the digestive tract, stools can be very dry and hard to pass. If the condition causes a prolonged lack of appetite, dehydration may occur, which can make the problem more serious. Give your vet a call. She will probably recommend adding water-soluble fiber to your dog's meals, an over-the-counter supplement, or medication.

## Picky Eaters

Cavaliers don't tend to be picky eaters. Usually, the opposite is true. They are little chow hounds, and you need to be vigilant and make sure they are not putting on extra weight. But if you have the rare fussy eater, adding unseasoned broth or a little bit of boiled chicken or liver to his regular food should arouse his interest and improve his appetite.

If your dog usually has a normal appetite but then becomes finicky, he may not be feeling well. Loss of appetite can signal a number of different problems. A trip to the vet is in order.

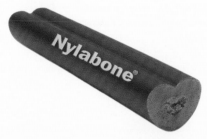

# CHAPTER 8

# CAVALIER HEALTH AND WELLNESS

Prevention is the best way to keep your pet in peak condition. For optimal health, your adult Cavalier will need to have a veterinary checkup on an annual basis and, of course, as needed throughout his life. As much as we think of our dogs as family, they are animals with the potential to pick up various diseases, as well as internal and external parasites. They can also suffer from allergies, eye conditions, ear problems, and other health issues.

## THE ANNUAL EXAM

Giving your Cavalier the best life possible includes routine health care. Years ago, vaccinations were given on an annual basis in part to ensure that dog owners brought their pets to a veterinarian's office for a yearly checkup. If you are following a different vaccination protocol, you still need to have your Cavalier examined.

When you make your appointment, be sure to tell the receptionist that you're bringing your dog in for his annual exam. That way she will be sure to give you an appropriate time slot.

When you arrive, a vet tech will have your Cavalier step on a scale to obtain and record his present weight. Keeping an eye on weight gain or

loss is very important as your dog ages. Obesity in particular can contribute to myriad health problems. Significant weight loss is also a red flag. After your Cav has weighed in, the vet tech will usher you into an examining room to wait for the vet, which should only be a few minutes.

When the vet arrives, she will give your pet a head-to-tail examination. Of course, your dog's vital signs—temperature, pulse, and respiration—will be checked. She will check the inside of his mouth looking to see whether the gums are red and/or puffy and whether there is plaque or tartar on his teeth. Depending on what is found, the vet may recommend a dental cleaning. She will look in your Cav's eyes for signs of an infection or any other abnormal condition and will also examine his ears, looking for irritation and to detect any unusual odor.

The vet will also run her hands over your Cavalier's body and check under his coat. She'll be looking for any possible rashes, new lumps, and perhaps fleas—although many monthly flea products these days do a good job of ridding your pet of these pesky pests. However, if she detects what appears to be pepper near the base of the tail or on the belly—this is flea dirt (feces)—your dog will need treatment to eradicate fleas. Your home may need to be treated as well.

The vet will draw blood to check for heartworms and, depending on where you live, may also check for Lyme disease. You should bring in a stool sample to check for parasites, and you may be asked to bring in a urine sample as well.

Vaccinations may be administered depending on the protocol you have selected: annual, every three years, or titer testing. I have my dogs' titers checked annually. Titer testing is a blood test that shows whether your pet still has enough antibodies from previous vaccines to ward off a disease. If protection levels have dropped on a particular vaccine—for example, distemper—I'll have the vet give the distemper vaccination only. It usually takes a few days to receive a titer level report, so you may need to make a second trip to the animal hospital. Yes, titer tests are a more expensive alternative to annual vaccinations. But I feel they're well worth the extra cost and prefer not to overtax my dogs' immune systems with vaccinations they may not need. If you have a wellness pet insurance policy, vaccinations are covered although not necessarily the titer tests themselves.

By the time your Cavalier reaches four or five, you should also have him checked annually by a board-certified cardiologist because mitral valve disease is a serious condition known to occur in the breed.

## PARASITES

Parasites are nasty little organisms that can make dogs miserable. Worms set up camp in their intestines and in the bloodstream, as well as in various organs. Fleas and ticks are external invaders that may cause severe discomfort, itching, and disease. There's no need to panic, though; just be aware and take appropriate action. Discuss potential prevention with your vet and also bring your dog in to be examined if you spot any of the signs of parasite infestation.

### Internal Parasites

Internal parasites can be found in the gastrointestinal tract or the circulatory system. Your vet will run annual (more if a problem is suspected) fecal tests and prescribe appropriate medication if necessary. Monthly preventive medications are available.

Giving your Cavalier the best life possible includes routine health care.

## Heartworms

Heartworms are parasites that ultimately live in your dog's heart. The parasite is transmitted into the dog's bloodstream through the saliva of a mosquito that is carrying immature heartworms, called microfilaria. This parasite then matures into adulthood in the dog's heart, which can cause respiratory and cardiac disease. Signs include coughing, lethargy, and abnormal breathing.

Treatment of adult heartworms is harsh and can have debilitating side effects. Because a heartworm infestation is a serious condition, the drugs used to eradicate it must be powerful. An arsenic-derived compound, or melarsomine dihydorcholoride, may be prescribed and hospitalization required. As the worms begin to die, the dog may actually get worse if the dead worms cause internal obstructions.

Because the treatments are so difficult and the outcome is not always positive, it's far better to use a preventive. Chewable ivermectin tablets are a popular choice among veterinarians. However, a blood test ruling out the presence of heartworms must be preformed before a dog is placed on a regular monthly preventive schedule.

## Hookworms

Hookworms are another common intestinal parasite that can cause diarrhea and blood loss. Severe anemia can result from a loss of blood in the intestines. Hookworms are not visible in the stool, however.

Your Cavalier can pick up this parasite by coming into contact with the stool of an infected dog. So if a doggy play date friend has contracted hookworms, it would be best to postpone your get-togethers until the problem has been eradicated. Also, try to stay clear of dog droppings in public parks, though this is often easier said than done.

## Types of Intestinal Worms

The following intestinal parasites can cause your dog discomfort and, in some cases, major health problems:

- heartworms
- hookworms
- roundworms
- tapeworms
- whipworms

Although some of these worms are visible to the naked eye, others can only be detected under microscopic examination. If you spot any signs of infestation, have your dog examined by your vet right away. Also check for parasites at your Cavalier's annual veterinary checkup. In many cases, monthly preventive medications are available.

Carry baggies with you and pick up after your dog immediately.

If you dog does contract hookworms, your vet will prescribe two treatments of an appropriate dewormer.

## Roundworms

Roundworms are the most common type of internal parasite found in dogs. They can cause loss of appetite, malnutrition, and diarrhea. They look like spaghetti when they pass onto the ground in the stool and if left unchecked can grow to 4 to 6 inches (10 to 15 cm). Once your vet has diagnosed roundworms, an appropriate medication will be dispensed to eradicate them.

## Tapeworms

Tapeworms are also very common. These intestinal parasites, which in one stage of their life cycle look like pieces of white rice, are frequently found near a dog's rectum or on the floor moving. Your Cavalier would need to swallow a flea with tapeworm larvae in it or eat a stricken small rodent to develop a tapeworm infestation.

The best form of prevention is to keep fleas at bay on your dog, in your home, and in your yard. Monthly topical flea and tick preventive medications with permethrin or fipronil are very effective. Also, go over your dog with a flea comb after a romp in the woods. If you do see tapeworms in your dog's stool or around his bottom, run a sample to your vet for confirmation and get your dog on the appropriate dewormer as soon as possible.

## Whipworms

Unlike other intestinal worms, whipworms live in the large intestine and burrow into the intestinal wall. Your Cavalier can contract whipworms from being around the stool of an infected dog and from ingesting food, water, or dirt contaminated with eggs. Whipworms cannot be seen in the stool, but weight loss and mucoid, sometimes bloody, diarrhea are clinical signs of infestation.

Repeat deworming may be necessary to effectively treat this infestation.

There are very good parasite-preventive medications on the market today for all types of worms. Discuss the options with your vet and try not to skip a dose. Also remember to bring a stool sample for examination during your dog's annual physical exams.

## External Parasites

There are several external parasites that can be found on or in your Cavalier's skin. They are listed and described below.

### Fleas

Fleas are the most common external parasite. If your Cavalier is scratching more than usual, examine him for fleas. Sometimes you can actually see these tiny pests on your pet's skin, rummaging through his hair. Or you may notice black pepper-like flakes near his tail (these are flea eggs). If you don't automatically spot fleas, comb your dog with a flea and tick comb. The teeth on these combs are closer together and can readily capture the tiny pests.

Once your pet contracts fleas, he may become very itchy and can lose hair typically near the base of the tail and down the hind legs. If you find one flea on your Cavalier, it's likely that there are plenty more waiting in your home! There are now several good flea products to help control fleas both on your pet and in your house. Some are oral medications and others are applied externally. Monthly topical spot-on products that are applied between the shoulder blades of your dog are very popular.

Flea collars are also an option. There are two types: one uses a toxic gas to kill fleas and the other is absorbed into the dog's subcutaneous fat layer of skin. The first is generally most effective around the head and tail. If you have more than one dog, I wouldn't use a flea collar because the dogs can grab hold of one during play.

Ask your veterinarian about the various products available

Check your dog for fleas and ticks after he's been playing outdoors.

and the pros and cons of each. If you do have an infestation, you may need to call in a pest company to treat your home. Be sure to wash your pet's bed and vacuum frequently. Also keep your lawn cut short.

## Mange Mites

There are two major types of mange in dogs: sarcoptic and demodectic.

Sarcoptic mange is contagious to other dogs and people. Clinical signs include itchy, irritated skin and hair loss. The ears and legs are usually the first areas to be involved.

Demodectic mange is not contagious to other dogs or people. This mite normally lives in the skin of all dogs, but in some young animals with immature immune systems, this mange mite will start to

proliferate and cause hair loss and itchiness.

Your veterinarian would have to perform a skin scraping to diagnose either of these two conditions. Topical medications are available to treat both.

## Ticks

Ticks are also very common and can cause diseases such as Lyme disease (lameness, swollen joints, possible fever, and poor appetite), ehrlichiosis (lethargy, weight loss, poor appetite, swollen lymph nodes, and nasal discharge), and Rocky Mountain spotted fever (fever, depression, nose bleeds or blood in urine, lethargy, and loss of coordination) in your pet, as well as in you. These diseases are treated with antibiotics; often a long course is needed.

Because they can carry disease, it's important to properly remove and dispose of ticks you may capture in your flea/tick comb. If a tick has already hooked into your pet's skin and is engorged with blood, use tweezers or a tick extractor (a tiny spoon with a V-shaped cutout in it) to carefully remove it. If done correctly, the tick's head will be removed with the body. Squeeze the tick with the tweezers to kill it. Fill a small cup with soapy water or alcohol and drop it in. Then flush it down the toilet. Afterwards, clean the skin with alcohol, and also disinfect your tweezers.

Good tick control is important to your Cavalier's health. There are oral and topical products to prevent and treat tick infestation. If you are uncomfortable with the chemicals used in flea and tick products and would prefer to try a natural alternative, seek advice from a holistic veterinarian. Visit the American Holistic Veterinary Medical Association website at www.ahvma.org to find a member in your area. Discuss these options with your vet.

### Ringworm
Ringworm isn't actually a worm at all; it's a skin fungus that can be contracted by pets and people. Possible signs include a rash, itching, and hair loss (usually resulting in flaky bald patches).

Once a diagnosis is made by your veterinarian by culturing an infected area of skin, ringworm will be treated with twice-weekly medical baths using a chlorhexidine or miconazole shampoo. Oral or topical antifungal medications may be prescribed. If you have multiple dogs, all of them must be treated. Dog crates and beds, cloth toys, blankets, carpets, and floors must be thoroughly cleaned because although the fungi live on the skin they survive by feeding on dead skin tissue and hair. This should eradicate the existing problem and prevent it from recurring.

## BREED-SPECIFIC ILLNESSES
As a breed, the Cavalier King Charles Spaniel is prone to several health problems. Some are more serious than others. It's important to be familiar with these inherited conditions prior to obtaining your Cavalier and to remain informed about them throughout his lifetime. (Note: The following conditions are presented alphabetically and not in order of prevalence in the breed.)

### Cataracts
Cataracts refer to cloudiness appearing over the lens of the eye. A cataract can be a small spot or grow large enough to cause blindness. Cataracts usually develop as a dog ages. However, as mentioned previously, juvenile cataracts also have been known to occur in Cavaliers. In less serious cases, a dog can adapt to his impairment. Surgery is available for more involved situations.

### Episodic Falling
Episodic falling (EF) is a syndrome often confused with epilepsy. Symptoms include muscle stiffness, rigidity in the back end,

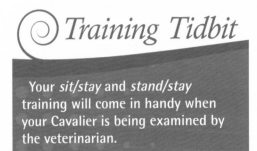

**Training Tidbit**

Your *sit/stay* and *stand/stay* training will come in handy when your Cavalier is being examined by the veterinarian.

Patellar luxation, or movement of the kneecap, is a common orthopedic condition of many small dog breeds.

falling, seizure-like activity, and collapse. Simple exercise or excitement can set off an episode, which may last minutes to hours. The affected dog remains conscious.

EF usually manifests itself before the age of five months but can occur later on and range in severity. Proper diagnosis is essential because drugs to control the problem are available and are different from those used for epileptics.

## Hip Dysplasia

One usually thinks of hip dysplasia as a condition afflicting larger dogs, but it is also present in the Cavalier. In fact, some believe that at least one third of all Cavaliers are affected. This type of dysplasia is caused by a poor fit between the ball and socket of the hip joints. It can cause mild discomfort in some dogs and can be debilitating in others. Treatments geared toward relieving pain and improving mobility include dietary modifications, medications, and surgery.

## Mitral Valve Dysplasia

Also known as mitral valve disease (MVD), mitral valve dysplasia occurs when there is a defect in one of the four valves of a dog's heart. The malformed valve is unable to close

# Veterinary Specialists

There may come a time when you need to seek the services of a veterinary specialist. There are usually three circumstances that warrant an appointment with a specialist.

1. You would like a second opinion on your dog's diagnosis. You may feel a little awkward telling your vet that you'd like a second opinion. Don't. She should understand and assist you in finding an appropriate specialist. Sometimes the vet may want input herself.

   When Rory started having cluster seizures, my vet called a neurologist immediately for his opinion on treatment. I thought it might take a few days to get some feedback but was very impressed when my vet called me within a matter of hours to share the specialist's recommendations. It was reassuring to say the least.

2. Additional help is needed to confirm a diagnosis. Because specialists have advanced training and access to all types of diagnostic tools, such as CT imaging, MRI scans, ultrasound, etc., they have the skills and equipment to determine exactly what the problem is. Plus they see specific types of conditions on a daily basis.

   A few years back, Woody developed a subtle limp. We thought it might be a problem in his knee. My vet suggested that we bring Woody to be examined by an orthopedic surgeon. To my great relief, it turned out to be a strain in his groin. (We had seen this specialist a few years prior for another problem with Woody—again a suspected knee problem which turned out to be a sprain.) To help Woody improve, I then took him to a canine rehab facility.

3. You may need to consult a specialist if your regular vet doesn't have access to the therapy your pet requires to fight his disease.

properly, and blood begins to flow backwards. Known as mitral regurgitation, this backflow keeps the proper amount of blood from circulating throughout the body and spills back into the heart. Over time the dog can develop congestive heart failure—fluid buildup in the lungs.

Although MVD occurs in a number of dogs after the age of ten, an unusually high percentage of Cavaliers develop MVD before they are five. It is the leading health concern in the breed.

Heart murmurs are an early sign that a dog may have MVD. But depending on its severity, dogs with murmurs can live to a normal age. More significant signs of MVD include coughing, inactivity, and labored breathing. Prognosis varies. Sometimes the disease progresses slowly and can be managed with diuretics to drain fluid from the lungs, as well as vasodilators, which help increase circulation by expanding blood vessels. In more serious cases, the dog is considered terminally ill and heart failure is imminent.

There is no cure for MVD and no way to prevent it other than breeding the healthiest dogs possible. It's heartbreaking to lose our dogs at any age, but to lose a young dog to a congenital defect is especially difficult. Those devoted to Cavaliers are working hard to alleviate the condition in the breed. For more detailed information on mitral valve disease, visit both national Cavalier club sites, and the Darcy Fund in particular at http://ackcsccharitabletrust.org/darcy. Darcy was a beloved Tricolor belonging to Kim and Jerry Thornton who died from chronic valvular disease in 2006. She was only six and a half years old. In honor of her memory, the Thorntons created the Darcy Fund to raise much-needed funds to support research into the causes and cures for this devastating disease.

## Patellar Luxation

Patellar luxation, or movement of the kneecap, is a common orthopedic condition of many small dog breeds. There is a genetic predisposition for this condition. Signs include limping and stretching of a hind leg. This can occur acutely with sharp pain or can be a chronic condition of intermittent lameness. Your veterinarian should be able to palpate your dog's leg and diagnose this condition. Treatment can consist of pain management and/or surgery. External factors such excessive weight can exacerbate the condition.

## Syringomyelia

Known as "neck scratcher's disease," syringomyelia is a serious genetic condition. It is caused by a malformation in the skull, which leads to fluid buildup in the spinal cord near the brain, and the fluid cannot drain properly.

Cavaliers with the condition scratch excessively at the back of their heads, hence the reference to neck scratchers. Other signs include scratching at the air when being walked, yelping in pain, and weakness or stiffness in the legs. Only an MRI can diagnose syringomyelia. Symptoms most often appear between six months and three years of age. Drug management can help in mild cases, but surgery is often recommended in more severe cases. Although it can stop the condition from progressing, it may not correct previous damage. Often more than one surgery is required.

## GENERIC HEALTH ISSUES

There are health issues that can affect any type of dog. Some are just more prone to them than others. Woody is plagued by seasonal allergies. His legs get itchy in early spring from the new grass and pollen and then the discomfort subsides in the fall. I usually use anti-itch sprays and/or antihistamines to keep him comfortable. Ear infections are very common in dogs with long floppy ears, especially spaniels. I clean my dogs' ears routinely and have medication at the ready if an infection crops up despite my preventive measures. Dogs may also be affected by more serious illnesses such as cancer. Traditional as well as alternative therapies are outlined below for some common canine health concerns.

## Allergies

Skin allergies plague many dog breeds. The most common clinical sign is itchy skin. Once the dog starts to

The Cavalier's long, floppy ears can be more prone to infection because they do not allow air to circulate as well as upright ears.

Some preventive measures can be taken. Good flea control reduces the risk of developing skin allergies. Bathing your Cavalier in a hypoallergenic shampoo reduces the risk of reactions to regular shampoos, which may be more irritating. Routine bathing also cleanses the skin and hair of irritants that may trigger allergies. Feeding a high-quality diet can alleviate allergic reactions to food. If your Cavalier is diagnosed with a food allergy, many hypoallergenic diet options are available. Discuss these options with your vet.

## Cancer

There are many types of cancer, with various treatment options and potential outcomes. In fact, dogs often tolerate cancer treatments and go about their daily lives better than people do. So if your Cavalier is diagnosed with a cancer, don't panic. Seek a second opinion. Meet with a canine oncologist. I'd also recommend consulting with a holistic veterinarian to find ways to bolster your pet's immune system to help fight the disease.

## Ear Infections

A mix of bacteria and yeast organisms normally lives in the ear canal. When there is an overgrowth of one or more, infections occur. Clinical signs include head shaking, scratching at the ears, red, irritated skin in the ear, and an odorous discharge.

If these signs occur, take your Cavalier to your vet to have his ears cultured. Once the yeast fungi or bacteria are identified, an appropriate medication will be prescribed.

Preventive care can help reduce the number of ear infections. Routine cleaning and hair removal are highly recommended. Special drying agents and antibacterial and cleansing solutions can also be purchased.

scratch, red areas may appear and hair loss often occurs.

Dogs can have allergic reactions to such varied things as grasses, trees, blankets, cleaning chemicals, and even other animals. They suffer from inhalant allergies as well and can react to molds, dust, and other irritants in their environment. Skin allergies may also occur from ingredients in a dog's diet, such as corn, wheat, certain meats, and other products. Fleas are another huge cause. If your Cavalier is allergic to fleas, one fleabite can cause painful scratching for months.

his head out of the car window.

Sometimes eye conditions may indicate other health concerns. Signs to look for include cloudy bluing of the eye, which may be an early sign of hepatitis; a pale color in the normally pink membrane around the eye, which may indicate anemia; and loss of glossiness, which may indicate a rundown condition.

If you believe that your Cavalier may have an eye infection or other condition, take him to your veterinarian for a professional eye exam right away. Left untreated some of these conditions may lead to blindness.

## Eye Conditions and Infections

Preventing eye infections can be as easy as keeping your pet's eyes clean. In fact, keeping the corners of your dog's eyes clean and mucus free is your first defense in your fight against eye problems. Using a sterile veterinary eyewash as recommended by your veterinarian will help.

Conjunctivitis is probably the most common eye infection and the easiest to detect. It includes redness around the eye and a yellow or greenish discharge. There are two types: allergic and bacterial. Allergic conjunctivitis is usually treated with topical cortisone, and bacterial conjunctivitis is treated with topical antibiotics.

Other eye problems can be caused by trauma, foreign bodies in the eye, or eyelid abnormalities. Keep your Cavalier away from situations where he could be subject to eye trauma, such as rough play, a fight with another animal, running underneath or into low-lying shrubbery or undergrowth, or letting your pet hang

## ALTERNATIVE THERAPIES

Alternative therapies are becoming much more mainstream these days for use on their own or in conjunction with traditional medicine. My dogs have had successful experiences with acupuncture, chiropractic, herbal supplements, and veterinary rehabilitation therapy. So I'm a big believer in investigating alternative therapies to assist in solving medical problems.

### Acupuncture

During acupuncture, certain physical locations on the body referred to as "acupuncture points" are either stimulated or made numb through the insertion of very thin needles. These points are selected based on the medical condition being treated and the desired effect. Acupuncture may be used as an alternative to traditional medical treatment to prevent disease and provide support to the immune system, balance energy, relieve pain, reduce muscle spasms, and increase circulation.

If you'd like

### Want to Know More?

If you want to know more about health care as your dog ages, see Chapter 13: Care of Your Cavalier Senior.

to find a veterinary acupuncturist, look for a practitioner trained by the Chi Institute (Traditional Chinese Veterinary Medicine, www.tcvm.com), the American Academy of Veterinary Acupuncture (www.aava.org), or the International Veterinary Acupuncture Society (www.ivas.org).

## Chiropractic

A veterinary chiropractor uses spinal manipulations to treat chronic pain created by neck and back conditions. During the initial evaluation, the chiropractor will review the patient's health history and current health status, inquiring about signs of lameness, difficulty in getting up or lying down, seizures or neurological problems, behavior changes, etc., and will review any prior X-rays and tests that may have been performed. After conducting her own physical exam, the chiropractor will recommend a specific course of treatment.

Chiropractic treatment is a bit controversial. I've had mixed experiences with human and canine chiropractic therapy, although I have heard many anecdotal success stories. To learn more about veterinary chiropractic medicine, visit the American Veterinary Chiropractic Association's website at www.animalchiropractic.org.

## Herbal Remedies

Many people are turning to herbal remedies

Acupuncture may be used as an alternative to traditional medical treatment to prevent disease and provide support to the immune system, balance energy, relieve pain, reduce muscle spasms, and increase circulation.

to solve health problems, both for themselves and for their pets. When Woody suffered from ongoing stomach upset in his youth, my canine nutritionist recommended slippery elm to help him. I'd never heard of it and was, to be honest, wary. But because medications were not working and he was obviously uncomfortable, I gave the slippery elm a try. To my amazement, it helped tremendously. So now I keep a bottle of capsules on hand and use it as a treatment for diarrhea for all of my dogs.

Herbal remedies can be helpful when a dog is under stress, whether it is caused by a trip to the vet, a thunder and lightning storm, a new pet in the house, and so on. One of my friends swears by lavender, and there are other herbal and homeopathic products available through catalogs, health food stores, and pet stores.

The production of herbal supplements is not approved by the United States Food and Drug Administration (FDA), and they can interfere with conventional medications as well as other herbs. So if you'd like to include them in your Cavalier's treatment plan, seek guidance from a holistic vet and/or canine nutritionist.

## Homeopathy

Homeopathy uses a distinctly different approach from traditional Western veterinary medicine and is somewhat controversial. The philosophy behind the use of homeopathy is that like cures like. Very diluted solutions of a compound are used to stimulate a healing response in the body. Some dog owners, who may find traditional pharmaceuticals are not helping their beloved pets, may turn to homeopathic remedies as an alternative.

Homeopathic substances are derived from herbs, minerals, and other natural substances. But be cautious—these remedies are generally not approved by the FDA and therefore have

Now more commonly used with pets, herbal remedies are helpful in alleviating pain, reducing stress, and boosting the immune system.

not been thoroughly researched and proven to be safe and effective in humans or animals. Before treating your dog with homeopathic remedies, consult with your veterinarian for a referral to a veterinary homeopath.

## Tellington TTouch

Tellington TTouch is a complementary protocol that involves precise finger and hand touches, passive movements, and guided exercises. It has been referred to as massage, but that is an inaccurate description. The specific circular

Chiropractic care and physical therapy can benefit dogs who suffer from musculoskeletal problems resulting from injury or old age.

touches applied with gentle fingertip pressure move the skin slightly in 1¼ inch (3 cm) circles. The TTouch system creates changes in brain wave patterns and improves circulation and coordination. It also helps reduce mental/physical stress and chronic pain, bringing on a sense of calm and well-being.

Tellington TTouch was developed by Linda Tellington-Jones for use with horses. Ultimately, the technique was used on other farm animals as well as pets.

In dogs it can help with separation anxiety, fear of thunder and lightning, aggression, and training issues.

## Veterinary Rehabilitation Therapy

Physical therapy is well known in human health care, but did you know that the term is legally reserved in most states for use only by licensed physical therapists who work with people? Veterinary rehabilitation therapy for animals is the equivalent of physical therapy because it applies many of the same techniques.

Your traditional veterinarian may recommend a rehabilitation vet soon after your dog has injured himself. Last year Woody pulled a groin muscle. After the problem was diagnosed and my vet prescribed pain medications, I also brought him to a new veterinary rehab center in my area. The vet treated him with a laser, recommended specific land exercises, and had him work out in the center's underwater treadmill. He wasn't too fond of the treadmill at first but after a few visits got the hang of it. Now he's back to living life in the fast lane—his usual M.O.

# EMERGENCY CARE AND FIRST AID

It's bound to happen. Your pet gets cut running through the woods during a hike, gets stung by a bee sniffing flowers in the garden, or sprains his paw chasing wildly after a squirrel. Woody managed to pull out two toenails in his puppyhood, once in the time it took me to walk to our mailbox and back. So knowing how to react and having a first-aid kit on hand is well worth it.

When an emergency occurs, it's best to be prepared. A muzzle is good to have available should your Cavalier get hurt. Sometimes dogs will bite when they are in pain. To protect yourself and to safely move or pick up an injured dog, you should use a muzzle.

Grooming shears or clippers are great to have to clear an area of injured skin. A Cavalier's long, silky coat can hide wounds or lacerations. A tourniquet is necessary only if your pet is bleeding profusely. Minor bleeding can be controlled with steady pressure and bandaging the area. Blankets are good to have set aside as well as to create a stretcher and/or to keep your pet warm when sick or injured.

As far as over-the-counter medications are concerned, you should contact your veterinarian for recommended dosages and the appropriate times to administer them. Buffered aspirin can be given when your pet is experiencing minor pain or has a mild fever. (Note: Never give your dog Tylenol or Advil.) An antihistamine like Benadryl is great to have at the ready for the occasional bee sting. Hydrogen peroxide can be used to cleanse wounds and induce vomiting. Cavaliers, like other dogs, may swallow harmful objects or poisonous substances. It's important to consult your veterinarian prior to inducing vomiting because some objects can actually cause more harm coming back up than passing through the gastrointestinal system. An antidiarrheal safe for dogs can be administered to your Cavalier for a mild case of diarrhea. Diluted iodine and triple antibiotic solutions are useful in cleaning and treating minor wounds and cuts.

To be completely prepared, you should have a first-aid kit for your dog stocked with the following items:

- bandage materials (gauze pads and tape)
- bandage scissors and small regular scissors
- blanket
- clippers and blades
- cotton balls and swabs
- exam gloves
- muzzle
- thermometer
- tourniquet
- tweezers
- antidiarrheal
- buffered aspirin

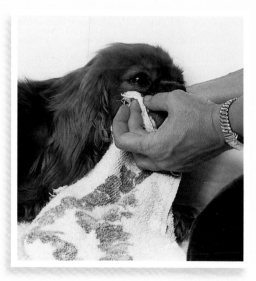

Responsible pet owners should become familiar with basic first-aid procedures that could help—or even save—a pet in need of immediate medical attention.

# Poisonous Plants and Flowers

Keeping our pets safe isn't always as easy as we might think because, unbeknownst to us, they can be surrounded by toxic substances everywhere, such as poisonous plants and flowers in our homes and gardens. If you love having houseplants in your home or flowers and plants in your garden as much as having companion animals, beware. It's best to find out which species are toxic if swallowed before decorating your house or landscaping with lovely but potentially dangerous greenery. Here is a partial list of some to avoid or to place strategically out of your dog's reach: aloe vera, amaryllis, crocus, chrysanthemum, daffodil bulbs, Easter lily, morning glory, peony, periwinkle, and tulip bulbs. For a more detailed list, visit the ASPCA website at www.aspca.org and look for poisonous plants in the Animal Poison Control Center section.

- antihistamine (like Benadryl; ask your veterinarian the dosage appropriate for your dog's size)
- hydrogen peroxide
- iodine
- triple antibiotic solution

## Bites

Bites caused by insects, snakes, dogs, and other animals require immediate attention. My dog Woody has a crazy habit of leaping into the air and catching bees mid-flight. So I keep an antihistamine at the ready in the kitchen cabinet right next to the sink. Sometimes insect stings and bites can cause severe reactions. If your dog seems disoriented or sick or has trouble moving or breathing, or there is severe swelling, take him to the vet immediately. Even if he seems fine, watch him for a day or so.

Bites caused by venomous snakes can be fatal and are therefore a very real and urgent emergency. Signs may include fang marks, swelling, skin discoloration at the site of the bite wound, restlessness, and/or weakness. Prompt examination and treatment are crucial. If you are able to bring the dead snake with you to the veterinarian for identification, that would be ideal; a picture taken at the scene is also helpful.

A dog who has been bitten by another animal or dog can have surface and deep penetrating bite wounds. If your dog was attacked and thrashed about by the other animal, spinal and tracheal injuries could have occurred. Bring your dog to a veterinarian immediately.

## Bleeding

Bleeding requires immediate attention. If your dog has a minor cut, cleanse the area with warm water, followed by an antiseptic. Use an absorbent gauze pad to stop the bleeding. Bandage the area firmly but not too tightly. For more severe bleeding, apply pressure and wrap the area. If the bandages get soaked with blood, do not remove them; just place additional bandages on top of the blood-soaked ones and continue to apply pressure. Seek veterinary assistance.

## Broken Bones

Fractures are typically caused by abnormal stress placed on the skeletal system. There are four commonly seen fractures in dogs: closed, compound, epiphyseal (growth plate), and greenstick (hairline). The first three types can be further characterized by whether they are simple fractures in which the bone breaks into only two or three pieces or in which the bone shatters into many pieces.

The symptoms and risks depend on what area and to what extent the bone is fractured. Fractures involving a joint are the most serious. A broken back may displace the spinal cord and cause complete paralysis. All fractures, however, are serious and should be treated at once. When a bone within a leg is broken, the dog will usually hold the entire leg off the ground. Usually no weight is placed on the paw. With a sprain or lesser injury, the dog may use the leg somewhat but walk with a limp.

## Frostbite

Frostbite is damage to the body's extremities caused by prolonged exposure to freezing conditions. Frostbite in dogs is usually characterized by white numb skin. To treat possible frostbite, you need to warm the area slowly. Do not rub or apply cold or warm water. For instance, if you believe that your dog's extremities (most likely the feet) have become frostbitten, wrap them in a warm blanket or hold them in your warm hands to thaw them. Once stable, take your dog to the vet for further examination and guidance.

## Heatstroke

Signs of heatstroke include a high rectal temperature, bright red mucous membranes such as the gums, excessive drooling, rapid panting, distress, vomiting or diarrhea, loss of coordination, collapse, and unconsciousness.

If your dog has heatstroke, remove him from the heat. Use cold compresses such as ice packs

Knowing how to recognize potential health problems and how to handle them is important to your dog's overall well-being.

# Disaster Preparedness

If you happen to live in an area prone to seasonal disasters such as flooding, hurricanes, or tornados, you may face a situation in which you may be requested to evacuate immediately. Being prepared ahead of time can help prevent tragedy from occurring. You should keep a disaster kit on hand containing everything you would need for your dog's care and have it handy in a sturdy container or duffel bag so you can quickly put it in your car.

The pet disaster kit should include the following items:

- Food and water for at least five days per dog, if you have more than one. If your Cavalier prefers canned dog food over dry kibble, be sure to pack a manually operated can opener. If your dog drinks tap water, be sure to bottle your own water and store it in a cool place until it is time to evacuate.
- Medications if your dog requires them. Store them in a waterproof container.
- A first-aid kit and a first-aid book for pets are highly recommended.
- Collars, at least two leashes, walking harnesses, car seat, and a travel crate or kennel to transport your dog safely. When you reach your destination, your dog may need to stay in his crate for a period of time, so you want to be sure that it is a comfortable and familiar place for him.
- Identification tags, current photos, vaccination records, and the name and phone number of your veterinarian in case you must board your pet.
- Paper towels and several highly absorbent cloth towels, as well as a sufficient supply of plastic garbage bags to collect pet waste.
- Grooming brushes and combs.

If you have to evacuate, leave early. Give yourself plenty of time to reach a safe destination. Take your dog with you. Never leave him behind because you have no way of knowing how long you may be gone or whether you will be permitted to return to retrieve him later.

Plan ahead. Have a list of pet-friendly accommodations along several different possible evacuation routes. Call ahead for reservations. If you plan to stay with friends or relatives, be sure that they are able to shelter you and your dog. If not, you may need to make other arrangements. If this is the case, prepare a list of boarding facilities, animal shelters, and veterinary clinics able to provide shelter in an emergency.

If your dog has heatstroke, remove him from the heat. Use cold compresses such as ice packs (in arm pit and groin areas, but do not pack the body in ice) or cold wet towels to cool the head and body. Offer small amounts of water after your pet has cooled down. Use a syringe if necessary. Do not immerse the dog in cold water. Then monitor your dog's temperature until it is normal. Normal rectal temperature of a dog is about 101.5° to 102°F (38.6° to 38.9°C). Watch that it does not dip below 100°F (37.7°C).Once stable, take your dog to the vet for further examination and guidance.

## Poisoning

There are many household items that can be poisonous to your dog if ingested. You should always be vigilant to ensure that nothing of harm is left within reach of your curious Cavalier. As a pet owner, you should familiarize yourself with potential hazards in and around your home. If you believe that your dog has ingested a potential life-threatening toxin, seek veterinary treatment *immediately.* If a container label is available, read the label directions and provide your veterinarian with as much information as possible regarding the toxin.

Symptoms can vary, depending on the type of poison. Signs include vomiting, convulsions, unsteadiness, lethargy, and unconsciousness.

The following is only a partial list of potentially dangerous poisons your dog could come into contact with: certain herbicides, fungicides, insecticides, rodent poisons, mold, mushrooms, blue-green algae, antifreeze, household chemicals, certain houseplants, human medications, and certain foods, such as bread dough, grapes, raisins, chocolate, and macadamia nuts. To learn more, research literature on pet health and poisoning.

## Planning for Unexpected Emergencies

How would you prepare for everyday emergencies? What would you do if you could not make it home when you intended to, or had to be away from home longer than expected? Who would you call to look after your adored Cavalier?

To ensure that your dog is taken care of properly when you cannot get home, you need to plan ahead:

- Speak with trusted, pet-friendly neighbors. If they are in agreement and can cover for you in your absence, make sure that they are comfortable with your dog and that your dog is familiar and comfortable around them.
- Provide friends and neighbors with a key to your home and a "to-do" list detailing your dog's eating, exercise, and sleeping habits.
- Make sure that you leave detailed instructions as to where to find your dog's collar, harness (if you use one), leash, dog food, and a pet emergency kit with any medication your dog may need to take while you are gone. Also, leave your veterinarian's name, address, and phone number in case your neighbor or friend needs to contact the clinic.

If you use a pet sitter, she may be able to help, depending on where she is located. You should discuss this potential situation with her in advance.

# CHAPTER 9

# CAVALIER TRAINING

There are ten basic commands your dog should learn to make your life with him more enjoyable: *come, sit, down, walk nicely on leash, heel, sit-stay, down-stay, wait, stand,* and *stand-stay*. Knowing and complying with these commands will contribute to raising a dog who is well mannered in the home and out in public. These behaviors will also come into play if you'd like to compete in canine sports, such as obedience, rally, and agility. There are also a few around-the-house commands I find useful: *let's go, off,* and *upstairs/downstairs*. And let's not forget tricks. What's life without a little fun?

## INTERMEDIATE OBEDIENCE COMMANDS

Several basic obedience commands were discussed in the puppy training section. In this chapter, we will cover intermediate commands such as *heel, sit-stay, down-stay, stand,* and *stand-stay.*

### Heel

Nothing looks snappier than a dog heeling by your side, gazing attentively at you. If you plan to participate in obedience and rally trials, a polished *heel* will be necessary. You can also teach your pet Cavalier to heel for regular walks, although controlled walking may be all you really need.

To teach heel, do the following:

1. With your dog positioned on your left side on leash, ask him to sit.
2. When he is sitting and attentive, say "Heel" and begin walking, starting with your left foot.
3. If he lunges to the front or lags behind, you can lure him into position with a small treat. Praise him for his compliance and give the treat.
4. Say "Heel" and walk off again. Each time you stop, ask your dog to sit. Reward him for his cooperation.

It can take a while for your dog to fully understand where the correct *heel* position is, but he will get it with praise and practice.

### Stay

The *stay* is a very useful command in everyday life and will also be needed if you intend to participate in obedience trials. It's usually taught in the following sequence: *sit-stay, down-stay,* and *stand-stay*. Be sure you have fully mastered one segment before you move on to the next.

When training your Cavalier, always remain calm, relaxed, and confident. If he isn't performing up to your standards, it could be that he just doesn't get it, his attention span has expired, or your techniques (body language, verbal commands) are inconsistent. Don't take it personally. End your session on a positive note and resume again at another time.

## Sit-Stay

The *sit-stay* is a very useful command around the house when you don't want your Cavalier underfoot. It is also necessary for obedience competition. Your dog should be on 6-foot (2-m) leash and wearing a buckle collar.

To teach *sit-stay,* do the following:

1. Ask your dog to sit on your left side.
2. Say "Stay" and move your left hand with your palm facing down toward your dog's face. Say "Stay."
3. Move out one step with your right foot and turn to face your dog.
4. Count to three (to yourself), then say "Good stay."
5. Return to your dog's left side, pat him on his left shoulder, and give the release command "Okay." Praise him. Allow your dog to get up and move around.

Repeat the above in slow increments, moving farther away from your dog. When you walk off, lead with your right foot. Soon your dog will realize that movement with your left foot means that he too should walk forward, and movement with your right

foot means that he should stay stationary. Eventually you will be able to step out to the end of the leash and walk in a full circle around your dog. When he has perfected this exercise, you can work on an off-leash *sit-stay.* To do this:

1. Give your command once and walk a few steps away.
2. If your dog gets up, walk back to him, and say "Sit," then "Stay," and try again.
3. If he has been good, return to the *heel* position, pat him on the shoulder, say "Okay," and release him.

Continuing to train and work regularly with your Cavalier will strengthen the bond between you and contribute to raising a dog who is well mannered in the home and out in public.

The *sit-stay* is an important intermediate obedience command.

4. Increase your distance and duration. When giving the stay command, always return to your dog and release him.

And here's some advice from my favorite trainer, Linda, if your dog is breaking the *stay:*

"If your dog breaks his *stay,* an immediate correction is in order. Make a loud sound (don't say "No!"—just a sound will do) to get his attention as you quickly (and I do mean quickly) go to him, hold his lead close to the collar, and take him back to the exact spot he was in to start. Repeat "Stay" and leave him again. Be consistent and correct him each time he breaks the command. (Note: The reason you do not want to use the word "no" if your dog breaks his *stay* is because he is probably breaking it to come to you and you never want to discourage a dog from coming to you. You just want to make a sound to get his attention.)

If your dog is getting proficient (in your eyes!) add distractions—that's the real test! Remember to take the *stay* command very seriously because it could save your dog's life some day. And take it nice and slow. This is a systematic process. Be consistent, add distractions, and don't get frustrated. Just remember to praise and have fun!

If you find your dog is breaking his *stay* a lot, it means you have gone too far too fast

## The Velcro Dog

If you are working on *sit* and *down-stays* in a class, don't be surprised if your Cavalier wanders over to you. By now you know just how much a Cav wants to be near his person. Keep practicing. You can be successful.

with this command. A good rule of thumb to remember is: Time is more important than distance. At first, when you put your dog in a *sit* and then tell him "Stay" you want to move only a couple of inches (cm) away from him. Don't increase the distance until he can sit in that position without breaking it for 30 seconds. Once you have accomplished that, you can start increasing the distance a little. Your goal is always a 30-second *stay*. If you get to a point where your dog starts breaking his *stay* again, you need to go back to the distance at which he can successfully stay in his spot for 30 seconds.

### Down-Stay

The *down-stay* comes in handy when you have guests, when you are in the waiting room at the vet's office, and in any other circumstance where you need your dog to remain under control and quiet. It is also necessary in agility, obedience, and rally competition.

To teach the *down-stay*, do the following:

1. Using a buckle collar and 6-foot (2-m) leash and with your dog on your left side, give the *down* command. If you need to review the *down*, go back to Chapter 4.
2. When your dog is lying on the ground, say "Stay," use your

hand signal, move out one step with your right foot and turn to face your dog. Count to three (to yourself), then say "Good stay."

3. Return to your dog's left side by walking around him, wait a second or two, pat him on his left shoulder, and give the release command "Okay." Praise him. Allow your dog to get up and move around.
4. As your dog remains in position, walk out a bit farther each time and increase the amount of time he needs to stay in place.

The *down-stay* should be easier to achieve in that your dog is now familiar with the *stay* command.

When you are working on the *stay* command and standing in front of your Cavalier facing him, *do not* stare at him. Eye contact (staring) can be very confrontational. It will probably make your dog nervous and cause him to want to get up and move away from you. Just relax and look to the side of him or up over him; you'll still be able to watch him without making direct eye contact.

### Stand

To stand on command is necessary in the conformation show ring and is also very useful at the vet's office.

To teach the *stand*, do the following:

1. With your dog on your left side, place him in a standing position
2. Say "Stand" and hold him in place for a few seconds.
3. Say "Good stand," then "Okay" and release. Build up the amount of time that you have him remain standing. You can give small treats while also saying "Good stand."

### Stand-Stay

Once your Cavalier

## Want to Know More?

For a refresher course on basic obedience commands, see Chapter 4: Training Your Cavalier Puppy.

has mastered the *stand,* you can add *stay* to it. Follow the steps as described above in the *sit/stay* and *down/stay* instructions. By now, your dog should understand that you want him to remain stationary, but the *stand/stay* may be a little more difficult to master because your dog is in a position that allows him to easily walk off. Be patient and consistent. With practice, he will get it.

## Wait

The *wait* is another useful command. While *stay* means "do not move until you are released," *wait* means "don't follow." I find it very helpful around the house when I'm walking out to the garage or into another room and want my dogs to wait for me where I left them. Or if I'm getting out of a car and want

them to remain there until I return. I teach my dogs to *wait* in the following manner:

1. Open a door.
2. Say "Wait" and close the door before your dog can scamper through.
3. Say "Good wait," then "Okay" and release. They get the idea in no time.

Linda, a private trainer, has a little different

During training, you can motivate your Cavalier to learn by rewarding him with a treat and praise when he obeys a command.

## Multi-Dog Tip

If you have multiple dogs and own a fenced yard, you can sharpen their response to the come command using the following game. Call one of your dogs by his name along with giving the come command, i.e., "Bailey, come!" When Bailey reaches you, praise him lavishly, engage him in a game with a favorite toy, and/or give him a treat. Chances are more than one dog will arrive at your feet, but pay attention only to the dog you called and then send them all off to play by themselves again. Repeat by calling a different dog's name and give only that particular dog attention. In time, each dog wanting to be the one to receive your attention should respond at top speed when he hears his name followed by the *come* command.

communication system with your Cavalier. Here are a few around-the-house commands that I find useful.

### Let's Go!

I use *let's go* when my dogs are on leash and we're about to take a nice walk around the neighborhood. I don't need them to heel, in fact, it would be rather difficult with so many. I just like to have two on my left and two on my right (I haven't included the puppy in the group walk yet.) Once collars and leashes are on and we're outside the gate, I say "Let's go." They get into formation and move forward in unison. If you're wondering how I walk four dogs without getting tangled in leashes, I'm pleased to tell you, we've got our system down and rarely have a problem. Turning around can be a little tricky, so each dog has a different-colored leash: Woody's is always green, Rory's is blue, Junie's is red, and Topo's is yellow. If someone steps out of line and starts to circle my legs, I know immediately who it is by the color of the leash and can straighten him out before we find ourselves in a predicament.

Perhaps this all sounds too easy. But keep in mind that I've taken each dog through numerous training classes and worked with them individually to walk nicely on leash. So extending their training to a group walk was not that difficult.

I also use *let's go* when the dogs are off leash in our fenced yard. Because we live in the country and have a large property, I often walk the perimeter with them. I say "Let's go!" and walk off in the direction I want to take. Since they all delight in walking with me, whether it be on leash or in the yard, I simply use the command as the action takes place so each new member of the pack learns quickly from watching the others.

meaning for the command. *Wait* means that you are to remain in that spot and you are not allowed to move until I give you another command. That other command will release you to either come to me or perform some other activity. *Wait,* in this sense, would come into play in agility. Your dog may have to wait for just a few seconds until you give him direction to take the next obstacle. Either response to the command is fine. Just be consistent with your training so as not to confuse your dog.

## OTHER AROUND-THE-HOUSE COMMANDS

You will undoubtedly come up with your own

If you don't want your Cavalier on the furniture, teach him your house rules from the first day. If you catch him in the act, firmly give the *off* command and remove him.

## Off

Because Cavaliers are consummate cuddlers and their people enjoy this trait, most are allowed on furniture. But you need to decide from the beginning whether your dog should have access to all furniture or will not be allowed on the furniture at all. And you must be consistent.

Let's say your grandmother's heirloom Queen Anne Chair sits in the corner of your living room and you'd rather not worry about it collecting dog hair or sustaining toenail scratches in the fabric. Teach your dog from Day One that he is forbidden on the furniture. If you catch him in the act of jumping on the chair, firmly say "Off"

and remove him. After several repetitions, he should get the idea. You can hasten the process by asking him to sit when he is back on the floor and then offering a food reward. Don't give the reward as soon as his feet touch the ground or he may jump on the chair just to get the treat when he jumps off! You can also place a scat mat on the chair to correct transgressions when you're not around to observe. It's a flat mat that gives an unpleasant sensation like static electricity when touched.

## Upstairs/Downstairs

As you and your Cav are headed up the stairs, use the word "upstairs." Praise as you go.

Because you are already in motion and your dog is complying with the action, it will be easy for him to learn the command. Then if you want him to climb up ahead of you and spare yourself the possibility of tripping, simply say "Upstairs" and off he should go. I'm assuming here that your dog already respects you as his leader and is happy to comply with your wishes. If you are having leadership issues, always climb up or down the stairs ahead of your dog.

Trick training can be a fun way to exercise your dog and stimulate his mind.

# TRICKS

Not everything in a dog's life has to have a serious purpose. There are plenty of tricks you can teach your little buddy. Not only are they fun for both of you, but they will also help stimulate his mind. Some tricks that come immediately to mind are: beg, paw/other paw, roll over, speak, etc.

Topo has an adorable habit of sitting up on his hind legs and pawing at the air. I took advantage of this natural behavior and added a hand signal so he will do it on command. It's a crowd pleaser every time.

Here's how to train your dog to do a few fun tricks.

## Roll Over

To begin, give your dog the *down* command, and when he is down kneel beside him. Hold a special great-smelling treat near his nose. Then slowly move it around and behind him while saying "Roll over." Your dog should move onto his side and then roll over on it. Praise and reward him when he does so. Be sure to practice on a soft surface such as a carpet or the lawn.

## Beg

Ask your dog to sit in front of you. Hold a tasty treat just above his head and say, "Beg." Most likely, your food-driven Cavalier will lift his front feet off the ground and paw at you. As soon as his he does, reward him with the treat and an enthusiastic "Good boy."

## Shake Paws

Begin by having your dog sit. Then say "Shake hands" or "Paw." Take one of his paws in your hand. Hold it for a few seconds, praise him, and give him a treat. Then let go of his paw. Try this a few more times. Eventually give the command and see whether he will

Once your dog learns all of his obedience commands, there's no limit to what you can do together.

lift his paw on his own. Dogs usually learn to shake quite quickly.

## Speak

There are a few ways to teach the *speak* command. Here are two. You can hold a very tasty treat in your hand within your dog's eye view. Say the word "speak." Then repeat it a few times with enthusiasm. If he's really interested in the treat, chances are he will bark with anticipation. Reward him by saying "Good boy" and giving him the treat.

Or you can start a game your dog really enjoys such as fetch. Show him a ball and get him excited by saying "Let's play! Want to play?" but don't actually throw it. If he barks say "Speak! Good boy, speak." Then toss the ball as his reward.

# CHAPTER 10

# CAVALIER PROBLEM BEHAVIORS

Just as parents wouldn't tolerate bad behavior in their children, neither should pet parents tolerate objectionable behavior from their dogs. If a problem arises, you can first turn to your dog trainer for advice. If the trouble is beyond the scope of the trainer's expertise, an animal behaviorist should be called in. Ask your vet for a referral or visit the Association of Animal Behavior Professionals (www.associationofanimalbehaviorprofessionals.com) or the Association of Companion Animal Behavior Counselors (www.animalbehaviorcounselors.org).

In nature, each member of a wolf or wild dog pack must be in a stable/balanced frame of mind, so that the pack itself will be in balance. It's essential to the well-being of the group to be in harmony in order to survive and thrive. There's no place for Type A anxious types. The same can be said for domestic dogs.

Many of the activities we label as problem behaviors are a direct result of the way we expect our companions to live, which can throw them off balance. What do I mean exactly? Think about it. Dogs are programmed to be with their pack, and yet how many nonpack dogs spend eight hours or more alone each day? This is not a natural state of being for them—and you're really asking for trouble with a breed as people-oriented as the Cavalier. Also, dogs are innately active animals. But how much exercise do we actually give them? Is a walk around the block every now and then even close to sufficient? When dealing with problem behaviors, first look at your dog's life from his point of view.

## AGGRESSION

Aggressive dogs are not born, they're created. In very rare cases, there can be an underlying psycho-physiological problem. But generally aggression generates from another issue. For example, it can stem from fear or a conditioned response to something that happened previously. You may see what you believe is "aggression" coming from your sweet little pup when it's really your puppy moving himself up to the leadership position in your pack because, in his mind, no one else has the role. The bottom line is that you have to determine what the cause of the aggression is and concentrate on fixing that issue first so that the aggression ceases.

Hopefully, if you have raised your Cavalier from a pup and firmly established yourself

Dogs need time with their people and exercise to help keep them out of trouble.

as his pack leader, aggression will never become a problem. This type of behavior is totally unacceptable in any breed but particularly contrary to the Cavalier's loving, devoted temperament. If your dog is growling or attempting to bite, it may be due to his confusion about his role within the family. Too much pampering may have given him the mistaken impression that *he* is the leader of your pack.

## Management Technique

You may encounter aggression in a rescued adult dog and not know the root of its cause. Once the reason is identified, you can start working on the real issue at hand. The good news is that dogs always want to go back to balance, and when they are behaving aggressively they are out of balance. With the proper strategy you can address the underlying issue. Once you do, you will see the aggressive behavior subside. Aggression is not a behavior you should attempt to correct on your own. Contact an animal behaviorist at the first sign of inappropriate growling or attempts to bite people or other dogs.

## BARKING

No one likes a dog who barks incessantly—especially the neighbors. Cavaliers don't tend to be yappers, but any dog may well complain by barking if he's left alone too long, too often.

## Management Technique

First, try to identify what's setting off the behavior. Are you leaving your dog alone for too long? Remember, this is a breed easily prone to separation anxiety. Spending more time with your pet should help, or if that's not possible, try hiring a pet sitter to break up the monotony of his day. Adopting a second dog to provide full-time companionship may also help in the long run. However, it would be best to solve the separation anxiety first before bringing in another dog. (Consult a dog trainer for detailed information on dealing with separation anxiety.)

Before you leave your dog for an extended period, do you give him ample exercise in the form of a structured walk? Dogs prone to separation anxiety are anxious when their owners depart. Exercise helps dogs relax. If you plan to leave your dog for a few hours, you will find that a brisk 30-minute structured walk before you go will drain your dog's energy and allow him to relax and rest in your absence. What is a structured walk? It's having your dog walk right by your side—he can be a little behind you but never in front. As you walk, there's no sniffing allowed. After you have walked a few minutes, you can give your dog a verbal command to let him know that it's okay for him to go ahead of you, sniff around, and relieve himself if need be. After a minute it's time to give him another verbal signal (like "Okay, let's go") and continue moving forward with your brisk walk.

This structured walk for your dog is comparable to your walking on a treadmill for a half hour. It gets your endorphins flowing and, in turn, it calms you down. It's also important to make your departure totally uneventful when you are finally leaving your house. Don't feel that you have to say goodbye to your dog or tell him you are so sorry you have to leave him. This will only raise his anxiety level because you will be giving off sad/worried/weak energy. When it's time to depart, just go. If you've ever watched a documentary on wild dog packs or wolf pack behavior, you will never see a pack leader turn and say to the pack before going off to hunt, "Okay, guys, I'm leaving now, but I'll be right back! Be good!" No, when it's time to go, the pack leader just confidently turns around and leaves.

It's also important to make your arrivals as uneventful as well. You don't want your dog to anticipate an excited arrival. Excitement is not a normal state for a dog. What we humans sometimes label as happiness or excitement in our dogs is really canine anxiety. Jumping, panting, circling, whining, and excessive barking are not found in members of a stable dog pack.

The anxiety we see in our domesticated dogs is almost always a result of a lack of exercise and structure in the dog's life.

If your dog won't stop barking when visitors stop by, teach the *enough* or *quiet* command. When there is a break in your dog's barking, say your selected word and immediately reward

## Multi-Dog Tip

Multiple Cavaliers can sound off like a chorus of hounds. Be sure to teach the *quiet* command to each of your dogs individually, which will come in very handy if your dogs all decide to sing together. (See Barking section for instructions.)

Some problem behaviors are caused by boredom and lack of sufficient exercise.

him with a treat for his silence. Timing is very important—you want to issue the command as soon as your dog stops barking, otherwise you will be rewarding the wrong behavior.

## CHEWING

Chewing can have a variety of reasons behind it. Boredom, teething, anxiety, and lack of exercise are all common causes.

### Management Technique

No one wants a dog to use his or her personal belongings as chew toys, so it's important to provide dogs with a range of appropriate toys of their own. Those that involve mental stimulation, for example, the type they must bat around in order to release treats, are especially good. So are the rubber toys, like

Nylabones, with holes that can be filled with foods such as kibble or peanut butter.

Teaching your dog a command is also helpful to break him of his inappropriate chewing habit. *Leave it* means don't pick it up. *Drop it* means let go of what is in your mouth. These commands can be taught by using treats that are of greater value to the dog than what he has his eye or mouth on. For example, when you catch your Cavalier chewing on a forbidden item, tell him to drop it. Praise him for complying, give him an exceptionally tasty treat, and then give him one of his acceptable chew toys.

## COPROPHAGIA

Coprophagia is the unattractive habit of eating feces whether it be a dog's own or those of

Chewing inappropriate objects should subside by adulthood. But dogs do occasionally revert to their puppyhood pranks. Be sure to firmly establish *drop it* and *leave it* commands early on. Puppies can begin to learn commands as early as 8 weeks of age.

another dog or other animals. In rural areas, deer and bunny poop appears to be a delicacy for many dogs.

## Management Technique

Eating feces can be caused by a multitude of medical problems, so the first course of action is to have your vet perform a complete physical examination and have your dog's stool tested to eliminate a medical issue. Once your vet has assured you that there are no medical problems, you will know for sure that you're dealing with a problem behavior.

Some dogs have no interest in this unsavory habit. Others who have never eaten droppings will learn to eat them from watching another dog do it. Dogs are genetically programmed to be able to survive in the wild by eating poop if other food is not available. Even though your dog gets ample food every day, he may still be a poop eater. It becomes a bad habit and one that is hard to break because food is in itself reinforcement.

There are products available that you sprinkle on the dog's food that are specifically

targeted for this behavior and claim that it makes the feces less palatable. Anecdotal evidence suggests varying degrees of success. Some people believe that adding papaya, yogurt, or cottage cheese to a dog's food will do the trick. But the one truly obvious way to assure that your dog won't eat his stool is to pick it up. I carry baggies in all of my coat pockets to have at the ready as soon you know what hits the ground. (Dealing with deer and bunny poop is a little more complicated, but I've been known to pick up piles of it as well.)

If the problem occurs when you're out walking, you can use the *leave it* command, but the command will have to be taught prior to using it on your walks. Unfortunately, there is no magical preventive when it comes to stopping this behavior. It will only be remedied by being one step ahead of your dog at all times and correcting his behavior.

## DIGGING

Digging is a common behavior for dogs. It occurs for a variety of reasons, such as for entertainment or seeking prey, attention, comfort, or escape.

## Management Technique

If your dog is digging just for the fun of it, try scheduling more play time with him. Make sure that he has mental stimulation

throughout the day. Teaching your Cavalier to play flying disc and to chase after tennis balls are good ways of providing entertainment. Also make sure that you are taking enough walks. A tired dog is a good dog. For those dedicated diggers, however, you may need to provide an acceptable digging space in the corner of your yard—a doggy sandbox, so to speak.

For dogs who dig due to prey instinct, it's best to have your yard searched for pests. If you discover a groundhog, for example, living on the other side of your fence, have him trapped and relocated by a wild animal service. I've rehomed several box turtles myself, although we're still not completely sure how one ended

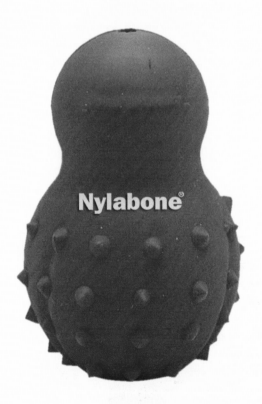

Rubber toys, like Nylabones, can be stuffed with food to keep your dog from becoming bored.

up in our pantry! I have a strong suspicion that Rory had something to do with it.

For attention seekers, turn your back when you see your dog digging—don't give him the attention he seeks! It's also important to make sure that your dog has enough one-on-one time with you during the day so that he doesn't feel the need to misbehave to get your attention.

For a dog seeking comfort or protection, see where he is digging. Is it in the shade? Near water? If your dog is digging to get comfortable, make sure that he has a cool, safe area to curl up and rest in when he's outdoors. A dog who is trying to escape his yard is giving you another sure sign that he is not getting enough attention. You know what to do.

## FEAR OF STRANGERS

It's hard to imagine the personable Cavalier being afraid of a stranger, but any undersocialized dog can feel insecure around new people and places. So be sure to get your Cavalier out into the world as much as possible as a youngster.

When we adopted Topo Gigio, he weighed a whopping 3 pounds (1.4 kg) and was irresistibly cute. (He looked like a miniature chocolate spaniel.) I dutifully brought him into stores, banks, libraries—any location where he would be welcomed and could meet new people. Because he was so tiny and adorable, strangers couldn't resist petting him on the head. None of my larger puppies minded this greeting, but Topo shrieked in terror. I tell you it was ear-piercing and quite a shock to me and friendly strangers. So I started carrying tiny treats in my pocket and asked people we met on our outings to offer them to Topo and not to pet his head.

At home, I'd have guests sit on our living room couch, give them a handful of treats, and then let Topo in to meet them. He soon

If you find your dog digging in your garden, give him his own digging area.

associated strangers with all these wonderful treats and lost his fear. Now two years old, he loves meeting new people and no longer shrieks—even if they pet him on the head.

Topo was obviously fearful about being touched on the top of his head. So the treat method I used worked well for him. But individual shy dogs can have different levels of fear/anxiety. If you happen to have a very anxious dog, the treat method will have to be tweaked. You must be careful to avoid having the treats reinforce his fear.

If your dog is extremely nervous around strangers, ask first-time visitors to ignore him (no touching, talking, or eye contact). Every so often, as your guest is ignoring him, have her drop a treat on the ground where your dog can see it falling from her hand. What usually

happens is that the dog will start moving toward the visitor and will sniff her shoes. Bingo! Once you see your dog finally start to use his nose, you're more than halfway there. At this point, your guest can slowly begin to interact with your dog. Watch their eye contact, though. Have your guest squat down and let your dog sniff some more. Tell her not to pet him on the head because it's a much too dominant behavior. Instead, she should do a scratch-type pet on your dog's chest or under the chin. Even better is to rub the dog's neck under the chin area and actually raise his head a little. This is a confident posture and helps the dog relax and feel more confident too.

On the other hand, if your dog only exhibits signs of anxiety (tail between the legs, shaking, avoidance behaviors), dropping treats is all the

Undersocialized dogs can feel insecure about new people and places.

visitor should do. Eventually, your dog will relax because he associates the positive treats with the new person who continually ignores him, which—to a dog—says that this human means no harm. Before you know it, your visitor will have made a new friend and your shy dog will be well on his way to becoming more self-assured.

## JUMPING UP

Jumping up is a problem for many dog owners. It's also one that frequently gets unintentionally reinforced by yelling "Get down," pushing the dog off, and even dancing around trying to avoid him. All of these reactions are giving the dog what he wants: your attention and a greeting! It's important to correct this problem with positive reinforcement and not force, which

has been more commonly used in past generations.

## Management Technique

Eye contact is one way dogs communicate. Because our eyes are up high, dogs often jump to get closer and extend a greeting. Therefore we must teach our dogs that this is not an acceptable behavior.

## Training Tidbit

Turning your back on your dog will discourage his jumping up "attention-seeking" behavior.

## Jumping on You

When our dogs are pups, we tend to pick them up or bend down to pet them and coo at them in high-pitched tones. Either response is very rewarding to a puppy. Later as they grow we may start pushing them away, which they interpret as play. So what should we do to diminish jumping and keep our dogs off us? Ignore them. That's right, when you come home and your Cavalier bounds over to greet you, ignore him. No talking, no petting, no eye contact—nothing. It even helps to turn your back on your dog and go about your business. (Note: A behavior that is not rewarded/reinforced will extinguish.)

Try it for a week. Come home and ignore your dog until he has given up on jumping. If you have children, instruct them to do the same thing. Explain to young children that when they run around, jumping and screeching, your dog will think they are the biggest and best squeaky toy ever invented. Instead, they should play "statue" and call to you for assistance. Pick up your Cavalier and give him a time out until everyone is back in a calm state.

## Jumping on Visitors

Greeting company is such an exciting experience that dogs can barely contain themselves. To keep your Cavalier from jumping on your visitors, keep a leash by the door. Before they arrive, tell your guests that you will be training your dog not to jump so they can participate appropriately. Before opening the door, tell your dog to sit. Once he's sitting, loosen up on the leash and keep it loose. Now invite your friends in. Tell them to ignore your dog unless he is sitting. If he is cooperating, they may approach and pet him. You can also give your guests some small treats to reward your dog if he remains sitting. If he breaks the *sit*, have them ignore

him again. If you have taught a reliable *sit/stay*, this would be a great time to use it.

Another effective approach is to set up a training session enlisting the help of a friend or two. While you are standing with your dog on leash in the street or in the yard, have one friend at a time walk toward your dog. As the friend approaches him and your Cav begins to jump up, have her immediately turn and walk away. Do this until your dog stops getting up. Once your friend can approach with your dog remaining on the floor, have her greet and offer

Ask your friends and relatives to help you correct jumping up by not encouraging this behavior and ignoring your dog if he does so.

## Finding a Pet Behavior Consultant

Some problem behaviors can defy even your most dedicated training efforts. Such issues can range from inappropriate barking or chewing to much more serious ones such as aggression. In these cases, you may not be able to handle the problem on your own and would benefit from seeking professional help. Behaviorists are experts in animal behavior and motivation and will be able to give you advice on how to best solve your pet's problem. You can get a referral from your veterinarian or from the following organizations:

- Animal Behavior Society, www.animalbehavior.org
- American Veterinary Society of Animal Behavior, www.avma.org/avsab
- International Association of Animal Behavior Consultants, www.iaabc.org

him a treat. This way, your dog learns through his own behavior that getting up or jumping causes what he wants (in this case attention from the person approaching) to go away. The dog learns that by remaining on the floor he can get what he seeks: the person's attention and treats. Do this with a variety of people and children as often as possible.

Using positive reinforcement, you can correct jumping up easily by reinforcing only your dog's appropriate behavior, in this case rewarding him when he remains on the floor. This means ignoring jumping up and all other enthusiastic greetings. When you come home and your dog is happy to see you and shows that enthusiasm by jumping up, running circles at your feet, and darting about the house, completely ignore him. Do not look at him, speak to him, or touch him in any way. Stare at the ceiling or turn your back to him. It may be difficult to ignore the adorable whirling dervish, but if you wait him out, he will realize that his jumping up is not getting him anywhere. When he does place all fours on the floor, reinforce the correct behavior with a barrage of calm petting and treats. Squat down and quietly say "Hello." Once the greeting is over, move on.

## LEASH PULLING

If you taught your dog to walk nicely on leash as a pup, leash pulling shouldn't be an issue. But if it is a problem, or you have acquired an adult dog who is pulling, try introducing or reviewing leash training or try using a head halter.

### Management Technique

A walk starts while you are still inside your house. Call your dog to come to you to put on his leash and/or halter. Don't bring the leash to your dog, and never chase after him. Once the leash is on, have your dog sit by the door. You can ask him to wait or just give him a hand signal to indicate that you want him to wait, then open the door and step outside. If your dog is calm and relaxed, you may invite him to join you. You can give him either a verbal command ("Okay" or "Let's go") or a hand signal. If your dog is not calm and relaxed, wait for him to become so. You want him to associate being calm with entering the

## Want to Know More?

To teach your dog to heel properly, see Chapter 9: Cavalier Training.

A dog who pulls on leash is difficult to control and poses a danger to himself and the person walking him.

outside territory and starting his walk.

The reason you are going through this ritual is because you are changing territories (your house is one territory and the outside world is another.) Dogs instinctively know that whoever crosses the threshold first is pack leader. By having your dog calmly sit and wait for you to cross the threshold first and then wait for your okay to move into the outside territory, you are claiming the new territory as yours. Dogs instinctively understand this. Once outside, begin your walk with your dog at your side. (Note: If he is accustomed to pulling you, it is important for you to have a training collar on him during his walk.)

Your dog will know how you are feeling by the messages you are sending through the leash. If you are anxious and stressed, you will send that energy to your dog, and it will cause him to want to move away from you. Keep your posture tall and confident and try not to stare at your dog as you are walking. Just look straight ahead and keep moving forward. Of course, you can glance at him from time to time, but your main objective is to remain calm and relaxed. You will find that once *you* relax, your dog will too. If your dog begins to pull, just stop walking. When he releases pressure on the leash, you can go forward again. He will soon learn that if he pulls, he won't get anywhere.

If you are walking on a sidewalk, teach your dog to sit whenever you come to a corner and have to cross the street. It is not necessary to do a lot of talking to your dog. (Dogs don't "talk" to each other when traveling in a pack.) In fact,

If your dog begins to pull on his leash, stop walking. He'll soon learn that if he pulls, he won't get anywhere.

sometimes talking to a dog will excite him and make him more difficult to control. Don't feel that you're being mean to your dog if you are not constantly talking to him. In the canine world, calmly traveling with the pack leader and enjoying the sights and sounds of nature are what life is all about.

Once you get back home, make sure that you enter the house first and then invite your dog in after you. What you are saying to your dog is "This is my territory and I am inviting you in." Now your walk is complete and your dog understands his place in the pack.

If you continue to have problems, speak with a trainer about possibly using a halter to correct this problem. The principle of using the halter is similar to that of leading a horse: Where the head goes, the body must follow.

Some people call head halters the remote control of dog walking. They fit on the dog's muzzle below his eyes and behind his ears at the top of his neck and fasten beneath his head. The head halter is a humane device because you are not inflicting any type of pain to correct pulling. A dog can also eat, drink, bark, and pant while wearing it.

Head halters must fit correctly in order to work properly. And since the concept is different from collars that go around the neck, it is best to have the trainer give you a demonstration before you get under way. Once your dog accepts the halter and you feel confident in its use, follow the trainer's instructions. At first, some dogs object to the new feel of a head halter. You can introduce it in short increments and give food rewards to start a positive association.

# NIPPING

Nipping may simply be a play behavior, or it can be the beginning of a more serious problem. Identifying the circumstances that motivate nipping can help you establish the cause of the problem so you can resolve it.

## Management Technique

Nipping is part of normal puppy play. Puppies enjoy wrestling with one another, and until they are taught some alternative play activities, they will often bite and nip their human playmates as well. Even though nipping is a natural behavior, it should not be encouraged. If your dog nips at your hands or clothing, you should immediately stop playing with him and ignore him. This will let him know that you do not enjoy this activity and will not participate. You can also teach the *no bite* command. Say the words "no bite," stop the nipping behavior, and give your pup an acceptable chew toy as an alternative. Here's another tip. When Woody was a pup, his nipping was so severe that I called him my snapping baby piranha. I sprayed my hands and arms with a bitter apple spray, which further helped reinforce the *no bite* command.

Adult dogs will most often display nipping as an attention-seeking tactic. Nipping often accompanies behaviors such as barking and jumping. Speaking to your dog, shouting at him, or pushing him while he is jumping and mouthing will only reinforce this behavior. If your dog nips at you when you arrive home, create a place to confine him while you are away so that he cannot accost you at the door. Refuse to open gates or doors until your dog has all four paws on the ground.

Some dogs will nip when they are guarding a valued resource such as food or their home. Territorial aggression should be addressed right away with training and behavioral modification. Nipping can quickly develop into biting if the behavior is tolerated or accidentally encouraged. It is natural for a dog to protect his food and home, but you will need to establish that you are his pack leader and there is no need to protect his food and toys or you from house guests.

Additionally, if your normally laid-back dog suddenly displays snapping or nipping

On the whole, most Cavaliers are well-behaved dogs.

behavior, there may be an underlying physical problem. Have your dog evaluated for injuries or illness under these circumstances. Pain and chemical imbalances can cause even the most tolerant dog to nip or display other uncharacteristically aggressive behavior.

## SEPARATION ANXIETY

When dog owners come home to a house that looks as if it has been ransacked—with pillows, cushions, and chair legs torn to bits—they often assume their pets have destroyed the furniture to retaliate for being left alone. What's actually often taking place is a condition referred to as separation anxiety, with an emphasis on anxiety. The dog is thoroughly distressed by being separated from his owner. He is not thinking, "Oh, no. My person has left me behind. How dare the master! I'll get even and chew up all the decorative pillows." More likely his thoughts are something like, "Oh no. Oh no. My pack leader has left without me. What should I do? I'm nervous left on my own."

Other signs of canine separation anxiety are: various vocalizations such as barking, whining, and howling; inappropriate urination and defecation; pacing and circling; and excessive licking and salivating. While any dog can suffer from this condition, those breeds with an especially high attachment to their people, spaniels among them, are often likely candidates.

### Management Technique

It's best to get your dog accustomed to being left alone from the get go. Cavaliers do well in crates and ex-pens—basically in small, confined spaces. They like their dens. If you have to leave for several hours each day, introduce your dog to a crate or ex-pen early on as explained in Chapter 4: Training Your Cavalier Puppy. Allow him to enjoy having his cozy space. This will make it less traumatic for him whenever you leave.

When my dogs were young, I'd collect my car keys and head for the door without a lot of fanfare. On my way out, I'd give them a few treats so they would associate my departure with something positive. At first, I'd only stay away for short spurts. Eventually, I increased the time I spent away from home. Having raised several "Velcro dogs," I'm pleased to report that none have suffered from separation anxiety. But if you are faced with this problem, here are some manageable solutions:

- Give your dog a treat, then leave the room for just a minute. Return. Repeat this until he takes your absence in stride. Next, offer a treat and leave the house for a few minutes. Return. Repeat this as needed, gradually lengthening the time you stay away. These exercises shouldn't be crammed into one day. Give your dog some time to adjust comfortably.
- Give your dog plenty of exercise early in the day, *e.g.*, a good vigorous walk or a game of

To prevent separation anxiety, give your dog plenty of exercise early in the day and make sure he has a variety of toys to play with when he's alone.

fetch in the yard. Remember, a tired dog is a good dog.

- Ignore your dog for 15 minutes before you leave and for 15 minutes after you get back home.
- Give your dog an interactive toy with food in it to keep him busy, such as a hollow rubber chew toy stuffed with peanut butter or kibble.
- Leave the radio or television on when you are not home.
- When you are at home, don't allow your dog to be by your side constantly. Teach him to remain quietly in another room some of the time.

- Practice obedience commands daily. Giving the *down-stay* command when you leave the room is a particularly good exercise in this situation.

If taking these measures doesn't solve the problem, talk with your vet and consider consulting a dog trainer or behaviorist because you may need a more comprehensive plan of action. Also, as a last resort, there are prescription medications available to treat separation anxiety, but these should be used in conjunction with behavior modification techniques.

# CHAPTER 11

# CAVALIER SPORTS AND ACTIVITIES

Although Cavaliers fall in the AKC's Toy Group, they are agile little dogs with plenty of gusto. Because of their intelligence, versatility, and willingness to please, they are capable of participating in myriad canine sports and activities.

Mabel, a Tricolor, enjoyed herding sheep in her youth. The first time the owner of the farm saw the little spaniel weaving and racing through her pasture, she thought a Border Collie pup had run amok. Surely, sheep herding is not the first sport that comes to mind when considering activities for your Cavalier, but don't tell Mabel—who at 12 years of age is still going strong—it couldn't be done.

## ACTIVITIES
Half the fun of having dogs in our lives is sharing various activities with them. For some folks that means hiking, doggy play dates, swimming at the beach, participating in pet therapy, etc. The possibilities are limitless. And the Cavalier is such a versatile little guy, there's not much he won't be happy to do with you.

## Camping
You may wonder whether a breed fit for a king would enjoy camping under the stars. Well, even a dog who lives primarily in the lap of luxury can adapt happily to the great outdoors, especially when camping with his beloved person. Just imagine, from your dog's perspective, the new sights, sounds, and smells of a campground, the hiking/walking trails, and the roasting of hot dogs.

Before heading out for that camping trip, you will need to plan ahead. First, has your dog been well socialized with other people and dogs? Has he had obedience training? If the answer to these two basic questions is no, then you'd best hold off on going. If you can't predict how your dog will react in this type of environment, then you're not ready for camping. But if your dog is well behaved, here's an idea: Take a test run. If you have the time before your camping trip and you have a backyard, start there. Pitch your tent, lay out your sleeping bag and your dog's familiar bed, and invite your Cavalier inside. Do not force him inside, but if he explores it on his own, toss in a few treats and praise him to let him know that the experience is a positive one. When he's comfortable inside, spend some time in the tent working up to about an hour in duration.

Before heading out for that camping trip, you will need to plan ahead.

Next, take your dog on several day trips, bringing along just enough equipment to replicate the environment you and your dog may experience while camping. Take it slowly and observe your dog for any signs of stress. Walk around the new area, getting him accustomed to it. Bring treats to reward him for good behavior. Once your dog has been desensitized to the simulated camping experience, you can try an extended stay.

As with any other travel plans, you will need to prepare for your trip in the same manner by ensuring the following:

• **Let a family member or friend know where you are headed:** If you're a serious camper and plan to enter a Bureau of Land Management campsite, stop in and register with the nearby park ranger station. Always check in with that family member or friend to let her know that you are okay or have returned home.

• **Vaccinations and license:** Make certain that your dog's vaccinations and license are current.

• **Identification, leashes, a harness, and tethers:** Ensure that your dog is under your control at all times. Do not allow him to wander. You should never underestimate the potential for danger. Keep your dog leashed while out for a walk or hike and tethered while at the campsite. Ensure that your collars and leashes are in good condition. Bring several. Use a specially designed tether that fastens around a tree or some other strong and stationary object. Tethers can also be staked to the ground, but they may not be as secure.

Also, be sure that your dog has identification tags on his collar with his name, your name, city and state of residence, your phone number, and if room permits, your veterinarian's phone number. If you know where you will staying in advance of your trip, you can make a temporary ID tag with your dog's name and the name of the campsite, as well as arrival and departure dates, to wear along with your dog's regular ID tag.

- **Appropriate bedding for you and your dog:** Bring familiar bedding for your dog, but also remember to place something (a plastic tarp, padding, or rug) under the bed to keep the chill of the cold ground from coming up through the bedding.
- **First-aid kit**: Bring along a doggy first-aid kit. For a list of essential items, see Chapter 8: Cavalier Health and Wellness.
- **Food and water:** Bring enough food (an extra two or three days' worth for good measure) and water from home for the duration of your camping trip. Never allow your dog to drink from natural water sources; they may be contaminated with unknown bacteria.

Your Cavalier can participate in activities with you in all kinds of weather provided he's prepared for it.

Because of their intelligence, versatility, and willingness to please, Cavaliers are capable of participating in myriad canine sports and activities.

- **Towels:** A few ultra-absorbent cloth towels and several rolls of paper towels are a must.

## Dog Parks

In theory, dog parks are a wonderful idea. What could be more fun for your dog than to run and romp freely with a bunch of his canine buddies? But there are some caveats to be aware of if you want your Cavalier to safely enjoy a dog park. First, the park should have separate large-dog and small-dog areas. I would not allow a toy breed to run with the "big boys," for obvious reasons.

You might want to observe the dogs playing in a park on a few occasions at different times of day before bringing your own dog. Are they well socialized? Playing nicely? Is there any aggressive behavior taking place? Dogs that have been left alone all day and are running around in a park after their owners have returned home from work may have too much pent-up energy to play properly.

You could select a quiet time of day and head to a park with your own friends and their dogs, assuming you already know the canine members of the group get along.

Proper socialization would be a primary concern, of course, but there are certainly a number of health concerns to consider as well. Be sure your dog is up-to-date with his vaccination protection. Presumably, dog owners who care enough to bring their dogs to a dog park also care enough to vaccinate them properly. But you can't know that for sure, so your dog should be protected before heading out to public areas.

As an alternative to public dog parks, you may want to organize your own doggy play dates if you have the space. I host them all the time, as my large property is fenced. This way I can screen our canine guests. I've also set up training classes by hiring an instructor and rounding up a group of my friends and their dogs.

## Walking/Jogging

Provided your Cavalier is in good physical shape, he will always be willing, able, and ready to walk when you are. If you're a heavy-duty jogger, one of the larger spaniel breeds would make a better running partner. But if you enjoy walking in neighborhood streets and/or parks, put on your sneakers or hiking boots, your dog's collar with proper identification tags, a comfortable walking harness and sturdy leash, and hit the trail and enjoy!

As you venture outside, consider your destination. Are dogs allowed where you plan to walk? Your neighborhood is likely a very safe bet, but what if you would like to travel to a nearby park? If you cannot call ahead or check the websites of parks in your area, you may upon arrival find signs posted with restrictions that pertain to dogs. In most cases, dogs must be walked on a leash and in all cases be under the control of the owner.

If you're planning a fairly long walk, bring water along. And regardless of where you walk, remember to carry several plastic poop bags so that you are equipped to pick up after your companion. Furthermore, be considerate and dispose of the waste properly. Parks often have poop container stations.

## CANINE GOOD CITIZEN TEST

After successful graduation from a basic obedience class and post-grad work in advanced training or participation in an AKC Canine Good Citizen (CGC) program, the final exam is the Canine Good Citizen test. This test is designed to demonstrate that your dog has been trained to be a reliable and respected companion and member of the community.

The test, administered by an AKC-approved CGC evaluator, is performed with the dog on a leash and wearing a buckle or slip collar. The Canine Good Citizen test is not a competitive program. Instead, the reward and recognition for you and your dog's hard work is a certificate of achievement officially recognizing that your dog has successfully passed the ten skills required of a well-mannered and outstanding canine citizen.

The test is evaluated on a pass/fail basis and consists of ten exercises.

### Exercise 1: Appearance and Grooming

The evaluator will inspect your dog to ensure that he welcomes being examined by someone other than his owner. The dog must appear to be in healthy condition, clean, and well groomed. The owner may be asked to present current health records and licenses, including a current rabies vaccination certificate. The evaluator will proceed to gently brush the dog, examine his ears, and handle each front paw to demonstrate the dog's willingness to accept handling from a friendly stranger such as a veterinarian or groomer.

## Exercise 2: Accepting a Friendly Stranger

The evaluator will approach you and your dog, greeting you in a natural, friendly manner while ignoring the dog. The dog should not demonstrate any signs of stress, such as aggression or shyness, and should not try to move toward the evaluator (especially not jumping up).

## Exercise 3: Loose Leash Walking

This exercise demonstrates that you have control over your dog and that he is attentive to you, your movement, and any change in your direction while he's walking on a leash. The dog must be positioned on the left side of the handler but does not necessarily need to be in the *heel* position. The evaluator will direct the handler to navigate a course with right and left turns, an about turn, and a full stop.

## Exercise 4: Walking Through a Crowd

This exercise simply demonstrates your ability to control your dog in public places and navigate through pedestrian traffic. During the exercise, you will be asked to walk your dog around and pass several small groups of people. The dog must remain polite and may show interest in the strangers but should

During the Canine Good Citizen test, a dog must sit politely for petting.

continue to walk with you without showing any signs of stress.

## Exercise 5: Sitting Politely for Petting

For this exercise, your dog must respond to the *sit* command while the evaluator approaches him and proceeds to gently pet him. Once again, the dog must show no signs of anxiety.

## Exercise 6: *Sit* and *Down* on Command and Staying in Place

This exercise demonstrates that your dog will respond reliably to the verbal commands for *sit*, *down*, and *stay*. After giving the command to *sit* or *down*, you will ask your dog to *stay*, drop the leash, walk away about 10 to 20 feet (3 to 6 m), turn, and return to the dog. The dog must remain in the *stay* position until the evaluator instructs you to release him.

## Exercise 7: Coming When Called

You will be asked to give your dog the *wait* command while he is standing or sitting. You will then proceed to walk about 10 feet (3 m) away from your dog, turn to face him, and call him to come.

## Exercise 8: Demonstrate Reaction to Another Dog

This part of the test demonstrates how the dog will react in the presence of another dog. In this exercise there will be a second handler and a '"neutral" dog, who will approach you and your dog from a distance of about 20 feet (6 m). You will be asked to shake the hand of the other handler, exchange greetings, and proceed on for another 10 feet (3 m). Your dog may show a casual passing interest in the other dog, but nothing more.

The Canine Good Citizen test encourages owners to foster and encourage good manners in their dogs. This attentive Cavalier awaits his next command.

## Exercise 9: Demonstrate Reaction to Distractions

The intent behind this exercise is to demonstrate your dog has been well socialized and distracting conditions, such as joggers, shopping carts, baby strollers, and loud noises, do not cause him undue trauma or nervousness. The evaluator will choose two distractions. Your dog may become startled but should not panic by showing any form of fear.

## Exercise 10: Supervised Separation

The rationale behind this exercise is to demonstrate that your dog is confident about

## Bentley the Therapist

Pet therapy is a wonderful experience for all involved. A Cavalier breeder shares this story: "A number of years ago, we were visiting a medical center for children with cancer and rare blood diseases. There was a teenage girl named Amy, who was wearing a very pretty scarf on her head, as chemotherapy had taken all of her hair. She was depressed and not really up for visitors, although she welcomed the dog. Bentley was happy to visit anyone. He thought she was very special and spent about a half hour with her, sitting on the bed and making her feel like she was the most important person he had ever met.

What I didn't know during the visit was that Amy is a gifted artist. She had not picked up her pencils in a month and was not interested in conveying her gift during her hospital stay—until she met Bentley. Her mother, who was Turkish and spoke very little English, came to summon me about 20 minutes later, when we were visiting another child on the floor. It was important that we come back to see Amy when we were done. Amy had asked her mother to get the drawing pad she had hidden under the bed and from memory, had drawn a perfect picture of Bentley, and I mean *perfectly*! I was blown away that she remembered half his tail was white and half was brown. To this day, I still keep that picture as a reminder of how Bentley helped a girl remember how special she was and for a few minutes forget about her disease.

being left alone with another trusted individual and will maintain good manners when you are not present. An evaluator will ask you whether you will allow her to watch your dog and then take the leash. You will move out of your dog's line of sight for about three to five minutes. During your absence, your dog should not show signs of constant worry such as whining or barking.

## THERAPY WORK

Cavalier King Charles Spaniels are consummate companions. They have an innate talent for sharing their affection and warmth with others and thus are very well suited to therapy work. Soft, cuddly, and empathetic, they provide comfort and love, especially for those who may be despondent or ill.

To become a pet therapist, your Cavalier must be well groomed, calm, and well mannered; have an outgoing temperament, tolerate other animals and people, especially children and the elderly; and have received obedience training and certification as a Canine Good Citizen (see section "Canine Good Citizen Test") before being accepted into a pet therapy program. Pet therapy is a rewarding activity in which you and your Cavalier volunteer as a team to bring comfort and joy to others.

Therapy dogs spread their affection in a variety of settings, including schools and libraries for "Children Reading to Dogs" programs, disaster stress relief, hospitals, assisted-living facilities, nursing homes, prisons, and shelters.

Children Reading to Dogs programs, which take place in schools and libraries, have really taken off in recent years. I've had the opportunity to observe some and find them quite touching.

At my local library, owners and dogs arrive before the children and select a spot on the floor. Soon children trickle in with books in hand and head to the dog of their choice. They plop down and begin to read. The purpose of the program is to encourage reluctant readers. And who better to listen than a loving, nonjudgmental dog. The day I was there, one particular dog placed his paw on a little girl's hip as she read to him. That small gesture nearly did me in. I'm certain Cavaliers must love participating in these programs as much as the children themselves.

## SPORTS

There are several sports well suited to the athletic Cavalier King Charles Spaniel. Among them are agility, canine musical freestyle (dancing with your dog), conformation, obedience, rally, and tracking.

## Agility

Agility is an active canine sport. Dog owners run alongside their pets, directing them over jumps, through tunnels and weave poles, up and down an A-frame, and on and off a seesaw. These and several other obstacles create a timed event that is lots of fun for both dogs and their people. The goal is to achieve the fastest time with the fewest penalty or fault points.

To the novice, an agility course looks like a colossal canine playground, but agility can provide a dog and his owner with an enjoyable recreational hobby. For the more serious minded, it can be a very demanding competitive sport. It's well suited for an energetic, physically active Cavalier who loves to interact with his owner. Your Cavalier needs to be confident enough to act independently yet reliable enough to follow direction. Because agility is physically demanding on both the dog and handler, Cavaliers and their handlers should be physically fit and healthy.

Agility classes are offered through dog obedience training centers, breed clubs, and through various agility organizations such as Canine Performance Events (CPE), the United States Dog Agility Association (USDAA), and the North American Dog Agility Council (NADAC).

The agility obstacle course consists of a number of obstacles depending on the level of competition, novice through advanced and masters level agility. There are two types of obstacles: noncontact obstacles or hurdles that the dog will jump over or pass through and contact obstacles that the dog will walk on or across or climb over. Agility training uses positive reinforcement and a motivational approach to build confidence while introducing the various obstacles through repetition and reward.

Training a dog for agility can be great fun. Dogs seem to love it, although the fancy footwork needed to run the course may sometimes make you feel that you have two

## Multi-Dog Tip

Not all dogs have the same interests and capabilities. If you have multiple dogs, experiment with various canine sports by taking a few classes with them. You may have one Cavalier who excels at agility and another who prefers the quieter pace of rally. If you'd like all of your dogs to play on the same team, try flyball. It's a fun, high-speed sport with two teams of dogs racing against each other and taking jumps along the way.

Sports like agility help your dog expend some of his excess energy.

left feet. A good grasp of the basic obedience commands, especially a reliable *stay* and *recall*, and the ability of your dog to focus his attention on you in a highly distracting environment are crucial. If you believe that agility might be an activity that interests you and is well suited to your dog, finding the right agility instructor is very important because the training involves teaching both the handler and the dog. Finding an instructor who has clear and effective communication skills, uses positive reinforcement, and actively competes would be a sensible choice because such an instructor can share knowledge based on hands-on experience with you. Agility should be fun—an enjoyable bonding experience for you and your dog.

To learn more about the different obstacles and the requirements for a dog your Cavalier's size, visit the website for the United States Dog Agility Association (USDAA) at www.usdaa.com and the website for the North American Dog Agility Council (NADAC) at www.nadac.com. You will see how the obstacles are set up and used in a standard course.

## CANINE FREESTYLE

If you love to dance and are looking for an enthusiastic partner who won't stomp on your toes, canine musical freestyle is a fun activity you can learn with your Cavalier.

Canine musical freestyle is a sport in which the handler (you) choreographs a dance routine for the dog and handler to perform together. There are two types of dance routines. The first is referred to as "heelwork to music," where the dog and handler dance in close proximity to one another. It derives its name from walking with your dog in a *heel* position, but with the introduction of some fancy footwork and music. The second is "musical freestyle," where the dog may perform at a distance and with a much greater repertoire of dance moves or, in dog-applicable lingo, "behaviors."

If you are not sure exactly what canine musical freestyle is, the best place to view the sport is on YouTube. Simply enter "canine musical freestyle" in the search engine, hit "go," and presto! You will discover a variety of video clips for your viewing pleasure.

A few organizations and their websites that may rouse your interest include World Canine Freestyle Organization (WCFO) at www.worldcaninefreestyle.org; Canine Federal Federation (FCC) at www.canine-freestyle.org; Paws 2 Dance (P2D) at bcfirst.com/paws; and Musical Dog Sports Association (MDSA) at www.musicaldogsport.org.

The sport is perfect for both low- and high-energy dogs, and the routines are customized to fit all types and sizes of dogs. Yes, it looks difficult, but take heart; the only prerequisite is basic obedience training. And if your dog likes to perform tricks, well then, that's a leg-up—forgive the pun!

## CONFORMATION

Conformation refers to a dog's overall appearance and structure as it complies with the American Kennel Club (AKC) standard for the breed. During a conformation show,

Conformation refers to a dog's overall appearance and structure as it complies with the breed standard.

If you eventually want to compete in a canine sport, take some classes. Aside from being fun, they're also a great way to teach your dog to listen to you in the midst of many distractions.

dogs are competing against the standard, not each other.

Dog shows headlined as "conformation events" are exhibits where breeders show their finest dogs and bitches alongside the favorites of other breeders. They are judged to be in outstanding conformance to the breed standard and thus regarded as having superior ability to produce quality offspring. Only dogs recognized and registered with the AKC are allowed to compete in AKC conformation dog shows. Each dog is presented to a judge by his owner, breeder, or a hired professional handler.

The judges are considered experts on all of the breeds they are asked to judge. Using their hands and comprehensive knowledge of each dog's bone and muscular structure, as well as bite (alignment of the teeth) and coat texture, the judge assesses each individual dog against the breed's standard. She also asks the handler to run around the ring so that she can view the dog as he moves to assess balance, gait, and personality.

There are three different types of conformation dog shows. The first is referred to as an all-breed show, which is a huge event where more than 150 breeds and varieties of dogs recognized by the AKC are eligible to be exhibited in the same arena. The second type

of conformation event is known as a specialty show, where entries are restricted to dogs of a specific breed or to varieties of one breed. For example, the Cavalier King Charles Spaniel Club, USA, and American Cavalier King Charles Spaniel Club, Inc., may hold specialty events just for the Cavalier.

Third are the group shows, which are limited to dogs belonging to one of the seven groups. The Cavalier King Charles Spaniel belongs to the Toy Group, so a group show would feature all of the different breeds that comprise the Toy Group.

To learn more about conformation events and how they work, visit the AKC's website and follow the link for conformation at www.akc.org/events/conformation/beginners.cfm.

## OBEDIENCE

There are two types of obedience competitions: traditional obedience and rally. (See "Rally.") Following directions from their owners, obedience dogs must complete a set of exercises that are scored by the judge on the basis of 200 points. (Rally is similar to obedience in that many of the commands are the same, but there are also signs throughout the course giving the handler instructions.)

There are three levels of competition in obedience. Novice is the first level; as the word implies, it is for the dog and his owner who are just starting to learn obedience. Some of the commands the team must master are heel on leash and figure eight, heel free, stand for examination, *recall*, a long (one-minute) *sit*, and a long (three-minute) *down*.

The second level of obedience involves more complicated exercises. It is called "Open." Here the dog is expected to learn a wider variety of tasks and must follow either verbal or hand signals. Open competition requires that the dog perform heel free and figure eight off leash, drop on recall, retrieve on flat, retrieve over high jump, perform a broad jump, and a three-minute-long *sit* and a five minute *down-stay*, both with the owner out of sight.

The third and highest level of achievement is called "Utility." The exercises require the dog to respond to commands given by hand signal only. These commands include *stand*, *stay*, *down*, *sit*, and *come*. Other advanced exercises include scent discrimination, directed retrieve, moving stand and examination, and directed jumping.

If you are interested in learning more about obedience competition, the AKC offers "A Beginner's Guide to Companion Events," which includes information about obedience, rally, tracking, and agility.

# RALLY

In rally, dog and handler teams follow a course that is predetermined by a judge and can vary from competition to competition. In rally obedience, you are allowed to talk to your dog, providing verbal encouragement and praise as you progress along the course. The training prerequisites for rally obedience trials are knowledge of the basic obedience commands for attention, *sit*, *stay*, and loose-leash walking in a *heel* position. This sport is suitable for all dogs and one in which your Cavalier could easily excel. For more information on rally obedience, visit the following websites: AKC rally at akc.org/events/rally/ and The Association of Pet Dog Trainers (APDT) rally at apdt.com/po/rally/default.aspx

A Cavalier who participates in activities is a happier and healthier pet.

## TRACKING

You may not think of your Cavalier in the same vein as the ultimate canine tracker, the Bloodhound, but any dog can be taught to use his nose and keen sense of smell to track a scent trail. Tracking can be an enjoyable recreational game of hide-and-seek, the foundation for canine search and rescue, or a competitive challenge where a Tracking Dog (TD) title or higher, such as Tracking Dog Excellent (TDX), is earned.

## TRAVELING WITH YOUR DOG

At one time or another, you may either elect to or find it necessary to travel with your Cavalier. Planning ahead is essential, particularly if your itinerary includes air travel and finding dog-friendly lodging. When traveling with your Cavalier, it will be expected of both you and your "royal" companion to demonstrate the proper social etiquette while on your journey. To ensure a stress-free trip, do yourself and your dog a favor by traveling only with a friendly, well-socialized, and obedient dog. For obvious reasons, namely, your dog's safety and the respect of others, keep your dog on a leash. Also, ensure that your Cavalier is polite—keep barking to a minimum. Plus, and this is important: Always and without fail, clean up after your dog.

Next, whether you are traveling by car, rail, or air, be sure to pack a pet travel kit, which should consist of the following essentials:

- any prescription medications your dog is currently taking and a veterinarian's

When traveling by car, your dog is safest in a travel crate secured by a seat belt in the back seat of your car or anchored in the rear cargo space of a minivan or sport utility vehicle.

prescription if you plan to be away for a long period and may need to refill the medication while you are gone

- bottle of dry shampoo or disposable bath wipes for quick cleanups
- bowls
- crate or kennel appropriate for car, rail, or airline travel
- enough food to last the duration of the trip, especially if the brand is difficult to find
- favorite toy or toys
- favorite treats
- first-aid kit
- flashlight for walking at night
- health and rabies vaccination certificate and any other health records that might be required, depending on your destination
- paper towels
- plastic "poop" bags for picking up after your dog
- recent color photo of your dog in case he gets lost
- slicker and pin brushes to keep his coat tangle-free
- soft crate pad, blanket, or similar bedding
- towel or towels for cleaning dirty paws if you experience inclement weather
- water (if traveling by car, it's always a good idea to bring some familiar water for your dog—some dogs will get sick from drinking unfamiliar water)
- your primary leash and collar with identification and license tags
- your veterinarian's contact information and a contact for a veterinarian at your destination

## By Car

Your Cavalier is safest in a travel crate secured by a seat belt in the back seat of your car or anchored in the rear cargo space of a minivan or sport utility vehicle (SUV). If using a crate

To ensure a stress-free trip, do yourself and your dog a favor by traveling only with a friendly, well-socialized, and obedient dog.

is not possible, then your dog should be in a doggy car seat or restrained with a seat belt harness that securely and comfortably keeps him in the back seat. You want to ensure that your Cavalier is not thrown about if the vehicle stops short or is involved in an accident. You also want to keep your dog from interfering with your driving. This is not the time to allow your Cav to snuggle in your lap.

Karen reports that her Cavaliers, Emma and Gracie, are great travelers. "We have a lookout seat that fits two dogs and they are really well behaved on car rides. Gracie falls asleep

Contain your dog in a safe and secure place at all times—whether on the road or in your lodgings. Otherwise, you run the risk he may get loose and become lost in unfamiliar surroundings.

shortly after the car starts to move and she and Emma snuggle up together. They have been to the Outer Banks in North Carolina and New Hampshire. They are great dogs to take on vacation. They like trail hiking in New Hampshire and playing on the beach in the Outer Banks. Emma goes crazy chasing after the ghost (sand) crabs, shoving her nose into the sand to find them. Gracie loves all the birds on the beach running up and down chasing after them. She'll even run through the water and get knocked down by waves just to chase them. They are so excited on the beach that I have to physically carry them off to go back to the house."

Once on the road, be sure to keep the interior temperature of the car comfortable. Plan to stop every two to three hours to let your dog out to stretch and relieve himself. Have some water available as well.

A word of caution, one you have likely heard before: *Never* leave your dog alone in a parked car on a warm or hot day, even in the

## Want to Know More?

For information on whether it's safe for your Cavalier to participate in a particular activity or sport, you should check with your vet. See Chapter 8: Cavalier Health and Wellness.

shade with a window opened. The interior of a car can heat up very quickly in a matter of minutes. Your dog could suffer the effects of severe heatstroke, which could lead to brain damage or even death.

## By Plane

Dog travel policies will vary depending on whether you are traveling within the United States or abroad. The complexities involving air travel are numerous, and several airlines require that you make reservations for you and your dog by phone. Each airline has requirements and restrictions, including the number of dogs allowed per flight and breed and weight for traveling in the cabin or cargo area. As such, it's best to check with the airline beforehand for any special customs regulations, quarantine pet restrictions, or breed-specific laws. It's also prudent to check with the appropriate embassy or consulate office of your destination for the regulations specific to that country.

Some airlines will require a certificate of health from a veterinarian within ten days of your travel date. This is true for travel to and from the United States. For United States residents returning home, you may need to obtain a certificate of health from an international veterinarian if you and your Cavalier have traveled outside the United States for more than ten days. For this reason, it's important to do your homework

early and get the name and recommendation of a veterinarian in the area where you and your Cavalier will be staying.

A good online resource is the Air Transport Association (ATA) website under Customer Services, Security & Airports, Passenger Info, and Air Travel for Your Pet at www.airlines.org/customerservice/passengers/Air+Travel+for+Your+Pet.htm. This site provides a wealth of information, plus links to airline websites, regulations, and FAA rules, as well as other quick links and resources.

## Lodging for Pets and People

Chances are your Cavalier is already accustomed to running around town with you, so he should make a perfect travel companion. He's compact and easily transportable, as well as hardy enough for sight-seeing excursions and other outdoor activities.

There are numerous books and online services available offering multiple listings for dog-friendly accommodations. As a matter of fact, the websites DogFriendly.com (www.dogfriendly.com) and PetsWelcome.com (www.petswelcome.com), to name just a few, publish pet travel guides and offer a wealth of information on where to stay with your dog. I also recommend a subscription to a wonderful magazine devoted to traveling with your dog, *Fido Friendly*.

## When Your Cavalier Must Stay Home

There may be times when it's just not possible or appropriate to bring your dog along when you travel. In those instances, there are many options to finding an appropriate caregiver. This decision is not altogether stress-free; it also takes some research and planning to find the right situation for your dog.

## Pet Sitters

It's no secret that your dog is happiest when he's home in familiar and comfortable surroundings. Hiring a pet sitter allows him to stay at home while you're away. I've been hiring live-in sitters for more than 20 years—long before the service became as popular as it is now.

We have a nice in-law suite I set up so that our sitter will be comfortable during her stay. But after watching television in the family surrounded by the dogs—all vying to be in her lap—she often falls asleep on the couch. I'm sure that our canine kids love the nighttime company.

Pet sitting services and fees can vary, so you should determine what your needs are before you enter a contractual agreement. You may want several visits a day or have the sitter live in as we do.

Finding a reliable pet sitter is akin to hiring a nanny. I check three references and conduct a personal interview. Then if the dogs and I have a good feeling about the person, I have her over a few times while I'm home so that the dogs get to know her.

When we leave for vacation, I always ask my sitter to call us to let me know she has arrived at the house and is officially on duty. I also leave a list of instructions, our cell and hotel phone numbers, and a list of emergency contacts. The nice thing about using the same sitter on a regular basis is that she already

knows the dogs' routine and takes charge with no problem. During the trip I may check in with her once in a while. But usually I assume that no news is good news. Once I get home, I call her to let her know that we're back and all is well.

There are two organizations that can provide you with valuable information on the subject. The first is the National Association of Professional Pet Sitters (NAPPS), which is a national nonprofit United States trade association for individuals with pet sitting businesses and Pet Sitters International, which is recognized as an authority on pet sitters globally. Both websites offer a wealth of information on the subject. Visit either www.petsitters.org or www.petsit.com and begin your search. If you are lucky enough to have a Camp Bow Wow in your area, it may offer an in-home pet care service, "Home Buddies by Camp Bow Wow." Visit the site at www.campbowwowusa.com/about.htm for more information.

Do not overlook your veterinarian's office or a local breed club for referrals on pet sitters. Family, friends, neighbors, and your breeder (if local) are also excellent resources.

## Doggy Day Care

Doggy day care or day camp is just what you imagine it would be—a place where healthy, nonaggressive, and well-socialized dogs can spend all or half a day, from morning to evening, romping and playing in a safe, well-supervised facility with indoor and outdoor play areas. There are usually two options: pet sitters who open their own home and yard to offer this type of service and franchises such as Camp Bow Wow or others like it that may be connected with animal welfare centers, dog training centers, or boarding kennels.

Whichever option you choose, do your homework. Visit each facility and interview the staff. Ensure that the environment is safe, secure, clean, well lit, and comfortably climate controlled and that the size and number of campers will not overwhelm your Cavalier. You also want to be certain that your dog will get lots of individual one-on-one attention from the staff. Then bring your dog for an introductory play session. If he appears stressed and does not engage with the other dogs, then this is clearly not the environment you want. If he immediately engages without a glance back, doggy day care/camp may be a wonderful boarding experience for him while you're at work or on a day trip. Some facilities may also offer overnight accommodations.

## Other Boarding Options

Traditional boarding kennels are another option. Time to research again and visit the kennels in your area. You will find that they range from rustic to luxurious. As with doggy day care/camp, you must visit each facility and interview the staff to ensure that the environment is safe, secure, clean, well lit, and comfortably climate controlled. Equally important, you need to know how the dogs are monitored in the evening hours and what security systems are in place in case of unforeseen events that may warrant evacuation.

Your veterinarian's office, a local breed club, family, friends, neighbors, and your breeder will once again be excellent resources for referrals. When you have selected a facility, a trial day and overnight stay is a good idea so that your Cavalier won't be terribly stressed when you go on vacation. If you plan to use kennels, I

If you can't take your Cavalier with you when you have to be away from home, a good pet sitter might be a viable option.

suggest getting your Cavalier accustomed to the experience from puppyhood. Some of my friends' dogs are perfectly happy to stay in a kennel. Mine would be dumbfounded and look at me as if to say "What, are you kidding?" Joking aside, dropping a dog off at a kennel for the first time as an adult can be stressful, especially for a Cavalier who is very attached to his home and family. So give considerable thought to how you plan to handle travel plans before you acquire your Cavalier.

# PART III

# SENIOR YEARS

# CHAPTER 12

# FINDING YOUR CAVALIER SENIOR

*Grow old along with me, the best is yet to be.*
—Robert Browning

According to CKCS breeders, Cavaliers begin to enter their senior years at the age of seven. In terms of rescue, ten years and beyond is considered the senior age range. Usually, when a dog is given up this late in life, his pet parents have hit on hard times be it divorce, job loss, or perhaps a move to a nursing home. So through no fault of their own, these senior dogs become orphans. They may be perfectly lovely companions, both well trained and well behaved.

## WHY ADOPTING A SENIOR IS A GOOD IDEA

Seniors have a quiet presence that appeals to pet owners interested in a more sedate companion. Perhaps they have already raised a few dogs from puppyhood while raising their families. It's wonderful for kids and dogs to grow up together. But now they are less interested in the puppy and young adult phase and just want a calm buddy as a companion.

Because of the breed's outgoing nature, a newly adopted senior Cavalier will most likely bond with his new person in no time. He won't need as much supervision as a younger dog and will be content to nap when no one is home. But like a dog of any age, he shouldn't be left alone for too long a period.

A senior will enjoy a stroll around the neighborhood but won't require as much exercise as he did in his youth. He will certainly love to accompany you on errands. I often see Cavaliers peeking out through car windows from their doggy car seats. Just remember to be aware of weather conditions. Never leave a dog of any age in a car in hot weather.

A senior will likely be a more welcomed guest than a younger dog when you visit friends and family by virtue of his calm demeanor. Just be sure to ask ahead to confirm that pets are allowed wherever you may be going before popping in. Though I tend to live by a "where I go, they go" attitude with my dogs, I never assume my beloved companions are automatically invited with me to other people's homes. So I will ask permission to bring them along and usually take only one or two and not the entire pack.

For some dog lovers, there is a special reward in reaching out to a senior in need. My friend Karen is a strong advocate of adopting pets

Through no fault of their own, many senior dogs become orphans.

from animal shelters and rescue groups. And she has a special fondness for seniors. While many people are uninterested in taking on an older dog because of the limited life expectancy and potential high costs of vet bills, Karen says "It can't always be about *you*. Sometimes you just have to do it for *them*." Then adds "They may be old but they still have lots of spirit and are very loving companions. You simply enjoy them and they enjoy you."

In addition, each situation is unique. Karen adopted Bancha from a shelter when the mixed breed was 11 years old. Karen thought she'd give her a nice family home for a year or two. But Bancha had other ideas. She lived to be 19½, and in all that time needed to visit the vet only twice.

## ADOPTING FROM A SHELTER OR RESCUE

It's very unlikely that a Cavalier would live that long, but the fulfillment of adopting a senior and giving him a happy retirement would be the same. Iris, a friend of Karen's, also has a soft spot for seniors. "With seniors it really

## Training Tidbit

Dogs are never too old to learn, and training keeps their minds active. Teach your new adopted senior some simple tricks or commands.

Cavaliers begin to enter their senior years at the age of seven.

However, a senior Cavalier who has spent his entire life with adults may be overwhelmed by the hustle and bustle of active youngsters. So if you have children, be sure to find out about your potential pet's background before you commit to adopting him.

## ADOPTING THROUGH A BREEDER

Aside from rescue groups and animal shelters, there's also the possibility of finding a senior Cavalier through a breeder. A young woman by the name of Laura has

is about quality of time, not quantity as with younger dogs," Iris says. "They are so easy to make happy, and their calm energy helps you keep calm and relaxed."

Because of their sunny, people-loving dispositions, Cavaliers usually adjust easily when rehomed. Rescue representatives report that Cavaliers are one of the most adaptable breeds when placed with a new family. They certainly miss their original owners but don't tend to pine; they look on the move as a new adventure.

In some circumstances, adopting a senior Cavalier is the perfect solution for the desire to have a pet. It can be an ideal arrangement for a senior citizen who just wants companionship but isn't up for training a puppy or may not have the stamina for the regular romps that younger dogs enjoy and require. In fact, many shelters have initiated "Seniors for Seniors" programs where they intentionally match a senior citizen with a senior dog. My friend and neighbor Glenn is 85 and his dog Artie is 14. The two of them walk four times a day regardless of the weather. Glenn is fond of saying "Artie dictates my schedule." I'm sure the bond they share and the daily exercise greatly contributes to their longevity.

Depending on the individual senior dog's background, he may or may not be a good choice for a family with young children. If he's been raised with kids, he may fit in beautifully.

Because of their affectionate dispositions, Cavaliers usually adjust easily when rehomed.

A senior won't need as much supervision as a younger dog and will be content to nap when no one is home.

the good fortune to be related to a Cavalier breeder who has a separate, fully decorated house on her property for the dogs. Laura shares the story of how Miranda, a senior Black and Tan and retired therapy dog, became her special companion. "Miranda was always my favorite Cavalier in the 'doghouse.' She always seemed to be in charge—she ran the show. She barked the loudest, jumped the highest, and put the little whippersnappers in line!

"Miranda was a good mommy to her babies. Her gentle and loving nature was carried on to create two more generations of therapy dogs. I dreamed that one day when Miranda was done being a mom and a therapy dog, my aunt would let her come live with me.

Two years ago, when Miranda was eight years old, that day came, and every one of my days has become better since. She is sweet, sassy, and sophisticated and loves to be petted and primped.

Miranda struts her stuff, attracting younger pups wherever she goes—some even call her a 'cougar.' She is my special girl, so gentle and affectionate with anybody who crosses her path. As the days go on, her hair has grayed a bit and her hearing has gone, but her spirit is as young as it's ever been."

## MAKING THE COMMITMENT

After making the decision to adopt a senior, what do you look for? Mostly the same characteristics you would seek in dog of a younger age. Is he friendly? Is he well mannered? Does he appear to have some training? Often the emphasis is on the dog, but you also have to look at your lifestyle. Would this particular dog fit in? Will he be able and interested in participating in the activities you enjoy, say walking in your local park or strolling on the beach? If you have other dogs or pets, will he get along with them? If you are interested in an individual dog, you may ask the breeder or rescue rep for a two-week trial period to see if everyone does indeed get along well.

With regard to caring for a new senior, it would be a good idea to have a geriatric exam and full blood work performed by your veterinarian. That way you can find out whether any underlying problems are brewing. Pay close attention to your new Cavalier's teeth and ask your vet whether a dental cleaning is warranted. Also discuss a good joint supplement.

You'll want to be sure he is on a high-quality senior diet. If you don't care for the food he's being fed, give him a week or two to adjust to your home and then gradually switch to a better diet.

Also be sure your house is set up to comfortably accommodate a senior. Buy a restful doggy bed (orthopedic types are wonderful for seniors who may have arthritis). You may want to place pet stairs up against your bed or couch and spare the dog from jumping

## Multi-Dog Tip

If you already have a dog at home, be sure to introduce your new senior Cavalier on neutral ground before bringing him into the house. And keep a watchful eye on all interactions. Supervise the dogs when they are together until you know they have accepted one another as part of the pack. You may want to give your senior a private spot away from your other dog(s) until he adjusts to his new home, as well as lots of time and patience until he seems comfortable and secure.

up to join you, which he will surely want to do.

People often think of seniors as being on the decline, with little zest. But this isn't always the case. A healthy senior Cavalier can still have plenty of spunk and be a welcomed addition to your family. If you provide good daily care and bi-annual veterinary exams, you can have many wonderful years together. Don't worry that your new dog will be depressed because he misses his first family. "Dogs adapt and bond with those who love and care for them," Iris says. "Seniors are so much more appreciative and needy, and bond so much faster."

# CHAPTER 13

# CARE OF YOUR CAVALIER SENIOR

If dogs have a single fault, it's that their life expectancy is so much shorter than our own. One day you have a gangly, energetic puppy scampering around the house and then in just a blink of an eye, it seems, your little buddy is slowing down and showing the signs of aging.

## WHEN IS YOUR CAVALIER A SENIOR?

There's something bittersweet about living with a senior dog. If you have raised your Cavalier from puppyhood, then you have probably been together for at least seven or eight years. The ebb and flow of your daily routine is well established, and the crazy puppy phase is a faded memory. You have formed a bond like no other, and you'd like to save this moment in time forever. And yet there are daily reminders that forever is not to be. You notice a few new gray hairs on your companion's face; perhaps his gait is a bit slower; he's napping longer or has trouble using his back legs to get up. The best we can do during our dogs' twilight years is to keep them as comfortable as possible and enjoy each day to its fullest.

I don't know about you, but making my companion animals happy makes me happy.

Such a simple equation, really. And dogs are so easy to please. A car ride to run errands with you is akin to a trip to Disneyland for a child. In our area, drive-through bank tellers hand out biscuits to canine passengers. So a bank deposit is a highlight of the day for my crew. And you can imagine the tellers' expressions when the six of us drive through. Of course, by now they are probably all familiar with my car and its "Fur Kids on Board" sign.

Whatever it is you and your Cavalier enjoy doing, continue to do it. He will appreciate the time together and so will you.

## FEEDING

As dogs age, their metabolism slows and they are less energetic. So weight gain, which can tax the body's organs and joints, is always a concern. There are too many tubby Cavaliers out there. You owe it to your canine companion to feed him appropriately, watch the type and number of treats he eats, and maintain a comfortable exercise program.

Seniors need less protein and calories than they did in their youth, so decreasing protein and fat and adding additional fiber will help with caloric intake and maintain a consistent

You owe it to your canine companion to feed him appropriately.

weight. Commercial senior diets are available to make this transition easier. If you are feeding a home-cooked or raw diet, discuss appropriate changes with a holistic vet or canine nutritionist. You should also discuss appropriate supplements, which may include vitamins to bolster the immune system, enzymes to aid digestion, or oils to improve a dry skin and coat.

A senior's taste buds may not be what they were either, so you may need to enhance the flavor of his food now. I find a little bit of meat or veggie baby food works well. Be sure that there are no onions in the ingredients.

If you have been feeding twice a day, making smaller portions and adding lunch back into his schedule may well be appreciated.

## GROOMING

Dogs should be groomed throughout their lives. It's especially important in their senior years because it will help you detect any body changes. You may even want to create a hand-drawn diagram and note any moles, lumps, or bumps. That way each time you groom, you can readily tell whether anything new has surfaced. Older dogs often develop lipomas—benign fatty tissue—but malignancies are also possible, so keeping a watchful eye is always a good idea.

Your senior Cavalier may not be as patient about grooming as he was in his youth, so keep at-home grooming sessions short and pleasant. Be sure that you are in a good mood before you start. Your empathetic Cavalier will certainly notice if you are feeling rushed or stressed and will feed off your anxiety, so wait until you can make the experience as relaxing as possible.

Be sure to have plenty of extra towels if you're planning to give a bath. Seniors usually have less body fat to keep them warm. Before you begin, warm your shampoo by holding the bottle in hot water or dilute it a bit so as not to shock your little friend. Give a gentle but quick and efficient bath.

Place thick towels on your grooming table to give your dog traction and to absorb any accidents if he has a weak bladder. Warm the towels with your hair dryer and towel dry your dog thoroughly before switching to your hair dryer.

Brush and comb your Cavalier as you have always done, but if he gets tired, skip nail trimming for another time—but be sure not to put it off for too long. The nails of geriatric dogs are thicker and more brittle. And because they are less active, their nails are probably not getting worn down naturally as they once were. So it's important to trim the nails routinely so that they don't curl back and grow into the paw pads.

If your dog is accustomed to visiting a dog salon, it's fine to keep up this routine. A groomer will try to make the experience as stress-free as possible by talking with your dog, keeping the session short, and allowing him to walk around a bit instead of spending longer periods in a crate. You may want to schedule your visit at a time when your groomer can complete the job in a short time and send your dog back home as soon as

Dogs should be groomed throughout their lives. It's especially important in their senior years because it will help you detect any body changes.

Your dog's overall quality of life should be the first and most important factor you consider as he advances in age.

he's ready. My professional groomer reports that the Cavaliers in her clientele are very agreeable about grooming. They accept most procedures without complaint but do not like having knots removed and cry out in protest. So keep up with your brushing at home to keep mats from forming. If your Cavalier no longer tolerates his trips to the dog salon, this might be a good time to experiment with having a mobile groomer come to your house.

## HEALTH CARE

Adult dogs should have an annual physical exam. Biannual exams are recommended for seniors. That way, problems can be detected at an earlier stage and chances for a positive outcome will be improved.

### Biannual Exams

Biannual geriatric exams are usually more involved than annual adult exams. Your vet will draw blood for a complete blood count (CBC). This test will detect the types and amount of blood cells in your Cavalier's blood system and can pick up on abnormalities. She will also run a chemistry panel, which measures enzymes, electrolytes, glucose, proteins, and other substances that can help identify diabetes, and liver and kidney disease, as well as a few hormonal diseases.

Senior Cavaliers over the age
of seven should have biannual
veterinary exams.

A urinalysis will be performed, which can give insight into numerous disease conditions. A heart test called an electrocardiogram may be included unless you are already visiting a canine cardiologist on a routine basis. Depending on your Cavalier's general health, X-rays may be included in the exam. Routine stool analysis certainly will. Keeping track of weight will be even more important with a senior pet, as obesity or unexplained weight loss may need to be addressed.

Old age is not a disease or condition in and of itself—it's merely a time of life. If your Cavalier seems a bit off, don't automatically attribute it to "old age." Many health problems can be controlled through diet and medication.

## Arthritis

Just like people, aging dogs can suffer from arthritis. This chronic condition develops as joint cartilage breaks down. This breakdown allows the bones to rub together, causing stiffness and pain.

Exercise is important in dealing with arthritis because it brings nutrients to the cartilage and strengthens the surrounding muscles, which in turn support the joint. Swimming is an excellent form of exercise because it is nonweight bearing. Walking at a leisurely pace is also helpful. Exercise should help your pet maintain a good weight. Being overweight only adds to the discomfort of arthritis.

Glucosamine and chondroitin supplements are often recommended. Glucosamine is found naturally in cartilage and helps cells that produce cartilage function properly. Chondroitin also works with cartilage-producing cells, as well as with cushioning and lubricating joint fluid.

There are various medications available to alleviate pain. Blood work should be done before starting these medications to make sure that there are no liver or kidney issues. The blood should be tested again two weeks later and then at six-month intervals. Side effects may occur, including vomiting, diarrhea, and inappetence. Discuss the various medications, their benefits, and their possible side effects with your vet. Acupuncture, chiropractic, and massage can also be very beneficial.

Just like people, aging dogs can suffer from arthritis.

A senior arthritic dog should have a comfortable orthopedic bed. To assist with mobility, you can place carpet runners on tile and wood floors or buy special rubber boots to provide more traction. A ramp up against the bed or favorite couch will make reaching these resting spots much easier on your pet. Visit www.SeniorPetProducts.com for additional ideas.

When Chelsea was 14, she began having trouble climbing the steps and was literally falling down on walks. I started her on a glucosamine/chondroitin supplement and within a week she ran through a park and jumped over a log. I was incredulous. So I give all of my dogs this same supplement as they approach their senior years. There are many supplements available. You may need to experiment a bit to find the one that works best for your Cavalier.

As Smokey entered his late teens, his back end had become very weak. One of his favorite pastimes in life was sleeping on the recliner. (Must be a guy thing.) But there came a time when he just couldn't climb up any longer. It may not seem like a very big deal to you or me, but I'm sure it was a huge quality of life issue to him. So I hired a canine massage therapist. Karen came to the house twice a month for the last six months of Smokey's life. He thoroughly enjoyed his massages, his mobility increased, and once again he was able to hoist himself into the recliner.

## Canine Cognitive Disorder (CCD)

Behavioral changes that come about with age can be caused by CCD. Some examples are housetraining accidents, confusion/wandering aimlessly,

### Training Tidbit

Use hand signals along with your verbal commands because the signals will come in handy if your Cavalier eventually suffers from age-related deafness.

increased whining/barking, restlessness during the night, no longer greeting owners when they return home, and walking away from being petted. As a comparison to a similar human condition, this disorder is sometimes referred to as a doggy Alzheimer's.

Smokey reached a stage in life where he would howl in the middle of the night. There was no apparent reason. He'd just wake up, give voice and wake us all up in the process. Commands to be quiet fell on deaf ears. Frankly, it was driving us crazy. Then we hit on an idea. We placed a T-shirt my husband had worn on Smokey's bed at night. My husband's scent on the shirt must have comforted him because Smokey gave up his nighttime vocalizations to our great relief.

We were lucky because the nighttime howls seemed to be his only unusual behavior. But symptoms can be more numerous and confusing to both the pet owner and the veterinarian. Thorough testing and detective work on the part of your vet will be needed to rule out other problems and definitively diagnose CCD. Medications are available to help your pet.

### Want to Know More?

For additional health concerns that affect Cavaliers, see Chapter 8: Cavalier Health and Wellness.

## Congestive Heart Failure

Congestive heart failure (CHF) is one of the most common heart problems found in toy breeds. It occurs when the heart is no longer pumping blood efficiently. Hence, the body is not receiving all the oxygen it should and fluid builds up in the lungs, stomach, and/or liver. Although there are several possible causes, valve disease is the most prevalent in adult dogs.

Symptoms include fatigue, panting, and coughing while in motion. If diagnosed early on, treatment includes diuretics and medications that improve blood flow. Dogs may live comfortably for years. Unfortunately, the outcome for more severe cases is poor.

## Cushing's Disease

Cushing's disease is caused when cortisol, a hormone, is overproduced. Symptoms include excessive drinking and urinating, hair loss, weight gain, a potbelly, and lethargy. Cushing's has three causes: a pituitary gland tumor, adrenal gland tumor, and long-term use of steroids. Treatment is dependent on the cause. Options include surgery, radiation, and medication to destroy cortisol-producing cells.

## Diabetes Mellitus

Diabetes mellitus, which is more common in older dogs, is caused by an inability of the pancreas to produce sufficient insulin. As a result, sugar in the bloodstream can't be utilized and builds up. The kidneys must work harder than normal to eliminate excess sugar from the body.

Congestive heart failure (CHF) is one of the most common heart problems found in toy breeds.

Early signs of the disease include increased appetite, consuming a larger volume of water, weight loss, and frequent urination. Diabetes can often be controlled with a modified diet and daily insulin shots.

## Kidney Disease

The risk of kidney disease is another health condition that increases with age. It can come on slowly or acutely. Some signs to be aware of are increased water consumption; various changes in urination: increased/decreased/lack of/ nocturnal and bloody; vomiting; weight loss; poor coat; lethargy; and diarrhea.

Because some of the above symptoms may also be attributable to other diseases, your vet will perform a complete diagnostic workup. Treatment and outcome vary greatly

## Multi-Dog Tip

You will probably find that your senior dogs like to snuggle together, but it's best to provide a bed for each and then allow them to select their own sleeping spots.

depending on the cause of the disease and the amount of kidney damage. Intravenous fluids, antibiotics, and specialized diets are all possible treatments.

## Nuclear Sclerosis

When an aging dog's eyes grow cloudy, it may be cataracts or it may be a condition known

Early signs of diabetes include increased thirst and appetite, frequent urination, and eventual weight loss.

# Age-Related Deafness

Age-related deafness is common in older dogs. Diane, who has bred Cavaliers for 15 years, shares some insight. "I've noticed over the years that a lot of Cavaliers start losing their hearing gradually between the age of seven and ten. Not all of them, but I think a significant number. With my old guy now, Bentley, who's 13½, I started noticing some subtle changes in his behavior at about the age of 7. He would snore louder, sleep sounder, and look startled when he woke up sometimes. As the years progressed, I noticed that I could say the word "cookie" standing behind him and there was no reaction. That's when I knew for sure.

"Because we did a lot of obedience when he was younger and he was a certified therapy dog for almost ten years, luckily, by accident, I had always trained him using verbal commands and hand signals. This has come in very handy over these last few years. We have a wonderful bond anyway, but this way, with a signal, he knows exactly what I want. We still sing together every morning on the grooming table when I put drops in his eyes. He gets up the same time every day, eats and sleeps, and plays on a structured schedule. I think that having a predictable routine helps them too. They almost know what is expected of them every minute of every day.

I also find deaf dogs bark a lot more than others. I think that it's just their way of making you notice them. It's not constant, just "Look, I'm here." The quality of life for an older deaf dog can be just as high as one who can hear if you take a few simple steps along the way."

as nuclear sclerosis. This is a common and normal change in the lens. Generally, it occurs in both eyes simultaneously. The lens actually becomes harder and thicker. Because it's not painful and normally does not affect vision, the condition is not treated.

## Urinary Incontinence

A valve at the end of the bladder is made up of muscle. Dogs are able to control this valve until they are ready to urinate in an appropriate location. Hormones, both estrogen and testosterone, affect the strength of the valve. As dogs age these hormones decrease and it becomes more difficult to control the valve, which causes leakage. And,

of course, spayed and neutered dogs have already lost the production area for these hormones.

There are medications available to treat hormone-related incontinence. Females tend to respond more favorably than males. As far as management, there are doggy diapers for both males and females. If you find that your pet is having accidents in his favorite resting spot, covering that area with a puppy piddle pad is another way to deal with the problem.

## TRAINING

It's best to begin your relationship with your new senior Cavalier the minute you take him home

Dogs need mental stimulation and physical exercise to stay healthy throughout their senior years.

from his breeder, the shelter, or his foster home. Don't overwhelm him by using a high-pitched voice or showering him with affection. Remain calm and establish yourself as his new leader immediately. Make sure that he walks next to you on leash en route to your car. Have him sit while you open the door. Wait until he is calm before inviting him into the car. Then either place him in a crate if he is accustomed to one or fasten him securely with a doggy seat belt.

When you arrive at your home do not bring him inside right away. Take a walk around the neighborhood to help him understand that you are his new pack leader and you're "traveling" to a new home.

Once you get back to the house do not just let him off the leash, allowing him to explore, as you would be telling him this is his house

and he is in charge. You need to enter the house first and then invite him in after you—and only when he is calm and relaxed. Make sure to keep him on his leash and introduce him to one room—preferably the kitchen. Because you have just taken him for a nice long walk, this would be the perfect time to give him water and food and show him where his resting place is. Later on you can put him back on his leash and introduce him to the rest of the house or the rooms that you want him to have access to. You do not have to give him access to all rooms for now (or ever)—it's completely up to you. It's a good idea to use a crate for at least the first week. After that, if you don't want to use the crate, you can replace it with a nice dog bed in the same spot.

If you have family members waiting for

you to arrive with the new dog, be sure that they too are calm. Excitement is not a natural greeting in the dog world. Explain, especially to children, that what the new dog needs is to know that this is a calm, secure environment. Later, after he has settled in, everyone can lighten up and play with him.

Prior to your senior Cavalier's arrival, you should have already considered the new feeding and housetraining schedule. Consistency is the key to a smooth adjustment. When will he eat? How often will he eat? Who will take him outside? Who will walk him? What will the walking schedule be? And so on. These decisions should be made before the new dog arrives at your home. Start working on basic commands immediately. Make him work for everything he receives using a *sit* command. Confirm the human hierarchy by having all of the family members go in and out of the door before the dog.

The best thing about adopting a senior is that housetraining is usually much easier and quicker. The difficult thing can be dealing with any previous behavior issues. If you know the dog you are adopting has a particular problem (dominance, separation anxiety, a particular phobia, fear aggression, etc.), consult with a behavior specialist before bringing the dog home so that you can have a plan ready to initiate on the first day. These problems can all be fixed because dogs live in the moment.

If your new Cavalier is a little gentleman already, so much the better. You are about to

enjoy his wonderful twilight years together. And there's no reason he can't continue to learn. Spend some time finding out what commands he already knows and then incorporate hand signals. For example, if you say "Sit" and he promptly replies, next time hold your arm straight at your side, and with palm facing up, raise your forearm up above your dog's head and say "Sit" simultaneously. Dogs respond better to body language than verbal commands, so your Cavalier will soon associate this action with the *sit* command. In no time, you won't even need to say the command. When my dogs are out on the deck, I can give the "Sit" hand signal through the window. Each will comply without hesitation. Understanding hand signals will be immensely helpful if your Cavalier eventually loses his hearing.

You might also want to add some fun activities to your senior's new life with you. Try hiding some biscuits in different areas of the house and ask him to find them using the *find it* command. Dogs catch on to this game in no time and really enjoy it. There are also interactive toys you can purchase. A ball with holes is a popular choice. You fill the ball with kibble and the dog pushes it around with his nose. As it rolls, pieces of kibble drop out, rewarding him for his efforts.

If your senior Cavalier hasn't had much previous training, there's no reason why he can't start now. Follow the instructions in Chapter 9: Cavalier Training. Just remember to keep sessions brief so as not to tire your dog or tax his patience.

# CHAPTER 14

# END-OF-LIFE ISSUES

Eventually, all dog owners have to face the sad reality that their beloved companion's time with them is coming to an end. Hopefully, your Cavalier has lived a long, healthy life well into his teens and you can take comfort in knowing that his passing is part of the natural cycle of life.

## HOSPICE AND EUTHANASIA

Probably the hardest part of sharing our lives with dogs is letting them go. So many questions race through our minds:

- Is our companion still enjoying life despite his infirmities?
- Could we be doing more to keep him comfortable and prolong his life?
- Is it the right time to euthanize?

Living with a terminally ill pet can be very stressful. If you need assistance physically caring for and coping with the infirmities of your pet, you can turn to animal hospice. The International Association for Animal Hospice and Palliative Care (IAAHPC) is one resource. This organization is dedicated to providing nursing and medical care for companion animals as they near the end of life and as they die. An Internet search will reveal additional hospice providers. Having a caring professional to lean on during your companion's final days may be just what you need to make this difficult time a little easier.

But also try to remember that dogs live in the present moment. They don't dwell on the past or worry about the future. If your vet determines that your Cavalier has a terminal illness, he won't go into a depression because he knows his time is running out. He has no idea! He just does what he always does—he lives in the moment and every day is a new beginning for him. The only reason a dog will show signs of low energy or depression (unless it is related to medications he is taking for his illness) is that the owners are feeling sorry for him and acting differently toward him, so he may react to their sadness.

The best thing for you to do in this situation—as difficult and heartbreaking as it may be —is to do what the dog is doing and live in the present moment with him. Enjoy the time you have left together. Take him to his favorite places, like the beach, the woods, the park, the pet store—wherever it is that makes him happy. Stay focused on the moment because that's how your dog lives. That's a good lesson for all of us.

It may be time when your Cavalier no longer enjoys doing the things he used to do.

## When to Euthanize

When your Cavalier's decline becomes more obvious, your vet can also help you make the painful decision about the right time to end his discomfort. I prefer to have a house call vet euthanize my elderly dogs. I want them to leave peacefully, resting on a favorite bed, in the comfort of their own home. Yes, it's a very emotional time for my husband and me. But knowing that we've done everything possible for our cherished companions, even to the very end, helps us get through it.

I can deal with arthritis, incontinence, and any other infirmity my dogs may suffer as long as they are enjoying life. Our Field Spaniel, Smokey, lived to be over 16. Since the average life expectancy for a Field Spaniel is 12, old Smokey was really getting up there. In his last year he developed bowel and urinary incontinence. Diapers solved these problems. His back end was weak from arthritis but his front legs and mental attitude remained strong. He wanted to go outside with the younger dogs. So a hind-end leash kept him marching.

As this stage of Smokey's twilight, I asked our house call vet to examine him—just in case I needed her advice on when we should euthanize. During her visit, she detected the light in his eyes, his interest in her, and the treats in my pocket. He was alert and happy. Clearly it was not his time. But a few months later, Smokey lost interest in eating. I couldn't tempt him with the tastiest of treats. And he didn't want to leave his bed. When he looked at me it was if he was trying to say "I've had enough, Mom. I'm tired. It's time to let me go." I called the vet. She came the next morning and confirmed that medically Smokey's body was shutting down. She administered the appropriate drugs with my husband and I petting Smokey and saying goodbye.

Our house call vet once told me she receives most calls for euthanasia in late summer and early fall. It's as if the dogs seem to know they won't have the strength to survive another winter. Smokey died in August. It was a peaceful end and gave me solace in that he had selected his own time.

Dogs rarely die on their own. Inevitably, most of us will have to make the decision to euthanize. How to say goodbye is a very personal decision. Many dog owners prefer to use the vet and hospital their dogs have known throughout their lives. Some opt to stay in the room, while others choose not to. If you feel that you would be more comfortable having a vet come to your home, it's best to find someone in advance when you are less emotional. Ask your regular vet and dog-owning friends for referrals. Or you can visit the following organizations' websites: American Association of House Call Veterinarians at www.housecallvets.com or In-Home Pet

The death of a beloved canine companion can be keenly felt by a child. If your Cavalier is declining, it is best to start discussing his inevitable passing.

Euthanasia Directory at www.inhomepeteuthanasia.com.

## GRIEF

After your companion has been euthanized, don't be surprised by the extent of your grief. The relationship we share with our canine companions is deep and profound. Some people, myself included, spend more time with their dogs during the course of the day than anyone else. And the attachment is so pure—there are no criticisms, arguments, or judgments between people and their pets—nothing takes place but unconditional love. So it's no wonder the loss is felt so deeply.

Friends and family members who have not shared their lives with animals may not understand the depth of your grief. But many will. I always appreciate receiving pet sympathy cards. To me, this small gesture demonstrates that the sender truly understands.

Recognizing the extent of grief people feel from pet loss, there are many books on the subject as well as pet bereavement programs. Large humane societies often offer the latter. Grief resources include the ASPCA National Pet Loss Hotline at 800-946-4646, the Animal Love and Loss Network at www.alln.org, the Association for Pet Loss and Bereavement at www.aplb.org, and the Pet Loss Support Page at www.pet-loss.net.

Losing a beloved dog can set off all kinds

of emotions and actions, from adopting a new dog right away to fill the sudden void to never owning another dog to spare ourselves repeating this terrible grief. Probably the healthiest reaction is somewhere in the middle. When people grieve they have very low energy. I remember when Chelsea died, I was so sad it was difficult getting out of bed. Had it not been for the fact that Smokey needed my attention, I don't know how long I would have wallowed in my grief. If you bring a new dog into your life at this stage of the grieving process, you won't be giving him a fair start. Low/sad energy will certainly be felt by the new dog or puppy and affect his own stability. It would be better to wait until you can smile when you think of

## Training Tidbit

If you have children and your elderly Cavalier has been trained to *down-stay*, allow them to read to him. It will be a nice quiet bonding activity for both of them.

your former dog and feel happy about all of the good times you shared with him. Once you have gotten through the severe grief, you will be better able to give a new dog or puppy a fresh and happy start in his new home.

One of the only reasons a dog will show signs of low energy or depression is that his owners are feeling sorry for him and acting differently toward him, so he may react to their sadness.

Your dog may grieve the loss of a canine friend.

Believe me, no one sympathizes more than I do when someone loses a dog. And yet I know I'll always have dogs in my life. The day-to-day enjoyment and enrichment each gives me outweighs the inevitable loss. I hope in time you feel the same way.

## Children and Grief

The death of a beloved canine companion can also be keenly felt by a child. If your Cavalier is declining, it is best to start discussing his inevitable passing. Use distinct words like death and dying. It's best not to use the phrase "put to sleep," as it may create fear when the child goes to sleep at night. Be as honest as possible. Don't say the pet ran away or went to live with another family because these fabricated stories can create a different type of grief. Try to explain that only the pet's body will be buried but his spirit will live on in your thoughts and memories.

Once your dog is gone, read children's books together on the process of loss and talk about your own sadness openly. Creating a memorial is also helpful. Plant a tree in your Cavalier's memory, or have your children draw pictures and create their own little book about their beloved pet. These rituals should help your child pass through the stages of grief.

## Grief and Other Dogs

Do dogs also grieve the loss of a canine friend?

I certainly believe that they do. Although dogs live in the moment and do not think about the past or look forward to the future, I'm sure that they miss the presence of their lost buddy.

When Chelsea died at the age of 15, Smokey and she had been together for 10 years. He became unusually clingy and, even more unsettling, began to mimic Chelsea's behaviors—acting in ways he never had when she was with us. As an example, Chelsea enjoyed rolling around on the carpet after meals to clean her face. Far less neat, Smokey never bothered—that is, until Chelsea passed on. I don't know what this means, but other pet-owning friends have had similar experiences with their pets.

My husband and I were too upset to adopt another dog right away, so I started hosting doggy play dates for Smokey. Interacting with his own kind definitely seemed to cheer him up. Seven months later, we adopted Woody to keep Smokey company. A field-bred setter,

## Multi-Dog Tip

If you have multiple dogs and elect to have your senior Cavalier euthanized at home, give the remaining dogs the opportunity to see and say goodbye to the deceased. Do not force them—let them decide how close they want to come to their departed friend.

Woody had enough energy to light a small city. So he kept all of us living in the moment.

Because Cavaliers love their people so and are always nearby, their passing will be keenly felt. The emptiness may seem overwhelming at times. But knowing that you gave your little companion the very best doggy life possible should help you through the sorrow. Over time, your sadness will be replaced by wonderful treasured memories—I promise.

*He is your friend, your partner, your defender, your dog.*

*You are his life, his love, his leader. He will be yours, faithful and true, to the last beat of his heart.*

*You owe it to him to be worthy of such devotion.*

—Unknown

# 50 FUN FACTS EVERY CAVALIER OWNER SHOULD KNOW

1. Cavalier-type spaniels were cherished pets of royal families long ago.

2. The Cavalier King Charles Spaniel received his name partly in honor of King Charles II, who adored his many toy spaniels.

3. Cavalier refers to the knights who served royal families.

4. Roswell Eldridge, an American, helped bring back the Cavalier from near extinction in the 1920s.

5. Cavaliers descend from sporting spaniels and still retain their hunting instincts.

6. Cavaliers are bred in four colors: Blenheim (red and white); Black and Tan; Ruby (solid red); and Tricolor (white, black, and tan).

7. The Cavalier is the AKC's 140th breed.

8. Breeders usually release their Cavalier pups at 12 weeks of age.

9. Cavaliers usually have small litters of just three or four pups.

10. Cavaliers have long ears, especially silky coats, and a plumed tail.

11. The Cavalier is a slow-to-mature breed.

12. The Cavalier is classified in the AKC's Toy Group.

13. The Cavalier should stand 12 to 13 inches (30.5 to 33 cm).

14. This toy breed should weigh between 13 and 18 pounds (6 to 8 kg).

15. Cavaliers have a big dog personality in a small dog package.

16. The Cavalier's silky coat is easily prone to matting.

17. There are two national Cavalier clubs: The Cavalier King Charles Club-USA, and the American Cavalier King Charles Spaniel Club.

18. The Cavalier has large, expressive eyes—a distinctive breed feature.

19. Cavaliers have very little concept of danger and need to have a safe, secure yard.

20. Cavaliers are not a breed that can be trusted off leash.

21. Cavaliers crave human companionship. They are the consummate lapdog.

22. Cavaliers make excellent therapy dogs because they are so loving.

23. Often referred to as a "Velcro" dog, Cavaliers will follow their people anywhere.

24. The breed is like potato chips—it's hard to have just one.

25. A very versatile breed, the Cavalier can participate in many canine sports.

26. The Cavalier is a clean little dog and easy to groom.

27. Cavaliers tend to get along well with other dogs.

28. The Blenheim is the most popular color in the breed.

29. Having two Cavaliers can help avoid separation anxiety.

30. The breed is very food motivated, hence easy to train with treats.

31. Cavaliers have a very merry disposition and a constantly wagging tail.

32. The Cavalier cannot be left alone for long hours.

33. Cavaliers are a wonderful combination of being both sociable and portable.

34. The Cavalier is usually not aggressive or territorial when confronted with unfamiliar dogs.

35. The Cavalier is not a yappy breed.

36. The Cavalier cannot be housed outdoors.

37. The Cavalier is very willing to please.

38. The fuzzy, bedroom slipper feet are a distinct feature as trimming is not allowed except beneath the paws in between the toes.

39. Cavaliers have quite a bit of feathering on their underbellies and legs.

40. The Cavalier is a wonderful companion for children and seniors plus every age group in between.

41. Queen Victoria had a favorite Cavalier-type spaniel named Dash who often appeared in paintings on his own and with his royal person.

42. The breed's history is closely tied to paintings of small, long-nosed toy spaniels from centuries ago.

43. Cavalier King Charles Spaniels and English Toy Spaniels are often confused, but they are two distinct breeds.

44. Although toy dogs, Cavaliers are capable of jumping on furniture

45. Toy Cavalier-type spaniels have long been referred to as "spaniel comforters."

46. Anne's Son won Best of Breed at the Crufts show in 1928 and became the model for the Cavalier King Charles Spaniel breed standard.

47. The first Cavalier King Charles Spaniel Club was formed in England in 1928.

48. The Cavalier was recognized by the American Kennel Club in January 1996.

49. The Cavalier never meets a stranger he doesn't like.

50. The Cavalier is one of the most popular dogs in England. Popularity is rapidly rising in the United States as well.

# RESOURCES

## ASSOCIATIONS AND ORGANIZATIONS

### Breed Clubs
**American Cavalier King Charles Spaniel Club (ACKCSC)**
http://www.ackcsc.org/

**American Kennel Club (AKC)**
5580 Centerview Drive
Raleigh, NC 27606
Telephone: (919) 233-9767
Fax: (919) 233-3627
E-Mail: info@akc.org
www.akc.org

**Canadian Kennel Club (CKC)**
89 Skyway Avenue, Suite 100
Etobicoke, Ontario M9W 6R4
Telephone: (416) 675-5511
Fax: (416) 675-6506
E-Mail: information@ckc.ca
www.ckc.ca

**Cavalier King Charles Club of Canada**
http://www.cavaliercanada.com

**Cavalier King Charles Spaniel Club-USA**
http://www.ckcsc.org/

**Federation Cynologique Internationale (FCI)**
Secretariat General de la FCI
Place Albert 1er, 13
B – 6530 Thuin
Belgique
www.fci.be

**The Cavalier King Charles Spaniel Club**
http://www.thecavalierclub.co.uk/

**The Kennel Club**
1 Clarges Street
London
W1J 8AB
Telephone: 0870 606 6750
Fax: 0207 518 1058
www.the-kennel-club.org.uk

**United Kennel Club (UKC)**
100 E. Kilgore Road
Kalamazoo, MI 49002-5584
Telephone: (269) 343-9020
Fax: (269) 343-7037
E-Mail: pbickell@ukcdogs.com
www.ukcdogs.com

## Pet Sitters
**National Association of Professional Pet Sitters**
15000 Commerce Parkway, Suite C
Mt. Laurel, New Jersey 08054
Telephone: (856) 439-0324
Fax: (856) 439-0525
E-Mail: napps@ahint.com
www.petsitters.org

**Pet Sitters International**
201 East King Street
King, NC 27021-9161
Telephone: (336) 983-9222
Fax: (336) 983-5266
E-Mail: info@petsit.com
www.petsit.com

## Rescue Organizations and Animal Welfare Groups
**American Humane Association (AHA)**
63 Inverness Drive East
Englewood, CO 80112
Telephone: (303) 792-9900
Fax: (303) 792-5333
www.americanhumane.org

**American Society for the Prevention of Cruelty to Animals (ASPCA)**
424 E. 92nd Street
New York, NY 10128-6804
Telephone: (212) 876-7700
www.aspca.org

**The Humane Society of the United States (HSUS)**
2100 L Street, NW
Washington DC 20037
Telephone: (202) 452-1100
www.hsus.org

**Royal Society for the Prevention of Cruelty to Animals (RSPCA)**
RSPCA Enquiries Service
Wilberforce Way, Southwater,
Horsham, West Sussex
RH13 9RS
United Kingdom
Telephone: 0870 3335 999
Fax: 0870 7530 284
www.rspca.org.uk

## Sports
**International Agility Link (IAL)**
Global Administrator: Steve Drinkwater
E-Mail: yunde@powerup.au
www.agilityclick.com/~ial

**The World Canine Freestyle Organization, Inc.**
P.O. Box 350122
Brooklyn, NY 11235
Telephone: (718) 332-8336
Fax: (718) 646-2686
E-Mail: WCFODOGS@aol.com
www.worldcaninefreestyle.org

## Therapy

**Delta Society**
875 124th Ave, NE, Suite 101
Bellevue, WA 98005
Telephone: (425) 679-5500
Fax: (425) 679-5539
E-Mail: info@DeltaSociety.org
www.deltasociety.org

**Therapy Dogs Inc.**
P.O. Box 20227
Cheyenne WY 82003
Telephone: (877) 843-7364
Fax: (307) 638-2079
E-Mail: therapydogsinc@
qwestoffice.net
www.therapydogs.com

**Therapy Dogs International (TDI)**
88 Bartley Road
Flanders, NJ 07836
Telephone: (973) 252-9800
Fax: (973) 252-7171
E-Mail: tdi@gti.net
www.tdi-dog.org

## Training

**Association of Pet Dog Trainers (APDT)**
150 Executive Center Drive
Box 35
Greenville, SC 29615
Telephone: (800) PET-DOGS
Fax: (864) 331-0767
E-Mail: information@apdt.com
www.apdt.com

**International Association of Animal Behavior Consultants (IAABC)**
565 Callery Road
Cranberry Township, PA 16066
E-Mail: info@iaabc.org
www.iaabc.org

**National Association of Dog Obedience Instructors (NADOI)**
PMB 369
729 Grapevine Hwy.
Hurst, TX 76054-2085
www.nadoi.org

## Veterinary and Health Resources

**Academy of Veterinary Homeopathy (AVH)**
P.O. Box 9280
Wilmington, DE 19809
Telephone: (866) 652-1590
Fax: (866) 652-1590
www.theavh.org

**American Academy of Veterinary Acupuncture (AAVA)**
P.O. Box 1058
Glastonbury, CT 06033
Telephone: (860) 632-9911
Fax: (860) 659-8772
www.aava.org

**American Animal Hospital Association (AAHA)**
12575 W. Bayaud Ave.
Lakewood, CO 80228
Telephone: (303) 986-2800
Fax: (303) 986-1700
E-Mail: info@aahanet.org
www.aahanet.org/index.cfm

**American College of Veterinary Internal Medicine (ACVIM)**
1997 Wadsworth Blvd., Suite A
Lakewood, CO 80214-5293
Telephone: (800) 245-9081
Fax: (303) 231-0880
Email: ACVIM@ACVIM.org
www.acvim.org

**American College of Veterinary Ophthalmologists (ACVO)**
P.O. Box 1311
Meridian, ID 83860
Telephone: (208) 466-7624
Fax: (208) 466-7693
E-Mail: office09@acvo.com
www.acvo.com

**American Holistic Veterinary Medical Association (AHVMA)**
2218 Old Emmorton Road
Bel Air, MD 21015
Telephone: (410) 569-0795
Fax: (410) 569-2346
E-Mail: office@ahvma.org
www.ahvma.org

**American Veterinary Medical Association (AVMA)**
1931 North Meacham Road,
Suite 100
Schaumburg, IL 60173-4360
Telephone: (847) 925-8070
Fax: (847) 925-1329
E-Mail: avmainfo@avma.org
www.avma.org

**ASPCA Animal Poison Control Center**
Telephone: (888) 426-4435
www.aspca.org

**British Veterinary Association (BVA)**
7 Mansfield Street
London
W1G 9NQ
Telephone: 0207 636 6541
Fax: 0207 908 6349
E-Mail: bvahq@bva.co.uk
www.bva.co.uk

**Canine Eye Registration Foundation (CERF)**
VMDB/CERF
1717 Philo Rd
P.O. Box 3007
Urbana, IL 61803-3007
Telephone: (217) 693-4800
Fax: (217) 693-4801
E-Mail: CERF@vmbd.org
www.vmdb.org

**Orthopedic Foundation for Animals (OFA)**
2300 NE Nifong Blvd
Columbus, Missouri 65201-3856
Telephone: (573) 442-0418
Fax: (573) 875-5073
Email: ofa@offa.org
www.offa.org

**US Food and Drug Administration Center for Veterinary Medicine (CVM)**
7519 Standish Place
HFV-12
Rockville, MD 20855-0001
Telephone: (240) 276-9300 or (888) INFO-FDA
http://www.fda.gov/cvm

# PUBLICATIONS

## Books

**Anderson, Teoti.** *The Super Simple Guide to Housetraining.* Neptune City: TFH Publications, 2004.

**Anne, Jonna, with Mary Straus.** *The Healthy Dog Cookbook: 50 Nutritious and Delicious Recipes Your Dog Will Love.* UK: Ivy Press Limited, 2008.

**Dainty, Suellen.** *50 Games to Play With Your Dog.* UK: Ivy Press Limited, 2007.

**Ewing, Su.** *Cavalier King Charles Spaniels.* Neptune City: TFH and Discovery Communications, Inc., 2007.

**Harris, Myra Savant.** *The Cavalier King Charles Spaniel.* Neptune City: TFH Publications, 2009.

**Morgan, Diane.** *Good Dogkeeping.* Neptune City: TFH Publications, 2005.

## Magazines

*AKC Family Dog*
American Kennel Club
260 Madison Avenue
New York, NY 10016
Telephone: (800) 490-5675
E-Mail: familydog@akc.org
www.akc.org/pubs/familydog

*AKC Gazette*
American Kennel Club
260 Madison Avenue
New York, NY 10016
Telephone: (800) 533-7323
E-Mail: gazette@akc.org
www.akc.org/pubs/gazette

*Dog & Kennel*
Pet Publishing, Inc.
7-L Dundas Circle
Greensboro, NC 27407
Telephone: (336) 292-4272
Fax: (336) 292-4272
E-Mail: info@petpublishing.com
www.dogandkennel.com

*Dogs Monthly*
Ascot House
High Street, Ascot,
Berkshire SL5 7JG
United Kingdom
Telephone: 0870 730 8433
Fax: 0870 730 8431
E-Mail: admin@rtc-associates.freeserve.co.uk
www.corsini.co.uk/dogsmonthly

## Websites
**Nylabone**
www.nylabone.com

**TFH Publications, Inc.**
www.tfh.com

# INDEX

Note: **Boldface** numbers indicate illustrations.

## A

accidents, housetraining, 71, 89
activities. *see* exercise; sports and activities
acupuncture, 125–126, **126**
adoption questionnaire, 86
adult Cavaliers. *see also* feeding; health issues; problem behaviors; sports and activities
  adopting from breeder, 82–85
  adopting from rescue or shelter, 85–89
  advantages of, 81–82
  age of, 82, 83
  annual exam for, 115–116
  feeding schedule for, 105, **110–111,** 111
  grooming, 90–101
  potential issues for, 89
  training, 134–143
  vital signs in, 125
aggression, 144–146, 157–158
agility, 169–170, **170**
air travel, 177
allergies, 123–124
  food, 112–113, 124
  vaccine, 57–58
alpha dog, 8, 39
alternative therapies, 103–104, 125–128, **126, 127**
Alzheimer's, canine, 194
American Cavalier King Charles Spaniel Club, Inc. (ACKCSC), 14, 15, 36, 85
American Holistic Veterinary Medical Association (AHVMA), 120
American Kennel Club (AKC), 7
  breed recognition by, 14–15
  events sponsored by, 15–16, 165–168, 169–170, 171–174
ammonia, 71
animal welfare groups, 210
Ann's Son, 13, 14
annual exam, 115–116
anxiety
  separation, 147, 158–159, **159**
  signs of, 147, 151
art, spaniels in, 10–11, 12–13
arthritis, 193–194

associations, 210
attention, need for, 23–24
attention-seeking behavior, 152, 157

## B

backyard breeders, 34–35
BARF diet, 108
barking, 146–148
bathing
  adult, 92–94
  puppy, 51
  senior, 191
beds, 41
  for camping, 163
  for seniors, 187, 194, 196
"beg," 142
behavior. *see also* problem behaviors
  attention-seeking, 152, 157
  ignoring unwanted, 152, 153
  reinforcing, 62, 154
behaviorists, 145, 154
birds, 31
bites and stings, 130
biting, 157–158
Black and Tans, 27
bleeding, 98, 129, 130
Blenheims, 11–13, 27
boarding kennels, 179
body structure, 25
bone meal, 110
bones, 108, 109
Bones and Raw Food (BARF) diet, 108
books, 212
bordetella, 54, 55
bowls, 44, 107
breed characteristics, 7–8, 23–25
  appearance in, 25–27, **26**
  pet suitability and, 27–31
breed clubs, 7, 13–15, 210
breeders
  adopting adult from, 81, 82–85
  adopting senior from, 185–186
  backyard, 34–35
  commercial, 36, 85
  experienced, 36
  finding right, 34, 36–38
  hobby, 36
  influential, 15–19
  paperwork from, 45–46, 85
  puppy mill, 35, 85

Rule of Sevens of, 38
talking to, 38–39
breed history
  dog domestication in, 8–9
  early development in, 9–11
  in England, 11–14
  influential people and dogs in, 15–19
  in United States, 14–15
breed standard, 25
  conformation to, **171,** 171–172
  for height and weight, 66, 111
  model for, 13
broken bones, 130–131
Brown, Sally Lyons, 14
Brown-Albrecht, Trudy, 14
brushes, 91
brushing
  adult, 90–92, **93**
  puppy, 52
  senior, 191
  tooth, 98–101, **99, 100**

## C

Caius, Johannes, 9
camping, 161–164
cancer, 59, 103, 124
canine cognitive disorder (CCD), 194
canine freestyle, 170–171
Canine Good Citizen test, 165–168, **166, 167**
canned foods, 107
carbohydrates, 104–105
car seat, 44
car travel, 43–44, **174,** 175–177
cataracts, 28, 58, 120
cats, 31
Cavalier King Charles Spaniel Club, 13
Cavalier King Charles Spaniel Club-United States, Inc. (CKCSC-USA), 14, 15, 36, 85
Cavalier Rescue USA, 85
Charles II, King of England, 11
chewing, 89, 148, 149
children and Cavaliers, 30–31
  bonding activity for, 205
  grief and, **204,** 206
  puppies and, 64, **64**
  seniors and, 185, 205
Children Reading to Dogs program, 30, 168–169

chiropractic, 126
chondroitin, 193, 194
chromodacryorrhea, 96
clothing, 41–42, **163**
coat, 26
   brushing, 52, 90–92, **93,** 191
   colors of, 27
   shiny, **104,** 105
trimming, 26, 52, 92, 93
cognitive disorder, canine, 194
collars, 42, 118
colors, coat, 27
combing, 90–92
*come* command, 71–73, **72,** 140
"comforter spaniels," 10
commands, obedience
   around-the-house, 135, 140–142, **141**
   basic, 61, 71–77, 135
   *come,* 71–73, **72,** 140
   *down,* 75
   *down-stay,* 138
   *drop it* and *leave it,* 148, 149
   *enough* or *quiet,* 147–148
   *find it,* 75, 199
   hand signals with, 194, 197, 199
   *heel,* 76, 135
   intermediate, 135–140, **137**
   *let's go,* 140
   *no bite,* 157
   *off,* 75, 141, **141**
   *sit,* 73–74, **74,** 109
   *sit-stay,* 136–138, **137**
   *speak,* 143
   *stand,* 138
   *stand-stay,* 138–139
   *stay,* 135
   *upstairs/downstairs,* 141–142
   *wait,* 139–140
commercial foods
   ingredients in, 109–110
   types of, 106–107
companionship needs, 23–24
conditioner, 92, 93
conformation, **171,** 171–172
   Cavalier wins in, 13, 15–19
   show-quality dog for, 39, 40
congestive heart failure, 58, 122, 195
conjunctivitis, 125
constipation, 113
contracts, breeder, 45–46, 85
coprophagia, 148–149
core and noncore vaccines, 54
corn, 112–113
coronavirus, 54, 55
crates, 42–44, **43**
   cushions for, 41
   interior design of, 67
   location of, **66,** 67

size of, 66–67
   travel, **174,** 175, **176**
crate training, 65–68, **66**
crying, 45, 46
Cushing's disease, 195
cushions, 41

**D**

dancing with dogs, 170–171
Darcy Fund, 123
day care, 178–179
deafness, age-related, 194, 197
demodectic mange, 119
denning instinct, 65
dental care, 98–101, **99, 100**
dental sprays and gels, 101
diabetes mellitus, 195–196
diarrhea, 113, 127, 129
diet. *see* feeding; food
digging, 149–150, **151**
disaster preparedness, 132
discipline, 61
distemper, 54, 55
documents
   adult adoption, 85, 86, 87–88
   puppy adoption, 45–46
dog food. *see* feeding; food
doggy day care, 178–179
dog parks, 164
dogs. *see also* multi-dog home
   Cavalier and other, **30,** 31
   domestication of, 8–9
   grief and, **206,** 206–207
   memorable, 15–19
   socialization with, 63, 64
dog shows. *see* conformation
domestication, 8–9
*down* command, 75
*down-stay* command, 135, 138
*drop it* command, 148, 149
dry foods, **105,** 107
   dental health and, 99
   for puppy, 50–51

**E**

ear care, 92, **94,** 94–95
ear infections, 94, 123, **124,** 124–125
ears, 26, **26**
ehrlichiosis, 119
Eldridge, Roswell, 12–13, 14
electric nail grinder, 97
emergencies, planning for, 133
emergency care, 53, **129,** 129–133
end-of-life issues, 200–207
   grief, **204,** 204–207, **206**
   hospice and euthanasia, 201–204
energy level, 7–8, **8,** 39, 49
England, breed history in, 10, 11–14

English Springer Spaniel, 9
English Toy Spaniel, 12
*enough* command, 147–148
environment
   adjusting to, 46, 89
   suitability of, 28
enzymatic cleaner, 71
episodic falling, 120–121
Eubank, Ted and Mary Grace, 16
euthanasia, 201–204
evacuation, 132
exercise, 28. *see also* sports and activities
   for arthritis, 193
   for problem behaviors, 145, 147, 158–159, **159**
exercise pen, 44
eye care, 92, **95,** 95–96
eye conditions and infections, 120, 125, 196–197
eye contact, 138, 152
eyes, 26, 38

**F**

facts, Cavalier, 208–209
falling, episodic, 120–121
fats, 105
fear of strangers, 150–152
feathering, 91
feeding, 102–113. *see also* food
   choices for, 106–109
   in crate, 67–68
   dog food labels in, 109–110
   health problems related to, 112–113
   housetraining and, 69, 71
   in multi-dog home, 107
   nutrition in, 104–106
   obesity and, 111–112
   puppy, 49–51
   schedule for, 50, 105, **110,** 110–111
   senior, 187, 189–190, **190,** 199
   special accessories for, 107
   teaching *sit* for, 73, 109
fees, adoption, 88–89
feet, 26
females, spaying, 58–59
Field Spaniel, 9
*find it* cue, 75, 199
first aid, **129,** 129–133
first-aid kit, 129–130, 163
flea collars, 118
fleas, 118–119
   allergy to, 124
   examination for, 115–116
   tapeworm and, 118
flews, 100
flowers, poisonous, 130
flyball, 169

food, 44, 106–109. *see also* feeding
  for camping, 163
  changing type of, 49–50,
    50–51
  commercial, 106–107
  dry, 99, **105**, 107
  noncommercial, 103–104,
    107–108
  toxic, 133
food allergies, 112–113, 124
food bowls, 44
food labels, reading, 109–110
Forwood, Lady, 14
fractures, 130–131
free feeding, 110–111
frostbite, 131
fun facts, 208–209
furniture, dogs on, 141, **141**

**G**

Garnett-Wilson, Barbara, 17–18
genetic health tests, 38
gingivitis, 99
glucosamine, 193, 194
grains, 112–113
Grandin, Temple, 8–9
grief, 204–207
  children and, **204**, 206
  dogs and, **206**, 206–207
groomers, 92, 101, 191–192
grooming, 90–101
  bathing in, 92–94
  brushing and combing in,
    90–92, **93**
  dental care in, 98–101, **99**, **100**
  ear care in, **94**, 94–95
  eye care in, **95**, 95–96
  for multi-dog home, 95
  nail trimming in, 96–98, **97**,
    **98**
  professional, 92, 101, 191–192
  puppy, 51–52
  requirements for, 28
  senior, 190–192, **191**
  supplies for, 44, 91
grooming table, 44, 51, 92

**H**

hair trimming, 26, 52, 92, 93
handling, acclimation to, 51
hand signals, 194, 197, 199
harness, 42, 162–163
head and neck, 25–26
head halter, 154, 156
health care
  adult annual, 115–116
  hospice, 201
  puppy, 52–58
  resources for, 211–212
  senior, 187, 192–193

spaying or neutering in, 58–59
vaccinations in, 54–58, **55**,
  115, 116
health certificates, 38, 177
health insurance, 41, 54
health issues, 28, 115
  alternative therapies for,
    125–128
  breed-specific, 120–123
  checking for, 51, 190
  dental, 99
  ear, 94
  emergency care and first aid
    for, **129**, 129–133
  food-related, 112–113
  generic, 123–125
  genetic tests for, 38
  laws addressing, 46
  obesity and, 111
  parasites, 116–120
  puppy-specific, 58
  senior, 193–197
  special diets for, 103–104, **108**,
    108–109
  veterinary specialists for, 122
hearing loss, 194, 197
heart, test for, 38
heart failure, congestive, 58, 122,
  195
heart murmurs, 58, 122
heart rate, 125
heartworms, 117
heatstroke, 131–133, 177

*heel* command, 76, 135
"heelwork to music," 170–171
height, 66
hepatitis, 54, 55
herbal remedies, 103–104, 126–
  127, **127**
*here* command, 71
hip dysplasia, 28, 38, 121
Holyoke Cavaliers, 16
home
  acclimating to, 46, 89
  bringing puppy to, 45–47
  puppy-proofing, **40**, 41
home-cooked foods, 103–104, 108
homeopathy, 127
hookworms, 117
hospice, 201–204
house call veterinarian, 202–204
housetraining, 68–71
  accidents in, 71
  adult, 89
  crate for, 65
  initial, 46
  procedure for, 69–71
  senior, 199
hunter, spaniel as, 9
hunting instinct, 7, 28–29, 31

**I**

identification, 44–45, 162–163
incontinence, urinary, 197
inhalant allergies, 124

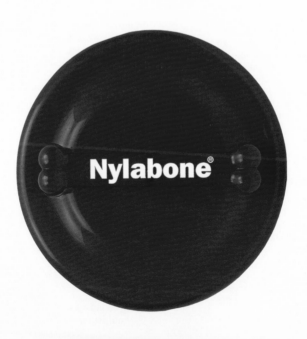

insect stings and bites, 130
intelligence, 29–30
International Association for
  Animal Hospice and Palliative
  Care (IAAHPC), 201

## J

James II, King of England, 11
jogging, 165
Johnson-Snyder, Meredith, 16–17
jumping up, 152–154, **153**
juvenile cataracts, 28, 58, 120

## K

Kennel Club, 13, 14
kennel cough, 55, 56
kennels, boarding, 179
kibble, **105**, 107
  dental health and, 99
  puppy, 50–51
kidney disease, 195–196
King Charles Spaniel, 12, 13

## L

Landseer, Sir Edwin, 12
lapdog, spaniel as, 10–11
Laughing Cavaliers, 17–18
leader, pack, 8–9, 145–146, 155
leashes, 45
  allowing off, 28, 29
  for camping, 162–163
  pulling on, 154–156, **155, 156**
  walking nicely on, 75–77, 140
*leave it* command, 148, 149
leptospirosis, 54, 55–56
*let's go* command, 140
lifestyle, suitability of, 23–24, 28
  adult dog and, 84–85
  senior dog and, 187
lipomas, 190
lodging, pet-friendly, 177
Lyme disease, 54, 56, 119

## M

magazines, 212
males, neutering, 58–59
mange mites, 119
Mary II, Queen of England, 11
massage, 194
mats, 91, 92
meat, 104
  in commercial foods, 107, 110
  raw, 108
meat meal and by-products, 110
Mech, L. David, 9
medical records, 45
medications, over-the-counter,
  129

microchipping, 44–45
minerals, 105
mites, mange, 119
mitral valve dysplasia (MVD)
  in adults, 116, 121–123
  susceptibility to, 28, 58
multi-dog home
  adult Cavalier in, 83, 89
  barking in, 147
  Cavalier sociability in, **30**, 31
  euthanasia and grief in, 207
  feeding in, 107
  grooming in, 95
  puppy in, 47
  senior Cavalier in, 187
  sleeping spots in, 196
  sports in, 169
  training in, 63, 140
  veterinary exams for, 55, 116
murmurs, heart, 58, 122
"musical freestyle," 171
muzzle, 129
MVD. *see* mitral valve dysplasia
  (MVD)

## N

nail clippers, 97, **97**, 98, **98**
nail trimming, 96–98, **97, 98**, 191
National Association of
  Professional Pet Sitters (NAPPS),
  178
neck, 25–26
"neck scratcher's disease," 28, 123
neighbors, meeting, 46
neutering and spaying, 58–59
nighttime puppy care, 46–47
nipping, 157–158
*no bite* command, 157
noncommercial foods, 107–108
nuclear sclerosis, 196–197
nutrition. *see also* feeding; food
  advances in, 103–104
  building blocks of, 104–106
nutritionists, 103
Nylabone products, 45, **45**, 67,
  109, **113**, 148, **150**

## O

obedience
  basic, 61, 71–77, **72, 74**
  competitive, 172–173
  intermediate, 135–140, **137,
    139**
  at veterinary exam, 120
obesity, 59, 111–112
*off* command, 75, 141, **141**
older Cavaliers. *see* senior
  Cavaliers
omega-3 fatty acids, 105
Orchard Hill Cavaliers, 18–19

organizations, 210
Ostmann, Karin, 17
over-the-counter medications, 129

## P

pack and pack leader, 8–9, 145–
  146, 155
paintings, spaniels in, 10–11,
  12–13
Pajaro, Rafael and Pam, **27**, 27–28
paperwork
  adult adoption, 85, 86, 87–88
  puppy adoption, 45–46
parainfluenza, 54, 56
parasites, 116–120
  external, 118–120
  internal, 116–118
parks, 65, 164
parvovirus, 54, 56
patellar luxation, 28, 38, 123
paw/other paw trick, 142, **143**
paws, 26
  handling, 96
  shake, **142**, 142–143
  trimming hair on, 93–94
pedigree document, 45
people
  fear of, 150–152
  influential, 15–19
  meeting new, 46
  sociability with, 23–24, 30–31
  socialization to, 64, 65
personality, evaluation of, 39
pet behavior consultant, 145, 154
PetFinder.com, 49
pet health insurance, 41, 54
pet-quality dogs, 39, 40
pets
  Cavalier and other, 31, 64
  Cavalier suitability as, 27–31
pet sitters, 24, 178, **179**, 210
Pet Sitters International, 178
physical appearance, 25–27, **26**
physical therapy, 128
picky eaters, 113
Pinecrest Cavaliers, 16
Pisanello, Antonio, 10
Pitt, Amice, 13
plane travel, 177
plants, poisonous, 130
plaque, 99
plastic crates, 42, **43**
play, 46, 157
poisoning, 133
poisonous plants and flowers, 130
positive reinforcement, 154
positive training, 62
preservatives, 107, 110
prey drive, 31
prices

adult, 83, 88–89
puppy, 39–40
problem behaviors, 144–159
aggression, 144–146
barking, 146–148
chewing, 89, 148, 149
coprophagia, 148–149
digging, 149–150, **151**
fear of strangers, 150–152
jumping up, 152–154, **153**
leash pulling, 154–156, **155,
156**
neutering and, 59
new adult with, 89
nipping, 157–158
senior with, 199
separation anxiety, 147, 158–
159, **159**
sleeping with humans and, 25
proteins, 104, 105, 110
publications, 212
pulling on leash, 154–156, **155,
156**
punishment, 61, 62
puppies
adopting two, 47
adults vs., 81
advantages of, 33–34
age of, 27, 36
basic obedience for, 71–77,
**72, 74**
bringing home, 45–47
classes for, 47, **76,** 77
crate training, 65–68, **66**
energy level of, 49
feeding, 49–51, 67–68, 105
finding, 34–39
geriatric dogs and, 203
grooming, 51–52, 92
health care for, 52–58
health conditions in, 58
housetraining, 65, 68–71
meeting needs of, 24
nipping by, 157
preparing for, 40–41
prices of, 39–40
selecting right, 39
socialization of, 63–65, **64**
spaying and neutering, 58–59
supplies for, 41–45
training, 42, 60–77
vaccination schedule for, 54
puppy kindergarten, 47, **76,** 77
puppy mills, 35, 85
puppy-proofing, **40,** 41

**Q**
quick of nail, 98
*quiet* command, 147–148

**R**
rabies, 54, 56
rally, 172, 173
Rattlebridge Cavaliers, 16–17
raw foods, 103, 108
*recall* commands, 71
rectal temperature, 125, 133
registration application, 45
rehabilitation therapy, 128
reinforcement, positive, 154
rescue organizations, 210
adopting adult from, 81, 85–89
adopting senior from, 184–185
resource guarding, 157
resources, 210–212
respiratory rate, 125
ringworm, 120
Rocky Mountain spotted fever,
119
"roll over," 142
roundworms, 117
Ruby Cavalier, 27
Rule of Sevens, 38

**S**
sales contract, 45–46, 85
sarcoptic mange, 119
scat mat, 141
schedule
daily, 33–34
feeding, 50, 105, **110,** 110–111
housetraining, 69, 70
setting up, 41
Secord, William, 10–11
semi-moist foods, 107
senior Cavaliers
adopting from shelter or
rescue, 184–185
adopting through breeder,
185–186
advantages of, 183–184
age of, 183, 185, 189
children and, 205
commitment to, 186–187
feeding, 105, 189–190, **190**
grieving after loss of, 204–207
grooming, 190–192, **191**

health care for, 192–193
health issues in, 193–197
hospice and euthanasia for,
201–204
in multi-dog home, 187, 196
puppies and, 203
training, 139, 184, 194,
197–199
separation anxiety, 147, 158–159,
**159**
shake paws, **142,** 142–143
shampoos, 93
shedding, 26
Sheeba Cavaliers, **16,** 17
shelters
adopting adult from, 81, 85–89
adopting senior from, 184–185
show-quality dogs, 39, 40
Sims, Joy, 18–19
*sit* command, 73–74, **74,** 109
*sit-stay* command, 135, 136–138,
**137**
size, 25, 66
skin allergies, 123–124
sleeping, 24–25, 46–47
slippery elm, 104, 127
snakebite, 130
snood, 107
sociability, 23, 30–31
socialization, 63–65, **64**
at puppy kindergarten, 47,
**76,** 77
to strangers, 150–151
soft-sided crates, 43
spaniel bowl, 107
spaniels, 7
as hunters, 9
as lapdogs, 10–11
spaying and neutering, 58–59
*speak* command, 143
special diets, 103–104, **108,**
108–109
sporting dogs, 7–8
sports and activities, 7–8, **8,**
160–179
affinity for, 28–29
agility, 169–170, **170**
camping, 161–164

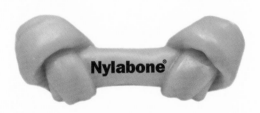

canine freestyle, 170–171
Canine Good Citizen test, 165–168, **166**, **167**
conformation, **171**, 171–172
dog parks, 164
for multi-dog home, 169
obedience, 172–173
rally, 172, 173
resources for, 210
for seniors, 199
therapy work, **27**, 27–28, **29**, 30, 168–169
tracking, 174
training for, 135, 172
traveling, **174**, 174–179, **176**
walking/jogging, 165
*stand* command, 138
*stand-stay* command, 135, 138–139
*stay* command, 135
    breaking, 137–138
    *down* and, 138
    *sit* and, 136–138, **137**
    *stand* and, 138–139
    *wait* vs., 139
Sterling, Bettina, 16
stings and bites, 130
strangers, fear of, 150–152
styptic powder, 97–98
supplements, 108–109
    herbal, 103–104, 126–127, **127**
    for seniors, 190, 193, 194
supplies, 41–45
    camping, 162–164
    disaster kit, 132
    first-aid, 129–130
    grooming, 52, 91, 92, 97–98
    travel, **174**, 174–175, **176**
syringomyelia, 28, 123

**T**
tail wagging, 23
tapeworms, 117
tartar, 99
tattooing, 44
tear staining, 96
teeth, care of, 98–101, **99**, **100**
Tellington-Jones, Linda, 128
Tellington TTouch, 127–128
temperament, evaluation of, 39
temperature, normal, 125, 133
territorial aggression, 157
tethers, 162–163
therapy work, 168–169
    resources for, 211
    suitability for, **27**, 27–28, **29**, 30
Thornton, Kim and Jerry, 123
ticks, 56, 116, 119–120
titer testing, 56–57, 116
toothbrush and toothpaste, 98, **100**, 100–101

Toy Group, 7, 8, 172
toys
    interactive, 148, **150**, 199
    puppy, 45, **45**
tracking, 174
trainability, 29–30
trainers, 62–63, 145
training
    adult, 134–143
    around-the-house commands for, 140–142, **141**
    basic obedience, 61, 71–77, **72**, **74**, 135
    crate, 65–68, **66**
    for feeding, 73, 109
    for grooming, 51, 52, 96, 101
    housetraining, 46, 68–71, 89, 199
    intermediate obedience, 135–140, **137**, **139**
    in multi-dog home, 140
    need for, 61–62
    off-leash, 28
    poor performance in, 136
    positive methods of, 62, 152, 153, 154
    professional, 62–63, 145
    puppy, 60–77
    puppy classes for, 47, **76**, 77
    resources for, 63, 211
    rewards for, 42, **69**, **139**
    senior, 184, 194, 197–199, 205
    socialization, 63–65, **64**
    for sports, 172
    trick, **142**, 142–143, **143**
    for veterinary exam, 120
traveling, 174–179
    by car, 175–177
    crates and supplies for, 42, 43–44, **174**, 174–175, **176**
    lodging for, 177
    by plane, 177
    without dog, 177–179
treats, 109, **111**
    obesity and, 111–112
    training, 42, 51, 52, **69**, **139**
tricks, 135, **142**, 142–143, **143**
Tricolors, **16**, 17, 27
trimming
hair, 26, 52, 92, 93
nail, 96–98, **97**, **98**, 191

**U**
undercoat, 26
United States, breed history in, 14–15
*upstairs/downstairs* command, 141–142
urinary incontinence, 197

**V**
vaccinations, 54–58, **55**
    annual, 115, 116
    controversy over, 56–58
    socialization and, 65
    types of, 54–56
"Velcro" dogs, 9, 138, 158
Venier, Erica and Rachel, 18–19
veterinarian
    annual exam by, 115–116
    bi-annual geriatric exam by, 187, 192–193
    euthanasia by, 202–204
    finding, 52–53
    first checkup by, 53–54, 55, 64
    training for visits to, 120
veterinary rehabilitation therapy, 128
veterinary resources, 211–212
veterinary specialists, 122
Victoria, Queen of England, 12
*The Vision of St. Eustace* (Pisanello), 10
visitors, jumping on, 153–154
vital signs, 125
vitamins, 105, 108, 110
vomiting, inducing, 129

**W**
wagging tail, 23
*wait* command, 139–140
Walker, K. Mostyn, 13
walking/jogging, 165
walk nicely on leash, 75–77, 140
water, 105–106, **106**, 163
water bowls, 44
weaning, 50
Websites, 212
weight
    overweight, 59, 111–112
    standards for, 25, 66, 111
Welsh Springer Spaniel, 9
Westminster Kennel Club Dog Show, 16, 18
wheatgrass, 108
whipworms, 118
wild animals, 31, 56
William III, King of England, 11
wire crates, 42–43
wolves, 8–9
worms, 116–118
wounds, 129–130

**Y**
yard, puppy-proofing, **40**, 41

# PHOTO CREDITS

## VETERINARY ADVISOR

**Wayne Hunthausen, DVM,** consulting veterinary editor and pet behavior consultant, is the director of Animal Behavior Consultations in the Kansas City area and currently serves on the Practitoner Board for *Veterinary Medicine* and the Behavior Advisory Board for *Veterinary Forum*.


## BREEDER ADVISOR

**Diane Zdrodowski** grew up with spaniels adopted from the pound as a child. She had always wanted a Cavalier, having met several at the home of her vet in CT, and then in the mid-1990s she acquired her first Cavalier, "Bentley," who would take her on a whirlwind trip through the dog world. He became a nationally recognized therapy dog and conformation dog, and introduced her to agility, rally, and obedience. Over the years, she acquired and bred Cavaliers and became involved in both national Cavalier clubs, holding positions of increasing responsibility. Currently, she is an Officer of the American Cavalier King Charles Spaniel Club (ACKCSC) and serves as the Recording Secretary and Membership Chairman, and is a Board Member of The ACKCSC Charitable Trust, which funds research for health issues related to Cavaliers. She also belongs to several local kennel clubs and is President of the Delaware Water Gap Kennel Club.

## DEDICATION

To my husband, Louis A. DiMare, Jr., who always has room in his heart for "one more." And to our canine family, Woody, Rory, Junior, Topo Gigio, and Lily—you're the best.

## ACKNOWLEDGMENTS

Quite a few people contributed to the creation of this book, and I must wholeheartedly thank them. My two fabulous research assistants, Debra Goetchius and Michelle Jay; dog trainer extraordinaire Linda Petrone; and my wonderful sounding board, Cavalier King Charles Spaniel breeder Diane Zdrodowski of Evanlake Cavaliers.

I must also thank all the Cavalier breeders, pet owners, and show and performance people who shared their knowledge of this wonderful toy spaniel with me. All of your contributions were invaluable.

## ABOUT THE AUTHOR

A lifelong animal lover, **Loren Spiotta-DiMare** has been writing about her favorite subject for more than 30 years. She's the author of *Beyond the Finish Line: Stories of Ex-Racehorses*; three pet-reference books, *Macaws, Siamese Cats,* and *The Sporting Spaniel Handbook*; and six picture books for children, *Madeline's Miracle, Rockwell: A Boy and His Dog, Chelsea & The New Puppy, Daniel, Dog Camp Champ! Norman to the Rescue,* and *Caesar: On Deaf Ears*; as well as the coauthor of *Everyone Loves Elwood*. Recognized by the Dog Writers Association of America (DWAA), the Humane Society of the United States (HSUS), the Doris Day Animal Foundation, and New Jersey Press Women, Loren's work has been published both nationally and internationally. A resident of Hunterdon County, New Jersey, Loren and her husband, Lou, share their home with five dogs and several pet birds. Loren's equine companion lives nearby.

Nylabone®

JOIN NOW
Club Nylabone
www.nylabone.com
Coupons!
Articles!
Exciting
Features!

He **Plays** Hard.
He **Chews** Hard.

He's a **Nylabone**® Dog!
Your #1 choice for healthy chews & treats.